1995

Pandora's Daughters

Pandora's

Translated by
Maureen B. Fant

with a Foreword by
Mary R. Lefkowitz

EVA CANTARELLA

Daughters

The Role and Status of Women in Greek and Roman Antiquity

The Johns Hopkins University Press
Baltimore and London

This book has been brought to publication with the generous assistance of the David M. Robinson Publication Fund and the Andrew W. Mellon Foundation.

Originally published as *L'ambiguo malanno*
© Copyright by Editori Riuniti, 1981

Second printing, hardcover and paperback, 1989
Third printing, paperback, 1991

The Johns Hopkins University Press
701 West 40th Street
Baltimore, Maryland 21211-2190
The Johns Hopkins Press Ltd., London

Library of Congress Cataloging-in-Publication Data
Cantarella, Eva.
    Pandora's daughters.

    Translation of: L'ambiguo malanno. 1981.
    Bibliography: p.
    Includes index.
    1. Women—Greece—History.   2. Women—Rome—History.
3. Civilization, Classical.   I. Title.
HQ1134.C3513   1987   305.4′2′0938   86-7292
ISBN 0–8018–3193–8 (alk. paper)
ISBN 0–8018–3385–X (pbk.)

Contents

Contents

Foreword

Until recently, histories of the ancient world made only occasional reference to women. The ancients themselves established the practice; even the wives of kings or aristocrats make brief claim to the attention of Herodotus or Polybius, and women are hardly mentioned at all by Thucydides, who concentrates on the activities from which they were by definition excluded, politics and war. But considerable information about the lives of ordinary women has nonetheless survived—although women themselves recorded little of it—in literature, papyri, and inscriptions. By turning their attention to these sources, scholars have begun to provide an account, though necessarily incomplete, at least for certain times and places, of how the other members of the ancient world's population lived.

Having edited a collection of ancient source materials *Women's Life in Greece and Rome* (Baltimore and London, 1982), Maureen Fant and I are aware of the obstacles involved in writing history from nonhistorical sources. For that reason, we thought it would be helpful to have this book available in English. For nonspecialists as well as for scholars, this book shows clearly how literary, anecdotal, and juridical sources should (and should not) be used to give an impression of what Greek and Roman men thought about women, and about the relative status of women in their lives. In it Eva Cantarella offers a particularly valuable assessment of the sociological information that can be derived from law codes, lawyers' speeches, records, and discussion of custom and legislation. Legal documents in particular constitute one of the most reliable—and underutilized—means of determining the status of women, as they draw attention to acceptable as well as to exceptional practice, without the distortions of personal bias or literary convention. In addition, Eva Cantarella provides a balanced assessment of one of the most controversial issues in women's history, the question of matriarchy in prehistoric Greece and Rome. She considers the original sources that have been used as evidence, not failing to take into account the historical contexts in which modern theories of women's societies have been produced.

The study of Greek and Roman women, as of any other aspect of the ancient world, has a certain relevance for our own time. At the very least, it helps to clarify and identify attitudes that persist: the notion that anatomy is destiny, that woman's place is in the home, that the motives of females who leave the home (for whatever purpose) are suspect, and that such women are aggressive or promiscuous—all these have analogues in antiquity. But as Eva Cantarella shows, in many respects the status of women in pagan antiquity was higher than it was for centuries afterward, and many of the attitudes that still keep women from reaching a status equivalent to that of men derive from the teachings of Christianity. It is also true, and remains so at present, that many women were able to lead happy lives within the confined role society assigned to them; but it is inevitable that we concentrate less on them than on the women who were not content, given that it was the discontented women whose attitudes and actions brought about the changes, for better or for worse, that affected the lives of women in future generations.

MARY R. LEFKOWITZ
Wellesley College

Translator's Note

The English translation of *L'ambiguo malanno* has been prepared from the author's revised version of the first Italian edition (published by Editori Riuniti in 1981), as has the French (to be published as *Filles de Pandore*). This version is not identical with the new Italian edition forthcoming from Editori Riuniti.

Unless otherwise indicated in the notes, the translations from Greek and Latin have been taken from *Women's Life in Greece and Rome* (Baltimore and London, 1982), with additional translations supplied by Mary R. Lefkowitz (Greek) and myself (Latin).

Naturally, some liberties of language must be taken when translating from Italian to English, but the text here is entirely Professor Cantarella's. The notes, however, have been substantially adapted for English-language readers. This work was undertaken by Mary R. Lefkowitz and Paula H. Morgan, with the assistance of Deborah Rae Davies.

I am obliged to Adrienne Mayor for her perceptive and sensitive copyediting.

MAUREEN B. FANT
Rome, February 1985

Preface

In the three years since the publication of the first edition of this book in Italy, investigations into women's life in Greek and Roman antiquity have proliferated to the point of making a simple translation from the Italian impossible. The most recent analyses of the female condition have explored areas that earlier studies, whose purpose was to reconstruct an initial overall picture, had inevitably left in the background. The more recent work has identified new problems and new areas to explore and, above all, refined the methods of investigations.[1] This book, therefore, had to be brought up to date, expanded, and reexamined. In other words, it had to be rethought, in the light of the most recent historiography. It is precisely this that I have tried to do before handing over the text to its foreign publishers.

Some topics have been developed, some points discussed in greater detail, some positions more fully documented. In doing this I have kept to the idea that inspired the original Italian version, namely, writing a book for a nonspecialist readership. Consequently, what we might call the more sophisticated problems, doctrinal and methodological debates, open questions or controversies, discussions of opinions different from those expressed in the text—in short, everything that would have interrupted the discussion and made the book more difficult to read—have been dealt with in the notes.

Finally, the title of the book has been changed, but not for reasons of principle. The new title reflects not a change of mind but simply the solution to a linguistic problem. The Italian title, *L'ambiguo malanno,* does not translate well into other languages. It is a translation of an expression used by Euripides in the *Hippolytus*— *kybdelon kakon.* Thus Hippolytus describes the female sex in general. An "ambiguous evil"—which is more or less the literal translation (though the "evil" that the word *malanno* can connote covers a wide spectrum, from nasty to malevolent)—could be misunderstood. The reference is not to the ambiguous evil of being a woman, ambiguous evil though it may be. Indeed, that ambiguity covers exclusion and power (albeit indirect power), marginalization and centrality (depending on the situation), and inferiority (cultural) and strength (sexual).

But in Euripides, the ambiguous evil is not being a woman but woman herself. That is why, to avoid any possible misunderstanding, it seemed wise to give up the Euripidean reference and to choose one from Hesiod. For Hesiod, women are by definition an evil: what else could they be, since they were sent to earth as a punishment for men?

There was once a happy time when women did not exist, but it came to an end when Zeus, angry because Prometheus had stolen fire from the gods, created Pandora, the first woman. He made her like a chaste virgin, full of grace and "cruel passion," but equipped her with a "thieving heart," an "ambiguous nature," full of lies and "tricky speeches"—in short, "a steep trap from which there is no escape." And from Pandora descends "the race, the cursed tribe of women, a terrible scourge installed among mortal men."

Hesiod's vision of women contains no ambiguity.

Eva Cantarella
Paris, May 1984

Pandora's Daughters

Introduction

The Weaving of Discrimination

I t is not only erudite curiosity that brings us to the history of women in Greek and Roman antiquity. The radical changes that have come about in the conditions of women's lives, the recognition of their full capacity to have subjective rights and to exercise them, the achievement of formal equality with men have not yet entirely wiped out the millennia-old web of discriminatory ideology whose origins and causes only history can help us understand and identify.

Observing the life and following the workings of social systems like the Greek and Roman helps to reveal, if not exactly when the division of sexual roles was born, then when this division was codified and theories about it formed and thus when it came to be viewed as not cultural but biological, a difference that was automatically translated as meaning the inferiority of women.

In the life of a society like the Greek *polis* (leaving aside for the moment its antecedents), rigorously determined and utterly inflexible sexual roles were the very condition of survival. It was not, therefore, accidental that it was in the *polis* that the concept of the "natural" difference and inferiority of women was theorized, and that Aristotle, identifying women with "matter" (as opposed to "spirit" and "form"), and consequently excluding them from the *logos,* the domain of "reason," furnished the theoretical justification for public life and private law.[1]

Many centuries had to pass before the "naturalness" of the inferiority of women was questioned. Christianity preached the equality of all men, but also the necessity of the subordination of women, and it even hardened the tones of a misogyny that was already widely present in ancient culture. Certainly, in many ways Christianity helped to modify the concept of marriage, which was linked for the first time with love, but Christian teaching contained a number of contradictions that confirmed the notion of female inferiority and "demonized" woman as a symbol and instrument of temptation and sin.

Although he wrote that there should no longer be "Jew, nor Greek, nor slave, nor free man, nor man, nor woman," Saint Paul elsewhere stated that "woman's head is man . . . man is the image of God, and the mirror of his glory, whereas woman reflects the glory of man." Saint Augustine postulated the existence of a natural order according to which woman was destined to serve man (*Quaestiones in Heptateuchum* 15), and Tertullian preached that woman was the "gate of the devil" (*De cultu foeminarum* 1.1).

Nor did the situation improve after the fall of the Roman Empire. The female condition in the barbarian kingdoms was one of total subjection. In A.D. 643, Lombard law codified the right of the males of a family to force a woman to marry, to accuse her of witchcraft, and to kill her if she should marry a slave (*Edict of Rotarit* 195, 197, and 221). In the Middle Ages, the need for an extended family group composed not only of parents and children but of grandparents, aunts and uncles, grandchildren, in-laws, and cousins, furnished with arms and holding offices within the group (whose power was not only private but also political and military), led to ever-stronger discrimination against women. Considered solely in her reproductive role, a woman was compelled to marry and pass from her father's family to her husband's, carrying with her a dowry that usually became the property of the husband's family. In the new family she was subject to the *ius corrigendi* of the husband, the right of corporal punishment. The situation was no better if she did not marry, because her only alternative was the convent.

The first agitations for reform, albeit at the theoretical level, began only toward the end of the seventeenth century. John Locke in England, Jean Jacques Rousseau in France, and Cesare Beccaria in Italy, though from different points of view, criticized the concept of society as a union of families rather than as a "union of men" (Beccaria, *Dei delitti e delle pene,* par. 39), and denounced the individual costs of a concept of that sort.

But not even the disappearance of the old medieval family liberated women, although the notion of her inferiority began to be questioned. Thomas Hobbes, in the seventeenth century, denied that there were differences "of strength and prudence" between men and women that would inevitably lead to male supremacy, using an example that should have proved that not all women could be subjugated, the Amazons, female warriors who according to legend lived in the furthest reaches of Anatolia, that is to say, at the edge of the known world.[2]

In the next century, social situations began to be discovered (and not only in mythology) in which the position of women seemed to be genuinely different from that of European women. J. T. Lafitau, the missionary, explorer, and ethnologist, published the results of his studies on the Iroquois Indians in 1724, and reported that in these tribes (where women had a very important role in both family and society), the original rule was the matrilineal. He compared his findings with certain statements of Herodotus and managed to conclude that the Iroquois were descended from the Lycians, who had had to abandon their land (present-day Turkey) following the chain of migrations caused by the expulsion of the Jews from Canaan.[3]

Nevertheless, the eighteenth century was far from benevolent toward women. It was in that century that the *médecins philosophes*, physicians who practiced medicine as a science able to explain man in his "physical" and "moral" entirety, proposed yet again in naturalistic terms the argument of the "difference" of women, with their "weaker nerve bundles" and "more abundant cellular tissue" because of the "uterus and the ovaries," as the most famous of these, Cabanis, wrote. And from these physical differences (maintaining that man was explicable in his entirety by anatomy), Cabanis deduced the existence of the "moral" difference of women, meaning by "moral" everything to do with the sphere of sensibility and consciousness. Because of the weakness and the richness of their cellular tissue, he maintained, women are not self-sufficient but always need to find protection, to be pleasing to others: "from this their capacity for dissimulation, their good manners, their caresses, in other words, their coquetry."[4]

It was only in the 1800s that the situation began to change. The ethnological explorers continued to signal the existence of societies where women had a determining role. It was discovered among the Baronda in Africa, for example, that the husband moved to the wife's village at marriage. In case of separation, the children remained with the mother. Moreover, women sat next to men in the tribal council.[5]

What is most interesting is that in those years the notion of a "female power" was not only conceivable in the context of a primitive people, but was seen as a stage of historical development through which all peoples had to pass, even the Greeks and Romans.

In 1861, the Swiss historian J. J. Bachofen stated this thesis in the famous *Das Mutterrecht,* and in the years to follow some anthropological research seemed to confirm it.[6] In 1865, J. F. McLennan, in turn, asserted the existence of a matrilineal organization.[7] In 1877, L. H. Morgan published *Ancient Society,* in which he compared the organization of the Iroquois and the gentile organization of the Greeks and Romans. Morgan formulated a hypothesis according to which all societies passed from the original phase of the *orda promiscua* to the higher phase of the *familia monogamica,* by means of a stage characterized by a matrilineal family.[8]

Although the anthropologists were talking about matrilineal descent and not about matriarchy, Bachofen's thesis seemed to be confirmed. It was taken up some years later by Friedrich Engels who, in the preface to the fourth edition of *The Origin of the Family, Private Property and the State,* cited Bachofen's interpretation of the *Oresteia* of Aeschylus as a description of the struggle between matriarchal and patriarchal law and the victory of the second over the first.[9]

The "historicization" of the concept of family was now complete and with it the "historicization" of the female condition. And if the matriarchal hypotheses have subsequently revealed their fragility in the face of tougher historical investigations and new data, this detracts nothing from the merits of those who questioned the hegemony of a model, revealing its "cultural" nature and thus admitting the possibility of other, different ones.

Problems of Method

The pages that follow do not claim to reconstruct the entire history of the women of Greek and Roman antiquity, but only to treat certain moments and aspects of this history. To write the history of women is not easy, because traditional historiography, always alert to politics, events, dates, and great personalities, has erased their passage, keeping at most the records of some characters whose lives were as exceptional as the mere fact that they entered into history. It is difficult, in other words, to reconstruct the life of the Greek or Roman woman who remained anonymous. Historians of different periods have access to precious documents. For the seventeenth and eighteenth centuries, for example, there are parochial records which, with tens of thousands of cases registered, have allowed the demographic history of the women of that epoch to be written, to know at what age they married, how many pregnancies were carried to term and how they were spaced, what the differences were between the conditions of the life of the woman of the bourgeoisie and the woman of the proletariat.[10] But the historian of antiquity has very few documents of this sort. With the exception of the historian of Greco-Roman Egypt, who can take advantage of a huge quantity of such documents as marriage contracts, wills, inheritance transactions of various types, or transcriptions of trials, the student of classical antiquity must deduce information from sources that are largely nonobjective. The narrator of the events of the epoch (whether real or imagined) inevitably transfers his own values to his account, his feelings, his "ideology": in some way, however much he tries to be objective, he interprets the facts. If it is true that the burden of the ideology on the female condition is such that there can be no history of women that is not at the same time the history of mental representations, it is also true that it is necessary to be able to distinguish these representations from reality; that it is necessary, whenever possible, to reconstruct the real conditions of women's life on the basis of documents that tell the facts as they are and not as they have been interpreted.

Recent studies of women's lives in antiquity have identified funerary inscriptions as a research area of particular interest. New work in this area has opened up avenues that allow better integration and evaluation of the literary sources.[11] Most important, they allow us to peer into the daily lives of unknown women, those women whom the other sources have stricken from the record.[12]

Another kind of source can make a fundamental contribution to the reconstruction of women's lives—the legal sources. Laws furnish objective and neutral indications of the lives of all women. Even when a discrepancy exists between the formal legal regulation and reality, that discrepancy can only be measured by first analyzing the rules of law. Custom may be more or less rigid than law. Depending on the case, custom can give women liberty and autonomy in reality greater or less than what is formally recognized; in other words, law can be more or less advanced than custom.[13]

How, then, do we assess the dimensions and the nature of the discrepancy? As often happens, the complexity of the facts offers no one single answer. The distance between law and custom can vary, even at the same time and place, according to the type of laws considered. Everyday family relations, for example, are more easily detachable from the abstract rigor of law than could be the case with public law.[14] The distance from the law, furthermore, can vary according to the social status of women, to which behavior it refers, and so on.

It is, however, a fact that law and custom are complementary. Only by examining them together and understanding how they interact can we obtain a picture of the female condition that is not abstract, schematic, and finally misleading. It is with this premise in mind that we will seek to evaluate the available legal information.

The rules of law, in their abstraction and generality, allow reconstruction of the conditions of all the women who have passed through history without entering it. And the lives of these women, or rather the "moments" of their story that we will try to reconstruct, may suggest reasons for their subjugation, the forms it took, and the theoretical constructions that justified it, under the rationale of being "natural" and inevitable, a rationale whose consequences are felt long after Greek and Roman times.

GREECE

One

Matriarchy in Prehistory, Myth, and History

The Neolithic Period

There was once a time in the history of humanity when houses were wooden huts, when weapons were slings and musical instruments pipes, when people began to ply rivers and lakes in dugouts, and when, according to an opinion widely held during the last century, institutions were dominated by women: in other words, when there was a matriarchy.[1]

Chronologically this phase would have coincided with a fundamental change in the condition of human life, the transition from nomadic to sedentary life and the introduction of agriculture, which took place in Asia about 12,000 years before the birth of Christ. Before then, it is said, men hunted and women gathered nuts, fruits, and roots, which supplemented but could not replace the food provided by men.

The life of these groups has been much discussed. According to some, their existence was difficult and precarious because of the constant need to move often without warning and the difficulty of obtaining food. Planning their future, even for the short term, would have been impossible. According to others, however, the Paleolithic Age was characterized not by scarcity but by abundance of resources. Food was easy to find, and there would have been plenty of time for rest. The wealth accumulated by more work would have been both useless (for people with no sense of possession) and troublesome (because it would have been difficult to transport). Only at the beginning of the Oligocene epoch, perhaps, might scarcity of wild game have led to a deterioration in the conditions of life. In any case, a change occurred at some point. In certain particularly favorable (largely for climatic reasons) areas of Asia, the bands of hunters and gatherers began to settle and cultivate the land around their settlements, creating the first village organizations. At that point the male-female relationship, which till that moment had been one of male dominance, slowly began to change.

The women, aided by their children (while the men continued to hunt), concentrated on agriculture and acquired competence and specializations that men did not. They became the principal suppliers of food, and, as they refined their agricultural and related skills, for example (for preserving the products of the fields) and weaving (which permitted garments obtained from animals to be replaced by ones obtained from vegetable fibers), they gained power.

Social and religious institutions reflected the change by leaning toward matriarchy. Fertility rites took on a central role in religion— for example, the *hieros gamos,* the sacred union of the goddess and her *paredros* (consort) in the bare earth where the plow had dug a furrow. Those are the rites that seem to be attested in Greek mythology by the unions of Zeus and Hera and Demeter and Iasion, and of which traces remain in the classical period in the Eleusinian mysteries. The female divinities began to take the upper hand, anticipating the cult of the Mother Goddess, the Potnia, who was to become the preeminent divinity in Mediterranean religion. Women became the exclusive receivers of mysterious powers, which they exercised by using "philtres" obtained from herbs: they became sorceresses exemplified by Circe, Medea, and Helen. The world saw a period, according to this theory, when power belonged to women.

The further development of agricultural techniques, the hypothesis continues, led to more changes in the relationship between the sexes. Cultivation became intensive—the spade replaced the hoe—

and the increasingly urgent need for irrigation and drainage led to a need for labor, especially male labor. The development of agriculture brought with it the development of trade, which in turn brought the need for protective buildings for the villages, which were increasingly exposed to raids by nomad tribes. The new wealth, then, brought conflict and agricultural villages found they needed leaders able to defend them militarily, which meant male leaders. Groups of relatives and followers soon formed around these leaders and enjoyed the benefits of being near the source of power. They were privileged groups with every interest in institutionalizing and consolidating the power of the leader. The democracy that had characterized the life of the matriarchal protoagricultural villages gave way to an unequal society in which women gradually lost their power. At least this is what is maintained by those who believe in the historicity of the matriarchy.

Flourishing in Asia between about 12,000 and 6,000 B.C., the matriarchy would thus have been a social organization characteristic of the Neolithic period. But humans arrived at the Neolithic period at different times in different parts of the world. In Europe, in particular (where in the fourth millennium there were still groups of Mesolithic hunters and fishermen, and where, in the Mediterranean region, Neolithic culture spread by sea from centers of diffusion most probably identifiable with Syria and Cilicia), the protoagricultural civilization can be placed in the fifth to fourth millennium: it has left traces in Cyprus, Crete, Phocis, Thessaly, the Argolid, Boeotia, Sicily, and Puglia, on the Adriatic coast of southern Italy.[2]

Social and religious institutions would have been characterized by female power at very different times and places. In the Mediterranean in particular, female power would have continued past the end of the Neolithic to the Bronze Age and the threshold of the so-called Hellenic Middle Ages (that is, Minoan and Mycenaean culture). It would have left traces even in the societies described in the Homeric epics.

At this point we should try to define what exactly is meant by the term *matriarchy*. Those who have spoken and continue to speak about the matriarchy attribute very different meanings to the word, depending on the case. One etymologically faithful definition is "female power," meaning not only power in the family but also political power, as in the Greek word *arche*. A second meaning, less exact but more widespread, is matrilineal law or society, that is, a society characterized by a predominance of women within the family, in which marriage is matrilocal (the husband goes to the wife's house), descent is according to the female line, and rights of succession belong to the women, but in which the political power can be, and usually is, in the hands of the men. A third, more generic meaning describes a society in which women have a position of importance in religion and society.

Clearly, the answer to the question Did the matriarchy exist? will vary according to how the term is used. When "female political power" is meant (as in nineteenth-century literature), the answer has to be No. In other words, no proof of the historical existence of that sort of matriarchy exists among ancient peoples or among modern tribal organizations.

If by matriarchy is meant "maternal law," then the answer can be different. Among certain "primitive" peoples, the existence of a "maternal law" in antiquity cannot be ruled out. Finally, if what is meant is a society characterized by a strong female presence in society and religion, the answer can be Yes, both for "primitive" peoples and for the ancient Mediterranean societies.[3]

Minoan Society: The Mediterranean Great Mother

In the Mediterranean, before the arrival of the European peoples of the Helladic group, a cult of a female divinity—mother and creatrix—was consolidated. In Minoan representations, her image appears flanked by two rampant animals or holding two serpents in her raised hands, or on a sacred boat. She was a goddess of land and sea, it can thus be presumed, an omnipotent mistress (*potnia*), symbol of the female generative force, the Mediterranean great mother. In this religion her consort, the *paredros*, would be a completely passive figure whose only function was that of satisfying her sexual needs. On these few facts alone (apart from the questionable interpretations of certain myths, to which we shall return) are based the hypotheses of those who maintain the existence of a matriarchal period in the Mediterranean, specifically in Crete, during the Minoan age (from the third millennium B.C.).[4]

But a dominant female in religion did not necessarily mean general female power; moreover, some of the greatest scholars of the history of religion have suggested that the Potnia had male divinities at her side. Even if she was the only divinity, the most this can mean is that women enjoyed an elevated social position. This theory is based on a number of facts. In the first place, in Minoan religion women fulfilled the socially privileged function of priestess. In the second place, as frescoes and iconography show, women attended public performances and participated in hunts. Third, in the palaces the area reserved for women was not segregated (as would be the case in Greek houses) but was in direct contact with the other parts of the house-fortress. This is a clear sign of a female freedom that was lost in later ages. Yet this is as far as we can go—it is very difficult to prove (as has often been attempted) that hereditary succession was matrilineal.[5] Traces of female-line descent are found in the law of Cretan cities, such as Gortyn, but as the laws of these cities are much later than the Minoan period it is not possible to say whether they represent a holdover from a more ancient female descent or new rights for women.

There is no proof that a Minoan matriarchy ever existed. Nor can it be said (though there is no proof to the contrary) that descent was matrilineal. Nevertheless, there are indications of a notable freedom, a certain dignity, and on the whole an elevated social position for women in Minoan times.[6]

The Mycenaean Kingdoms

The reading of the documents written with the syllabic characters known as Linear B (deciphered in 1952 by Michael Ventris, who proved that the language was a form of Greek) allowed reconstruction of the life of the Mycenaean kingdoms (named for the most powerful of them) of the first Greek populations on both Crete and the mainland in the second half of the second millennium B.C.[7]

Mycenaean society, as it emerges from the documents and archaeological and iconographical evidence, was quite different from Minoan. First of all, Mycenaean religion worshipped numerous male gods, such as Zeus, Poseidon, Ares, Hermes, and Dionysus, as well as female deities. Although the iconography still documents a large female presence in public life, the architectural remains indicate that the areas of the palaces reserved for the women were more separate from the rest of the building complex than on Crete. The tablets record, moreover, the existence of salaried female workers and, at Mycenae, female tasks and male tasks. The men (besides holding all positions of command) did the work of sheep rearing and artisanship and they managed the female labor groups. Women handled, stored, and distributed cereals; they were employed in ancillary jobs; and their only artisanal jobs were those related to making cloth. Hence, in the organization of female labor at Mycenae, we can identify certain characteristics of female labor that were to remain constant in later Greek society.[8]

The complicated system of land concession generally excluded women. The few women who did manage to own (sometimes vast) parcels of land were priestesses, from whose privileged status it is impossible to draw general conclusions.

Given the present state of our knowledge of Mycenae, we can conclude that Mycenaean society (the earliest Greek society we know) assigned women a different place than did the Minoan. The strong presence of male divinities indicates a reduction of the female role, as might be expected given the society's military organization. Even if they were freer than Greek women of later epochs, the women of Mycenae began to correspond to the model to which we find them perfectly adapted in the Hellenic Middle Ages.

Myths of Matriarchy: Amazons and the Lemnian Women

Proponents of the matriarchy theory have often based (or at least supported) their arguments on certain myths that are supposed to represent the memory of situations in which power, including political, was in the hands of women. The most important of these myths are those of the Amazons and the Lemnian women.

The Amazons were a warrior people whose only men were slaves. They conceived their children with strangers and killed boys at birth or, according to another tradition, blinded them. So that their daughters might handle the bow and spear without impediment, they cut off one breast—whence their name, *a-mazon,* without breast.

The Lemnian women once had husbands, but, punished for an offense against Aphrodite with a foul odor (*dysosmia*), they had been deserted by their men for Thracian slave girls. In revenge, the Lemnian women cut the throats of every man on the island, and from that moment Lemnos was a community of women alone. They were governed by the virgin Hypsipyle, until one day Jason and the *Argo* landed and that was the end of female power. The Argonauts married the Lemnian women (the foul odor disappeared the moment they welcomed the men) and Jason married Hypsipyle. From that time a festival acting out the events was periodically held on Lemnos.

Both the Amazons and the Lemnians were cruel women, and the Lemnians were savages who devoured "raw flesh." Both the Amazons and the Lemnians, furthermore, were communities of women only—in neither story do women rule over a normal society, which would be a requirement of matriarchy. Moreover, the rule of the Lemnians took place at a time that was, as it were, pathological for the group, and as such destined to disappear at the first chance to return to normality (that is, with the appearance of men).

Rather than representing a moment of matriarchal power, these myths seem intended to exorcise the possibility of female power. Modern interpretations have been very different from those of the nineteenth century, which used the myths for historical reconstruction. The myth of the Amazons has been read as a monstrous representation by the Greeks of a barbarian and savage world, the opposite of "culture": it is therefore no accident that it should be made up solely of women.[9] The rite in which the myth of the Lemnian women was represented has been interpreted as a "cathartic" release of tension between the sexes, which would have had the function of preventing this tension from becoming a true conflict.[10] It is not without significance, moreover, that the women of Lemnos had a foul odor. Even during the festival of the Thesmophoria in the high classical period in Athens, when the women were temporarily separated from the men, they were said to have eaten garlic. But at Lemnos, where the separation (at least in intention) was to be definitive, their odor was nauseating. There are other myths that signal the unnaturalness of separation from men; for example, the myth of the daughters of Proetos, who refused to take husbands even though they were sought as wives by all the Greeks. For having thought so little of Hera (the patron goddess of marriage) and Dionysus (the initiator god) they were afflicted with an illness that made them lose their hair and their skin to become covered with white spots. A foul odor or other repulsive illness was, in other words, the regular punishment for refusing men, indicating the pathological and negative aspect of such behavior.[11]

Interpreting Myth: Forgotten History or Unthinkable World?

Myths, of course, are susceptible to many interpretations. The polemic on the meaning of myths and the way they should be studied has been going on for centuries. Bernard Le Bovier de Fontenelle (who published in 1686 the *Histoire des oracles* in which he maintained that pagan oracles expressed not the will of the gods but that of those in power), in a work called *De l'Origine des Fables* (1724), confronted the problem of considering myth as one of the "errors of the ancients." From the similarity between the South American Indian belief that the souls of the dead went to certain lakes and the Greek belief that they went to the banks of the Styx and the Acheron rivers, he intuited the importance of the comparative study of myth. This idea was suggested during the same period by Lafitau.

Giovanbattista Vico, in the *Scienza Nuova,* had insisted on the historical credibility of myth as the "mirror of history." As such, myths were indispensable for understanding the past. Voltaire, however, had written in the *Essay on Manners* (1756) that in order to understand pagan civilization it was not necessary to study myths, "absurd fables which continue to infect the youth," but rather contemporary "savage" societies. The polemic was continued into the nineteenth century, when Max Müller pointed to the path that J. G. Frazer would follow. Frazer, observing the myths of peoples still capable of creating them, maintained that it was possible to explain a Greek myth, for example, in terms of a Polynesian one.

Today the prevalent approach is the "structural" method, according to which mythology is a "tradition consisting of an ensemble of tales that have more affinity with one another than with any other discourse or form of thought with which they were able to associate tricks of chronology or casualness of information."[12] In other words, the myth is autonomous and its relation to reality (natural or social as the case may be) is not direct and immediate but mediated to such a point (and this is our problem) that it can represent institutions that are the *opposite* of the real ones. This means that even if a myth is sometimes connected to a historical event, it reworks this event and reinscribes it in different structures. The matriarchal myths, if this is true, could mean exactly the opposite of what the nineteenth-century scholars held them to mean and what some feminist literature still tends to attribute to them. Such myths may well describe a world turned upside down, a world so different from the real one as to be unthinkable. And certain myths of the origins of cities seem to confirm this interpretation.

Women and the Origin of Cities

The origin of many Greek cities of Italy is linked in the mythological account to women. Caulonia was supposed to have been founded by Caulon, son of the Amazon Cleta, who, on her way to Troy to attend the burial of Penthesilea (who had been killed by Achilles) was caught in a storm and washed up on the shores of Italy. And Caulonia is one of the places where nineteenth-century scholarship thought it saw a matriarchy. Tarentum was founded by helots who, during the war between Sparta and Messenia, married free Spartan women and were driven out at the end of the war. Epizephyrian Locris was founded by slaves from Locris in Greece, who, while their masters fought at the side the the Spartans, had relations with the women of Sparta. It is notable that women and slaves are featured in the origins of certain cities.[13]

Nothing could be more unthinkable for a Greek than a slave with power. "Naturally" different from the free man, and thus an *object* rather than a *subject* of law, the slave could not ever have any power. The association between slaves and women in these myths is therefore very significant. Women too were excluded from every sort of participation in the life of the city, this "men's club," as the *polis* has been called. The myths that represent situations in which power rests with women and slaves, therefore, refer to reality, but power, by definition, belongs only to men.[14]

Female Initiation Ceremonies

So-called primitive societies have rites that mark an individual's entrance into the group and determine his or her position within it. Rigorously regulated by the groups to which the initiate is being admitted, these rites are celebrated according to customary rules, known only by the members of the group. The rites represent an essential moment in the life of the individual, the moment that symbolizes and brings about access to the knowledge of the collectivity, the awareness of being part of it, and the corresponding certainty that whoever is not a part of it is different.

When the rites are for initiation into a political group, consequently, they are a symbol of access to power. Their importance for our purposes is evident. Given that even the Greeks, as "primitives," celebrated "initiation," the participation or exclusion of women is an unmistakable indicator of the female condition and clearly demonstrates the exclusion of women from Greek public life and their relegation to the role of reproducers.

Although there were initiation ceremonies for women in Greece, they were separate and different from the men's. The reason is clear. The initiation ritual served to signal the place that the individual occupied in the community and to "transform" him or her according to the role that the community offered or, rather, required. The place and role of women obviously differed from the place and the role of men. Let us discover what these initiations rites entailed.

In the Doric areas (especially Sparta), unlike in the Attic areas, initiation rites survived well into the classical period. The initiatory nature of Spartan education is abundantly clear. Beginning at age seven, young Spartan boys were introduced into groups of their contemporaries and by means of a series of experiences and rites eventually became *omoioi* (equals)—full citizens destined to rule over those who were not, namely, the *perioikoi* and the helots.

At age seven, boys were taken from their families and put in a "flock" (*ageia*). After their heads had been shaved, they were prepared for the harshnesses of life. At age twelve they entered a new, more difficult phase. Provided with a single garment, the same for all seasons, they slept on a straw pallet that they made themselves. At twenty, they became *eirenes* and supervised the younger boys.

After a homosexual experience (all the boys were at a certain point chosen as *eromenoi* by adult *erastai*; see chapter 6) and having learned to survive in any circumstances (their provisions were limited to force them to steal, and if they were caught they were punished for their ineptitude), the young Spartans were capable of being what they had been trained to be—warriors.[15]

Female initiation rites also existed at Sparta. Their rites were based on the male ones, but differed in a very important way. Not even at Sparta could women participate in the governing of the city. Though compared with other Greek women Spartan women were freer and better trained physically, they still had only one function, that of producing sons for the city. It is no accident that the girls passed through only two principal groups, those of *parthenoi* (virgins) and married women. For the male, the achievement of citizenship was marked by a series of stages; for the woman, the end state was marriage, and only one stage preceded it—virginity.

Young Spartan girls were placed under the protection of Artemis, the virgin goddess. When they reached a certain age (presumably puberty) they passed to the protection of another goddess, Helen, to whom was entrusted the task of making them into women in her image. The passage from the protection of Artemis to that of Helen coincided with the celebration of an initiation rite which by means of a period of segregation, disorder, and reversal of the sex roles signified their entry into the world of adult, marriageable women.[16] The Spartan female initiations were probably not very different in substance from the Athenian, which we are able to reconstruct in greater detail thanks to the testimony of the chorus of Athenian women in Aristophanes' *Lysistrata*. The women thank the *polis* for their education and relate its stages.

> When I was just seven, I was *arrephoros*,
> then at ten, I was *aletris* for the *archegetis*
> then I carried the orange robe as *arkios* (bear) at Brauronia
> and finally, having become a beautiful girl,
> I was *kanephoros*, with a necklace of dried figs.[17]

The verses describe certain religious ceremonies which, at the end of the fifth century B.C. when Aristophanes was writing, were entrusted to the girls. The *arrhephoroi* were four virgins, chosen from the noblest families of the city, charged with weaving the *peplos* for Athena. The *aletrides* ground the grain for the sacred bread for the goddess. The "bears" were the priestesses who celebrated a rite intended to expiate an offense against Artemis. Once upon a time a she-bear who had sought refuge in the temple of the goddess was killed. The angry goddess sent a famine, and an oracle ordered the sacrifice of a girl as propitiation. That sacrifice was recalled by the bear-priestesses. The *kanephorai* were the girls who carried the baskets containing the offerings at the Panathenaic festival.

Even if the passage in Aristophanes refers to the era in which it was written, it is not difficult to see behind it the basic lines of an ancient initiation system in which all the girls, as they reach puberty, pass through four steps characterized by particular symbolic rites and functions. Taking the information given by Aristophanes together with other sources, it is possible to identify some of these rites.

During the first stage the *arrhephoroi* were secluded for a certain time on the Acropolis where, dressed in white, they performed the typical female art of weaving. The second level of initiation, also segregated, provided for the learning of the basic female function of baking bread. The third step was characterized not only by the usual period of segregation but also by a symbolic death and resurrection, typical of many primitive initiations. The girl passed through a symbolic death, and after participating in an orgiastic festival, was finally ready to enter the ranks of adult women. She was readmitted to the community wearing new insignia.[18]

When in history were these rites performed? Attica was first inhabited in the Neolithic period, when it was the site of a Mycenaean settlement. It is very difficult to establish which period contained the roots of what Aristophanes described, but we may say that however far back in the history of Attica it is possible to take these rites, women never had a dominant role. The place that the collectivity assigned them, as seen in the initiation rites, was not very different from the place they held during the historical period; that is, as weavers and bakers and organizers of family life, sent off at a tender age to begin to learn their functions as wives and mothers.

Conclusions

Minoan society certainly afforded women an elevated position. It was a society whose religion recognized female divinities and assigned women priestly functions; it was a society in which women participated in social life. But there is no proof of the existence of a matriarchy in the etymological sense. There are no clear traces of female political power or "matrilineal descent." If it is true that some evidence might be made to support the latter, it is also true that this evidence is very problematic. Minoan "maternal law" cannot be ruled out, nor can it be proved.

Superimposing itself on a pre-Greek people, the Mycenaean society, though it perpetuated certain Minoan elements, introduced many new and different ones. To the cult of the Potnia it added male gods; women were excluded (if they had ever been admitted) from the administration of property (at least at the mass level).

Although they were still free in their movements and not entirely shut out of religious and social functions, Mycenaean women lived in a transitional situation. Women's status, as the military nature of the society rose, began to decline. The Greek society that emerged from the collapse of the Mycenaean palaces eliminated the dual value system and followed a path which is traced in the next chapter.

Two

Origins of Western Misogyny

The Homeric Poems

THE HOMERIC WOMAN

The first documents that describe in detail the life conditions of Greek women are the Homeric poems. Here we will consider them as "historical" documents, whether or not the events narrated really happened or the characters really lived, or whether or not the Trojan War was really fought. Their historicity, of course, has proponents on both sides; some have even attempted to pinpoint the war in time and space, and others (such as M. I. Finley) maintain that the events are poetic invention. But for our purposes, the question is irrelevant—the poems do not interest us as a record of events, but as a document that transmits the memory of a culture.

At least until the eighth century B.C., Greek culture was preliterate, which is to say it was transmitted orally, not by written documents. The Mycenaeans had a form of writing (Linear B) but they used it only for administrative purposes—registering the operations of their complex bureaucratic organization, troop movements, organization of labor on public utilities, concession of land to private citizens, and so forth—not for the transmission of the society's cultural heritage, history, and values. Mycenaean civilization, then, was essentially an oral civilization, and because Mycenaean script disappeared with the collapse of the palaces, the civilization that emerged from their ruins and solidified in the centuries to follow was also oral. At least until the eighth century, when the Greeks began to use a new alphabetic script borrowed from the Phoenicians, the memory of the Greeks, the record of the deeds of their ancestors, the spread and transmission across the generations of models of behavior and of social and religious rules, was entrusted to poetry.[1]

For all the centuries of the so-called Hellenic Middle Ages, the *aidoi* and *rhapsodoi,* singing the deeds of their ancestors, fulfilled not only a recreational function but an important pedagogical one as well. They taught the Greeks what to feel and think, what they should be, and how they should behave. As men learned from the *epos* to adapt themselves to the model of the hero, so women listening to the poets learned what sort of behavior they should adopt and what they should avoid.[2] It is in this sense that the *Iliad* and the *Odyssey* are considered historical documents.

Even if the situations described are not true, they must be realistic. The characters surely behave according to the rules of real society; the ethic that inspired their deeds must be that which the poetry, almost institutionally, taught and transmitted. The society described in the *Iliad* and the *Odyssey* is, in other words, a mirror of Greek society in the centuries between the end of Mycenaean civilization and the eighth century—and the female condition which they suggest is the true condition of the women who lived in those centuries.

According to current thinking, the Homeric woman enjoyed a respect and freedom that the Greek woman of the classical period (segregated, disparaged, and without rights) did not. At the end of the last century, Samuel Butler, an English translator of Homer, proposed that the attention paid to feminine themes and the depth of psychological analysis of the characters in the *Odyssey* was such as to suggest that it had been written by a woman. He went so far as to identify the author as a noblewoman of Trapani, Sicily, who would have been autobiographically described in the character of Nausicaa.[3] One need not go quite that far to notice the periodic reappearance in literature of the notion of an *Odyssey* dominated by female figures in high relief, who might be taken as indicative of the consideration in which the Homeric woman was held. One is tempted to compare, for example, Athena, the goddess who protects Odysseus and Telemachus in their plan to regain power, to the figure of Beatrice in the *Divine Comedy*,[4] or to suggest that in the Bronze Age communities existed in which regal power was entrusted to a woman, in which marriage was matrilocal and descent matrilineal.[5] To examine this hypothesis we will compare the situations described in the poems and the "values" they transmit, with reflections, on the one hand, of the virtues or qualities women ought to have, and on the other, of the rules of behavior that the members of the Homeric family, and in particular the women, ought to follow.

THE MODEL AND THE SUPPOSED REALITY

First of all, a woman had to be beautiful. Homer lingers over this attribute when he presents a female character: her beauty makes her like a goddess.[6] When she is as beautiful as Helen, she can be forgiven anything. Speaking of Helen, the old Trojans seated by the Scian Gates watching the battle say the following lines:

> No one could find fault with the Trojans or well-greaved Achaeans
> for enduring sorrow for so long a time for the sake of a woman like
>   Helen
> —she looks dreadfully like the immortal goddesses.
>
> (*Il.* 3.156–58)

Moreover, women had to take care of their looks and worry about their clothes; these are the qualities with which a woman conquered "glorious fame" (*Od.* 6.25–30). She had also to excel in domestic jobs, and above all be obedient.

> "Mother . . . , go inside the house and tend to your own work,
> the loom and the distaff, and order your women to attend
> to their work; the bow is the concern of men, and to me
> most of all, since the authority in the house belongs to me."
>
> (*Od.* 21.350–53)

So says Telemachus to his mother Penelope, and Penelope obeys. Even Andromache, one of the characters frequently cited to illustrate ancient female power, is no less under the thumb of her husband than Penelope is under that of her son in the absence of Odysseus.[7] It is true that in the relations between Hector and Andromache, the relationship between spouses that emerges differs from the normal relationship of a hero and his woman. Their more human relationship is certainly unusual in the poems.[8] But, as Hector reminds his wife with the same words Telemachus uses to his mother, Andromache's place is still the house, her work is only domestic work, and it is unseemly for her even to think about things that are reserved for men, such as war (*Il.* 6.490–93).

Rigorous respect for the division of roles and obedience, then, are the virtues one expects from a woman, together with modesty and fidelity—all the typical virtues of a subordinate woman. Perhaps we can go further. The Homeric woman is not only subordinate but also victim of a fundamentally misogynist ideology. Behind the screen of paternal affection, already fragile enough, the Homeric hero mistrusts women, even the most devoted and submissive of them.

Odysseus waits till he has killed the suitors before he reveals himself to his wife, although he had made himself known to Telemachus, Euryclea, and Eumaeus.

> For this reason do not ever be too kind to your wife
> or tell her the whole of your plan, however well you know it,
> but tell her part of it, and leave the rest hidden.
>
> (*Od.* 11.441–43)

This is what Agamemnon had advised Odysseus in the underworld. Agamemnon (having been killed by his wife Clytemnestra) had good reason to think that way, but was now generalizing from his personal experience:

> But I shall tell you something else, and you take it to heart
> Bring your ship back to your homeland secretly,
> not openly, since women can never be trusted.
>
> (*Od.* 11.454–56)

Not even Penelope, whom even Agamemnon praises for her fidelity, is above suspicion. Athena counsels Telemachus, who is at Sparta seeking news of his father, to go home at once. Penelope's father and the suitors insist, in fact, that she choose a husband. But the reason for the haste is not, as one might think, that his mother needs help in averting a marriage. The danger is something else.

> Do not let her take treasure from your house against your wishes
> Since you know what sort of instincts lie in the hearts of women.
> A woman wishes to increase the household of the man who wins her,
> and no longer remembers the children of her old marriage
> or her first husband, now dead, nor does she ask about them.
> But go yourself, and entrust everything
> to the maidservant who seems to you most trustworthy,
> until the gods show you a noble bride of your own.
>
> (*Od.* 15.19–26)

Weak, fickle, opportunistic, perhaps even incapable of lasting feelings, she was destined for marriage. Her interests, her emotions, are bound up in this destiny. That is what woman is, and it should not be surprising as she was taught to put marriage above everything else. But women, of course, have no sense of proportion. Even the best of them, even those who make good use of their training, can be dangerous. It is likely that they will go overboard and, if married more than once, they forget the dead husband, the children of the first bed, everything of their previous life. In any case, they need to be kept under control.

The admired, respected, powerful female figures often mentioned are, in fact, quite difficult to pin down. The virtues women were supposed to have were not ones that would make protagonists of them. Quite the reverse: their qualities had to be utilized exclusively within the limited circles of their attributions and their role, never venturing into the world outside. Only one female figure has a different role—Athena, the goddess who advises Odysseus and Telemachus in typically masculine matters, which are those related to power. It is significant that Athena is the goddess born from the head of Zeus, the *parthenos,* the virgin who by refusing marriage never assumes a female role. The only woman who has a constant influence and who is recognized as a counselor and protector is a nonwoman.

The other female characters are either mythical (in this case insidious and dangerous, like Circe and the Sirens)[9] or socially and intellectually pallid, subordinate images, shut out from and in most cases ignorant of the male world. Neither consoler nor counselor, the Homeric woman was only the instrument of reproduction and preservation of the family group.

Though both men and women in Homer were quick to tears, women's tears were quite different from men's. Women's are not violent manifestations of a strong, energetic, heroic character. They are drawn-out, consuming sobs, moans, and useless laments—yet another proof of their impotence.[10] Ideologically relegated to the inside of the *oikos* (despite some freedom of movement), outside of the *oikos* the Homeric woman does not exist. In this light certain very unusual features of Penelope's personality can be explained.

The bride of Odysseus has entered history by virtue of her fidelity, but her behavior casts doubt on her legendary virtue. Exaggerated fidelity, in fact, is only one of her cloaks: more than once she appears quite eager to marry, and above all she behaves with reproachable coquetry. She deceives the suitors for a good four years, making promises to each one (of the 108!) and sending them notes.[11] If she does not decide to remarry, it is because she is afraid of being criticized by the people, who have remained loyal to the memory of Odysseus. Furthermore, doubts about the paternity of Telemachus are expressed more than once and by more than one person. Even Athena, Nestor, and Odysseus are not sure—and Telemachus himself shows some perplexity when interrogated about his parentage. My mother says I am the son of Odysseus, he answers, but "I don't know. No one by himself can know his own seed."[12]

Mater certa, in other words, *pater semper incertus*. But that this principle should be repeated so often, and always with regard to Penelope, is very odd indeed. Perhaps this is simply what men thought of women and not only strangers but also their fathers, husbands, and sons. Penelope's ambiguities are perhaps due to two contradictory facts. On the one hand, there was the need for epic poetry, given its function of cultural training, to propose a model of woman that was the symbol of all the virtues that a woman could have. On the other, there was a misogynist ideology that mistrusted women profoundly.[13] Penelope can be read as the product of these two opposing needs; she is an image of both the "should be" and the "is" (in the eyes of men, of course) of the Homeric woman.

WIFELY DUTIES

That the first duty of a woman was to be faithful to her husband will not be surprising, and *epos* lets us know what happens to adulteresses. First, of course, there was Clytemnestra, the adulteress by antonomasia, but another wife, a goddess this time, also breaks the conjugal bond. This was Aphrodite, as beautiful as her husband Hephaestus was ugly and lame. Zeus, Hephaestus' father, one day lost his temper with him because, during one of the countless fights between himself and Hera, Hephaestus had tried to defend his mother, attempting to pull her away from her husband's blows. And so Zeus grabbed his son by the foot and hurled him down from Olympus. Hephaestus fell all day and finally landed on Lemnos, where he was rescued by the Sintii.

It is no wonder that Aphrodite, so beautiful and adored that all the gods desired her, had an affair with Ares, the god of war. Hephaestus knew of it because the Sun had played the spy. Hephaestus prepared an invisible net as thin as a spider's web and stretched it over the bed where it would trap the lovers. When the lovers were successfully entangled, Hephaestus, the "glorious cripple," called all the gods to witness the adultery. He did not let the adulterers go, but said:

> My trap and chains will hold them there, until
> her father gives me back the whole of the bride-price (*eedna*),
> which I entrusted to him for the sake of his wanton ("dog-faced")
> daughter,
> because his daughter is beautiful, but not faithful in heart.
>
> (*Od.* 8.317–20)

The punishment of the unfaithful wife was repudiation, accompanied by restitution to the husband of the *eedna*, the price he had paid to the wife's guardian, a tangible sign of the woman's new status (socially determined according to the value of the *eedna*), and signal of the husband's power over her.[14] The corporal punishment with which the husband kept the members of his *oikos* in line, including the wife, for offenses other than adultery, does not appear for unfaithful wives. Zeus, for example, was always striking Hera, sometimes even with a whip; he even punished her much more severely, as when he chained and hung her with two weights tied to her feet (*Il.* 15.16–21).

Obviously, this does not mean that Greek husbands made a habit of hanging their wives. The Zeus–Hera relationship is one of particular conflict and violence, which certainly cannot be taken as a model marriage. Yet their marriage presents a picture of conjugal relationships that the public somehow accepted. Evidently the public was used to considering such punishments as a non-pathological aspect of the relationship—in other words, they could laugh at Zeus' excesses, but they were not shocked.

The Homeric wife had to accept more than physical punishment. She had to tolerate her husband's relations with a concubine and other women, such as prisoners of war (who were awarded to heroes as part of their booty) and household slaves. The man's children by these women, though illegitimate (*nothoi*), were not treated differently than the legitimate ones (*gnesioi*), as in the classical law of succession. The *nothoi,* in fact, often lived at the father's house, and at his death shared in the inheritance along with the legitimate children, although their status was lower. Instead of a share of the inheritance (which was divided equally among the legitimate offspring) they received goods of substantial value, such as a house or a female slave: they had, in other words, rights that were different from and less than those of the legitimate children but they were rights nonetheless.

The wife, with all her many duties, did not even have the privilege of ensuring that her children would have exclusive rights to their father's estate. This did not mean that the husband had no duty to them. The hierarchy of women, with the wife in the top position and concubine below, had to be both fully visible from outside and perceptible by the wife in the context of conjugal relations. Nevertheless, the concubine enjoyed a certain prestige, or at least a certain social position. Although it is not technically precise to speak, as has been done, about the Homeric male's polygamy, given that there was only one wife, concubinage was still a recognized bond. But the hierarchy had to be respected. Only his

31

wife could appear socially at the side of the Homeric man, and he could not neglect her for the concubine.[15]

Failure to observe these marital duties, moreover, was not dealt with by concrete and physical punishments like those that guaranteed the wife's observance of her duties. Offenses by the husband against the wife were sanctioned only at the social level. Finally, if the man had duties toward his wife, albeit only social and moral ones, he had none toward his concubine or any of his other women. The prisoners of war, loved and respected in words, in reality were neither more nor less than slaves. And the household slaves, the maidservants, had to be obedient, and perhaps were even expected to show sexual fidelity to the master, who had not only the authority to inflict corporal punishment but also the right of life and death over them. Odysseus, on his return to Ithaca, had twelve maidservants who had been unfaithful to him put to death by hanging.

CONCLUSIONS

Attempts to demonstrate that the poems contain traces of matriarchal organization (such as the statement that the Homeric woman enjoyed certain privileges and a greater social dignity than that enjoyed by the woman of the classical period) seems to be in contrast with the values and rules of heroic behavior.

The fact that there are some references in the poems to female characters endowed with some power does not mean anything. These isolated references are absolutely unreconcilable with the general picture of both family and political organization. The position of women in the Bronze Age was far from privileged: it was a position of immutable subservience to a family head whose powers as husband were limited only by the competing power of the father. In examining the condition of Penelope (the woman who should transmit regal power)[16] we see how fantastic is the image of a Homeric woman who was, if not powerful, at least free. In the first place, Penelope cannot refuse to marry the suitors—it is not for her to decide whether to remarry. It is not really clear to whom this privilege belonged, given that certain passages attribute it to her father, Icarius, and others to her son, Telemachus. But one thing is certain: the decision did not rest with Penelope, who could only, after others had decided that she should marry, choose the suitor she liked best. Telemachus went so far as to say that he did not dare turn his mother out of the house, forcing her to remarry. This shows that he had the power to do so. This is the only consideration he shows for his mother, whom he is constantly reminding that he and he alone is in charge of the house while Odysseus is away.

This, then, is the domestic place of the Homeric women—not only of Penelope but of all the women who appear in the context of a family group.[17]

The situation is different with respect to such figures as Circe and Calypso, "independent" witches and nymphs with magic powers. These characters (the Sirens and malicious fairies) from tales perhaps told for centuries by sailors and eventually collected in the great Homeric poem have been said to embody a memory of vanished female powers.[18] In the poems, however, they are mythical figures for whom it is impossible to construct a historical account. The status of the wives, mothers, sisters, and daughters of the Homeric heroes is, in fact, quite different from that of the nymphs and fairies. The true female condition in Homer was this: total exclusion from political power and participation in public life; subordination to the head of the family and submission to his punishment; and finally, ideological segregation. Forbidden to think about anything but domestic matters, the woman cannot even talk about male matters. Faithless, weak, fickle, she was regarded with suspicion. The roots of Western misogyny go back to a more remote epoch than is usually thought—they are already well fixed in the oldest document in European literature.[19] Nor is it possible that the poems express an individual position, the misogyny of a single poet (or two).

Although the epics represent the confluence of songs that were handed down and reworked for centuries, and the didactic and socializing function of epic poetry requires that the tales both express and, at the same time, contribute to forming public opinion, the distrust of women that the poems express is matched in the literature of the period immediately following. The most important example is the poetry of Hesiod.

33

Hesiod and Semonides

PANDORA

In both the *Theogony* and the *Works and Days* Hesiod (ca. 700 B.C.) tells the story of the creation of the first woman.[20] Angry because Prometheus had stolen fire from the gods, Zeus decided to punish men by sending them misfortune: Pandora, the first woman. Her name meant that every god had given her a gift—beauty, charm, grace, skill in women's work, but also "a bitch's mind and a thieving heart" and "lies and tricky speeches." When Pandora reached earth, everything changed. Before she arrived men lived happily, untouched by troubles and diseases, but from that moment on:

> The other thousand miseries fly around among men. The earth is full of evils, and the sea is full of them. Diseases come to men in the day, and at night uninvited, bringing evils for mortals in silence, since Deviser Zeus took away their voices. So there is no way to escape the mind of Zeus. (WD 100–114)

But what is more interesting in the story of Pandora is the description of her nature. Created from "earth and water,"[21] Pandora was a product of Hephaestus' craftsmanship. She was made "like a chaste virgin," and Athena gave her the ability to seduce.[22]

Thus, Pandora was constructed, this "evil so beautiful" from whom descends the "cursed race, the tribe of women."[23] To bring evil to men, she uses her ability to seduce, which is no small thing. Seduction and beauty constitute enormous power, as described with indisputable grace in a fragment of the *Anacreontica*:

> Her beauty gives her a power to equal any shield or any weapon. A beautiful woman can conquer iron and fire. (*Anac.* 24.9–13)[24]

But the gallantry of this unknown poet is certainly not the norm. Hesiod saw the power of beauty quite differently:

> Don't let a woman with an alluring behind deceive you with her charming lies, while she pokes into your granary. A man who believes women believes cheats. (WD 373–75)

For Hesiod beauty and charm can only be dangerous. The use women make of them (given the reason they were created) is inevitably to do harm to men. To Pandora Aphrodite gave "grace," "cruel passion," and "worries that gnaw at the limbs" (*charis, pothos argaleos,* and *guiokoroi meledonai*), but Hermes gave her "a thieving heart" (*kuneos noos*) and in her heart put "lies" (*pseudea*) and "tricky speeches" (*logoi aimulioi*) (*WD* 59 ff.). Furnished with these gifts, Pandora is inevitably a "terrible scourge" (*pema mega*), a "steep trap from which there is no escape" (*Th.* 592 and *WD* 83).

WOMEN AND ANIMALS

Like Hesiod, Semonides (seventh century B.C.) holds that women (or at least some women) were made from earth and water.

> Another [woman] the Olympians moulded out of earth, a stunted creature; you see, a woman like her knows nothing, bad or good. The only work she understands is eating; and not even when the god makes cruel winter weather does she feel the cold and draw a stool near to the fire.
> Another he made from the sea; she has two characters. One day she smiles and is happy; a stranger who sees her in the house will praise her, and say, "There is no woman better than this among all mankind, nor more beautiful." But on another day she is unbearable to look at or come near to; then she raves so that you can't approach her, like a bitch over her pups; and she shows herself ungentle and contrary to enemies and friends alike. Just so the sea often stands without a tremor, harmless, a great delight to sailors, in the summer season; but often it raves, tossed about by thundering waves. It is the sea that such a woman most resembles in her temper; like the ocean, she has a changeful nature. (fr. 7.21–42)[25]

But if women made of earth or born from the sea are a misfortune, still worse are the other women who, according to their nature, derive from animals, the characteristics of which they retain:

> One he made from a long-bristled sow. In her house everything lies in disorder, smeared with mud, and rolls about the floor; and she herself unwashed, in clothes unlaundered, sits by the dungheap and grows fat. Another he made from a wicked vixen; a woman who knows everything. No bad thing and no better kind of thing is lost on her; for she often calls a good thing bad and a bad thing good. Her attitude is never the same. . . .
> Another he made from a bitch, own daughter of her mother, who

35

wants to hear everything and know everything. She peers everywhere and strays everywhere, always yapping, even if she sees no human being. A man cannot stop her by threatening, nor by losing his temper and knocking out her teeth with a stone, nor with honeyed words, not even if she is sitting with friends, but ceaselessly she keeps up a barking you can do nothing with. . . .

Another he made from an ash-grey ass that has suffered many blows; when compelled and scolded she puts up with everything, much against her will, and does her work to satisfaction. But meanwhile she munches in the back room all night and all day, and she munches by the hearth; and likewise when she comes to the act of love, she accepts any partner.

Another he made from a ferret, a miserable, wretched creature, nothing about her is beautiful or desirable, pleasing or lovable; she is mad for the bed of love, but she makes any man she has with her sick. She does great damage to her neighbours by her thieving, and often eats up sacrifices left unburned.

Another was the offspring of a proud mare with a long mane. She pushes servile work and trouble on to others; she would never set her hand to a mill, nor pick up a sieve nor throw the dung out of the house, nor sit over the oven dodging the soot; she makes her husband acquainted with Necessity. She washes the dirt off herself twice, sometimes three times, every day; she rubs herself with scents, and always has her thick hair combed and garlanded with flowers. A woman like her is a fine sight for others, but for the man she belongs to she proves a plague, unless he is some tyrant or king (who takes pride in such objects).

Another is from a monkey; this is the biggest plague of all that Zeus has given to men. Her face is hideous; when a woman like her goes through the town, everyone laughs at her. She is short in the neck; she moves awkwardly; she has no bottom, and is all legs. Hard luck on the poor man who holds such a misery in his arms! she knows every trick and twist, just like a monkey; she does not mind being laughed at, and will do no one a good turn but considers, and spends the whole day planning, how she can do someone the worst possible harm. (fr. 7.2–20, 43–82)

Sow, vixen, bitch, ass, ferret, mare, monkey: each worse than the last. Only one woman escapes:

Another is from a bee; the man who gets her is fortunate, for on her alone blame does not settle. She causes his property to grow and increase, and she grows old with a husband whom she loves and who loves her, the mother of a handsome and reputable family. She stands out among all women, and a godlike beauty plays about her. She takes no pleasure in sitting among women in places where they tell stories about love. Women like her are the best and most sensible whom Zeus bestows on men. (83–93)

Does the bee-woman really exist? If she does, she is very rare and one suspects that Semonides does not believe in her at all.[26] This explains how he can calmly and without fear of inconsistency conclude his catalogue by asserting that

Zeus has contrived that all these tribes of women are with men and remain with them. Yes, this is the worst plague Zeus has made—women; if they seem to be some use to him who has them, it is to him especially that they prove a plague. The man who lives with a woman never goes through all his day in cheerfulness; he will not be quick to push out of his house Starvation, a housemate who is an enemy, a god who is against us. Just when a man most wishes to enjoy himself at home; through the dispensation of a god or the kindness of a man, she finds a way of finding fault with him and lifts her crest for battle. Yes, where there is a woman, men cannot even give hearty entertainment to a guest who has come to the house; and the very woman who seems most respectable is the one who turns out guilty of the worst atrocity; because while her husband is not looking . . . and the neighbours get pleasure in seeing how he too is mistaken. Each man will take care to realise that the fate of all of us is alike. Yes, this is the greatest plague that Zeus has made, and he has bound us to them with a fetter that cannot be broken. Because of this some have gone to Hades fighting for a woman. (96–118)

Three

Exclusion from the *Polis*

The Greek city represents the perfect realization of a political plan to exclude women.[1] The cities of Greece began to have written laws, given them by more or less legendary personages, in the seventh century B.C. Athens, of course, occupies a very special place among these cities.

The Athenian legal experience has always been considered paradigmatic of the Greek legal experience for two reasons: the incomparably greater quantity of documents that allow reconstruction of its institutional history than for other cities, and the political, military, and cultural predominance of Athens over the Greek world. Therefore, though we will keep the variety and diversity of the Greek experience in mind, we will assume Athens as the model of the non-Doric Greek city, pointing out, where the sources permit, the similarities and differences between the Athenian model and the Doric.

Beginning in the seventh century, the Greek city defined itself as a political community by means of the exclusion of two classes of people, slaves and women.[2] Although the forms of exclusion of women were legally different, the theoretical justification was the same: the "nature" that made women and slaves different from, respectively, free man qua male and free man in the sense of human being. The "difference" of gender was what prevented free women from being part of the *polis*.

The exclusion of the female slave was not linked specifically to her sex so much as to her servile status. She was "different" from both free men and free women and equal to slaves of the male sex. The life of female slaves was harsh. Expected among other duties, to satisfy the sexual needs of the family's men, a female slave could be sold at any moment and thereby taken away from the family that she had perhaps constructed with another slave. Their children, of course, belonged to the master. To follow the course that led to the exclusion of women, however, it is more useful to concentrate on free women and the codification of their difference. The Greeks identified this "sexual difference" over the centuries, beginning when Hesiod envisioned a dangerous and faithless first woman "made from earth and water," up until the construction of the model of the "woman-matter" endowed by Aristotle with a solid and, one might say, undying theoretical constitution.

We will return to the theoretical justification of exclusion after looking at the laws with which the *polis* progressively identified itself as an association intended to respond to the needs of males.

The First Legislators

THE LAWS OF DRACO

The idea that women's lives should be aimed at reproduction rested on a centuries-old tradition. At least since the collapse of the Mycenaean palaces (and possibly longer, but the Mycenaean documentation contains very little information on the private sector), the Greeks worked out and translated into rigorous laws an ideology that centered the life of women around childbearing functions. Yet in comparison with what was to come in the centuries to follow, the so-called dark ages were characterized by a certain flexibility that allowed women some freedom of movement and the right to participate (except in political life) in at least some aspects of social life.

It was with the birth of the *polis*, then, that the situation changed and moved toward the path that led, in the classical period, to the total segregation of the female sex. The opportunities to live side-by-side with men in certain "external" moments, to see and know persons and facts outside the family circle ceased to exist in the seventh century B.C. Women were increasingly excluded; not only were they closed off figuratively in the narrow confines of their domestic role, they were actually confined within the walls of the house (in a part of the house called the *gynaecaeum*). A series of laws limited the few freedoms they had.

The legislators who gave the Greeks the first written laws were concerned first with regulating female sexual behavior, thus demonstrating that they considered respect for that fundamental law, an orderly reproduction of family groups and thereby of citizens, to be absolutely necessary to the life of the nascent city. To prove this, we need only examine the legislation of Draco, the first Athenian lawmaker, once thought to be legendary but now more widely considered historical.[3]

In the last decades of the seventh century, Draco gave the Athenians their first laws. The most important and the only one to have come down to us forbade private revenge and established that anyone who killed another man would be punished with a penalty (death or exile) to be inflicted by a tribunal specially constituted for the purpose. The penalty would be determined according to whether the homicide was willful or involuntary.[4] But there was one exception. In violation of the new fundamental principles that signaled the birth of a genuine penal law, he established that a citizen who had killed a *moichos*, a man caught in the act of sexual relations with the former's wife, concubine (*pallake*), mother, daughter, or sister, could not be punished because he had committed a legitimate—or *dikaios*—homicide, provided that, as in the Homeric period, the *moichos* did not pay his debt to society by offering a *poine*, acceptance of which was left to the discretion of the offended party. For the infant city, the offense was too great to be punished under the terms of the new law, in which the guilt should have been declared and the penalty imposed by a tribunal. *Moicheia* was a crime of such gravity as to be excluded from the application of the new principles. This was true not only in the legislation of Draco but throughout the entire history of Athenian law. *Moicheia* went beyond what today is called adultery. It included any extramarital sexual relations with married women, unmarried women, or widows. One characteristic of the Draconian legislation underscores the Greek attitude toward women. The law concerning *moicheia* contains a provision that strikes us at first glance as unusual: though it allowed killing a man who had committed adultery (as we will call illicit sexual relations for convenience), it did not allow the killing of the woman. She was subject to another punishment, namely, repudiation (if married) and being forbidden to participate in sacred rites. Moreover, if she should participate in rites, any citizen could punish her at his pleasure, as long as he stopped short of killing her.[5] But this provision is unusual only at first glance. From Helen to Clytemnestra and on until the fifth century B.C. and the wife of Euphiletus (accused of having killed Eratosthenes, his wife's lover, and defended by Lysias, who invoked the sanctity of the law of legitimate homicide), the woman was never considered an adulterer but rather "adulterated." She was *moicheutheisa,* or "corrupted" as Lysias says, which is to say seduced. She was a victim even if she had consented, because in the final analysis she was unfit to make up her own mind, whether for good or bad.[6]

It was, in other words, the incapacity of her sex (which we will see again in the justification for keeping women under permanent guardianship) that saved the woman from the death that her accomplice risked. Even if he was not surprised *in flagrante delicto* and thus could not be killed, he still risked being exposed to a public action, the *graphe moicheias,* which could be invoked against him not only by the head of the woman's *oikos* but by any citizen. Any good citizen would be interested in seeing that no woman in the city should break the rules of the organization and morals of the family. Other, more humiliating punishments were also possible, such as *paratilmos,* shaving of the pubic hair (which was a female practice and thus disgraceful for a man), or *rhaphanidosis,* being sodomized with a radish.[7]

THE LAWS OF LOCRIS AND GORTYN

How did other Greek cities view adultery? The statements by Lysias and Xenophon that the legitimate killing of the *moichos* was the common rule are probably generalizations.[8] At Locris, for example, a law attributed to Zaleucos prescribed that the adulterer be blinded,[9] and at Lepreon, the *moichos* was led through the city for three days and exposed to public derision, after which he was *atimos* (without civic rights) for the rest of his life.[10] We do know that all the cities, even if they did not provide for legitimate homicide, considered *moicheia* a crime to be punished with the heaviest penalties. There was perhaps one exception: Gortyn, a Doric city of Crete, not far from Phaistos. From the seventh century B.C. on, Gortyn had a code of laws inscribed on slabs of stone. Parts of these laws, datable to the fifth century, established that the adulterer should pay a fine according to the status of the man and the woman, and the place in which the crime took place.[11]

The law has generated debate. According to some, even at Gortyn it would have been possible to kill the adulterer, and the sums established by law would not have been of the fines, but the measure of the *poine* fixed by the city, which would have allowed the culprit to escape death by giving a satisfactory alternative to the injured party.[12]

But even if that were the case, there would still be a fundamental difference between the law of Gortyn and that of Athens. In Athens the plaintiff could refuse the *poine* and choose to kill the *moichos*. At Gortyn, however, the *poine* would have been imposed by law. It seems quite likely that at Gortyn adultery was punished by fine. Furthermore, this is perfectly consistent with the characteristics of a system, like the Doric, in which the family–state relationship—and consequently women's status—was very different than in the Ionic cities. The scanty but important documentation of Spartan women's life serves to demonstrate this, though it must be kept in mind that the sources, being Athenian, tend to interpret tendentiously a situation that was upsetting to their eyes.

Brought up outside the home, used to the outdoors and the stadia and palaestrae, Spartan women were considered by the Athenians to have sexual habits that were at best liberal and probably libertine.[13] Both Plato and Aristotle attributed the decline of the city to this fact.[14] Furthermore, women had great authority over their children and influence over their husbands in Sparta.[15] According to Plutarch, when a foreign woman told Gorgo, the wife of Leonidas, "the women of Lacedaemon were the only women in the world who could rule men," the Spartan woman replied, "With good reason, for we are the only women who bring forth men."[16]

For our purposes it is not important that this information is fragmentary and incomplete or sometimes wholesale invention. Quite apart from Athenian reactions and inferences, it is certain that Spartan women's lives were unlike Ionic women's and that their relationship with men was very different.[17] It is thus not surprising that the law of Gortyn, a Doric city, considered and punished adultery very differently than Athens. Procreation was still women's main function, although the Spartans, unlike the Athenians, put the interests of the city ahead of those of the integrity of the family group. Because the first interest of the Doric city was that the children be citizens—and not that they be legitimate—at Gortyn, and probably at Sparta too, adultery was a less serious crime than at Athens. It was still a crime, but not so grave as to warrant the killing of a citizen.

These, then, were the first written Greek laws to regulate the life of women. They dictated a code of behavior that unequivocally shows the centrality of the biological function, which was governed by the *polis* in such a way as to guarantee the replacement of citizens. In the Ionic cities, the laws ensure that this replacement took place in the context of family groups and their inheritance.

The Classical Period

Marriage, prescribed by the first laws as the center of female life, remained the focal point of the *polis*' defense and the reinforcement of its economic, social, and political security. We will therefore use marriage as the primary point of reference as we try to follow the life of Greek women in the classical period. We begin with their birth, assuming they escaped the fate of being "exposed."

EXPOSURE OF FEMALE INFANTS

Exposure (*ektesis*) of newborns was a practice allowed by law and accepted without difficulty by the social conscience. Despite Aris-

43

totle's proposal to ban it, it was still practiced in the Hellenistic period.[18]

Posidippus (a New Comedy playwright who lived between the third and second centuries B.C.) observed that "a poor man brings up a son, but even a rich man exposes a daughter."[19] Indeed, girls were exposed much more frequently than boys were. Girls, after all, were an expensive and unremunerative investment, not only because of the cost of supporting them as children but also because of the expense of providing them with dowries. When a girl married, the family lost her just when she was ready to fulfill her biological function of reproduction. A daughter, in other words, did not "repay" what was spent on her if she married, and if she did not marry, she continued to be a burden on the family economy.

That is why (as among all peoples who practice infanticide), girls are the most common victims. In Greece, the custom was to put the infant into a crockery pot (called *chutra,* whence the verb *chutrizein,* "to put into a pot") and abandon it on a roadside usually not far from home.[20] The exposure of infants in Greece had the socially, and thus politically, useful function of regulating the number of the members of groups and, above all, regulating the ratio between the sexes in such a way that there would not be an excess of women who would remain unmarried.[21] The need to marry off all eligible women gave rise to the activities of the matchmaker, a figure widely found at Athens.[22] Even more significant was a practice that was forbidden by a law attributed to Solon, but which, one infers from the very fact that it had to be forbidden, was widespread, and perhaps never completely wiped out,[23] that is, the drastic but effective practice of a father's selling as a slave the daughter he risked seeing turn into a "white-haired virgin."[24]

ENGAGEMENT, MARRIAGE, AND DIVORCE

Brought up at home by slaves if their family was well-off (in Greece, when economic conditions allowed, women did not raise their very young children themselves), girls did not stay long in their father's house. Betrothed at sometimes extremely young ages (in one famous case, at five),[25] they waited for marriage (at age fourteen or fifteen; the man would usually be about thirty)[26] without receiving any education, either at a school or at home. If the family was well-to-do, they learned only women's work. Their pastimes, which were certainly not aimed at intellectual development, consisted of such toys and games as dolls, hoops, balls, tops, and swings.

The ceremonies that accompanied marriage, or at least the most sumptuous, lasted for three days. On the first day (*proaulia emera*), the father of the bride made offerings to the gods, the bride sacrificed her toys to Artemis,[27] and the bride and groom bathed in water drawn from a spring or sacred river.[28] The second day (*gamos*), the father of the bride held the nuptial banquet, at the end of which the bride was taken to the husband's house.[29] The third and last day (*epaulia emera*), the bride, in the new house, received the wedding gifts.[30]

Yet none of these ceremonies constituted a legally valid wedding. Beginning in the age of Solon, the event that made a marriage valid sometimes took place many years before the actual wedding. This was the *eggue,* or "promise." It was the *eggue,* in other words, and not the wedding ceremonies, that under the law made the difference between simple cohabitation (*suneinai*) and a true marriage (*sunoikein*).[31] The *eggue* did not signify the beginning of the marriage (which was only when the couple began to live together) nor was it legally binding (in the sense that it obliged a couple to go through with the marriage); the promise was a "condition of legitimacy" of the marriage itself, and consequently the legitimacy of the offspring depended upon it.

At Athens, the existence of a blood relationship between the bride and groom was not an obstacle to marriage, not even when the relationship was quite close, such as uncle and niece or even brother and sister. There was, however, one distinction: although marriage between consanguineous brother and sister (with the same father) was allowed, marriage between uterine siblings (same mother) was prohibited.[32]

The logic of this rule, according to some, can be explained by history. The ban on marriage between uterine siblings would be the remnant of a matrilineal system in which the children of the same mother could not marry because they were members of the same family, while there would have been no obstacle to marriage between consanguineous siblings, because they belonged to different families. But I believe there is another explanation. When a girl married her father's son, the dowry stayed in the family. The financial advantage was, perhaps, the true reason for allowing the breaking of a taboo that could cause all the anguish dramatized in the story of Oedipus.[33]

The rule and its logic are not very informative. Far from being a personal relationship inspired by an emotional choice, marriage usually took place for social and financial reasons, for example, the necessity of keeping the family fortune intact (in marriage between siblings) or the desire to establish or maintain bonds with other families (in marriage with outsiders). In any case, it was the family that was valued, not the bride.

Closed off in the internal part of the house to which the men did not have access, the married woman had no chance to meet persons other than members of the household. In Athens, men even did the shopping.[34] Wives (and, for that matter, mothers, sisters, and daughters) could not attend banquets.[35] Nor does it appear that they were allowed to attend the theater.[36] "My sisters and nieces," says a client of Lysias, "have been so well brought up that they are embarrassed in the presence of a man who is not a member of the family."[37] Only the women of the poorest classes moved among men with a certain freedom, going to the market to sell bread or vegetables, or, in the demes of Attica, working the land and taking the animals to market.[38] But for the women of the wealthiest classes, there was only one chance to meet outsiders. Certain ceremonies (public festivals and funerals) were the exceptions. The women were allowed to leave the house for these gatherings and young Athenians took advantage of them to arrange clandestine meetings. For example, Eratosthenes met the wife of Euphiletus at her mother-in-law's funeral; he became her lover and was killed by her husband.[39]

The empty life of the Greek woman of the upper or middle class, deprived of interests or gratifications, was not even repaid by the knowledge that her relationship with her husband was exclusive. This was not necessarily because he had a relationship with another man, though that happened often enough (see chapter 6); quite frequently he had relationships with other women that were socially and even, in part, legally recognized.

The Athenian system provided for three possible ways to dissolve a marriage (apart from death, of course). The first, and certainly the most frequent, was repudiation by the husband, called *apopempsis* or *ekpempsis*. A husband could repudiate a wife at will, without justification. The only difficulty for him was that he had to give back the dowry. Another legal method was abandonment of the "conjugal roof" by the wife, called *apoleipsis*. Even when there were serious reasons, it was sometimes physically blocked by husbands (such as Alcibiades) who stopped their wives from going to the archon to request the needed authorization.[40] Finally, by the so-called paternal *apheresis,* the wife's father, for reasons of his own (usually to do with family property), might interrupt his daughter's marriage.[41]

At Athens what marked a woman's definitive passage into the husband's family was not the marriage but the birth of the first child. Only when she gave her husband a child, did a woman enter irreversibly into the new *oikos*. Her father could end the marriage at any time up till that moment. In special cases, the woman's nearest relative had the right to do so too. The reasons for this will become clear as we look at the condition of the so-called heiress (*epikleros*), the woman who found herself the only descendant of a family without males (*oikos eremos*).

HEIRESS

In Athenian law of succession, males enjoyed a more privileged position than females, given that the existence of male offspring and descendants excluded female offspring and descendants from succession. The only privilege the woman (called, in this case, *epiproikos*) had a right to was a dowry, a complex of goods which, at marriage, became the property of her husband. She received the dowry in lieu of sharing the family inheritance.[42]

Sometimes, of course, there were no male descendants. Although a woman, by herself, could not inherit the patrimony (*kleros*), she was nevertheless the means by which it was transmitted to the family's males. The concern on the part of her relatives that she not marry an outsider thus becomes obvious, as does the reason why she might be made to marry her nearest relative. In fact, the hand of an heiress was often sought by several aspirants, each claiming to be her nearest relative. The solution proposed by Athenian law was that the woman be "awarded" by a special judgment to the litigant who proved that he was her nearest relative.

In Athenian law, the judiciary action that put an end to the controversy in the matter of property was called *diadikasia*. And the judgment that resolved the dispute among the various aspirants for the hand of an heiress was simply an application of the *diadikasia* called, in this case, *epidikasia*. Family concern that the inheritance not end up in alien hands appears in another even more important law. If the heiress was already married when her father died, but did not yet have children (which would have bound her irrevocably to her husband's *oikos*), her nearest relative had the right of *apheresis* in place of the father.[43]

There were only two provisions in this complex of laws that worked in women's favor. The first law, attributed to Solon, concerned the fate of a poor heiress. With no parents to give her a dowry, the heiress without money risked not finding a husband. And so grave was this danger for a woman that Solon maintained that the nearest relative, if he did not wish to marry her himself, should be obliged to provide her with a dowry.[44] Another law, also attributed to Solon, concerned the wealthy *epikleros* (married, therefore, for her money), who risked being ignored by her husband after she had produced an heir. The husband was obliged by law to have sexual relations with her at least three times a month.[45] This is how Athenian legislation responded to the needs of the *epikleros*. It assured her a husband, necessary for a dignified place in society, and guaranteed her a "ration" of sexual intercourse with a man she had not chosen.[46]

WIFE, CONCUBINE, AND HETAERA

Demosthenes says that the Athenian man could have three women: the wife (*damar* or *gyne*) "for the production of legitimate children"; the concubine (*pallake*) "for the care of the body," that is, for regular sexual relations; and the hetaera (*hedones heneka*) for pleasure.[47] This division of three female functions (in itself extremely revealing of the male–female relationship) poses certain problems that arise from the difficulty of defining the boundaries of the role of concubine. In daily life, a man's relationship with a *pallake* (who was sometimes received into the conjugal home) was substantially identical to his relationship with his wife. It was subject to legal regulation which, on the one hand, required the concubine to be faithful, as though she were a wife (whence the Draconian right to kill her lover "legitimately"), and, on the other hand, granted certain rights of succession to her children, though not the same as those accorded legitimate children.[48]

This does not mean that Athenian law authorized bigamy, which a passage from Diogenes Laertius is often used to support. Diogenes writes, in fact, that the Athenians "because of the scarcity of men, wished to increase the population and approved a law whereby a man might marry one Athenian woman and have children by another."[49] Even recently the passage has been considered a proof of the fact that the Athenian law, albeit temporarily and in exceptional circumstances, allowed bigamy.[50] It actually means something very different: it means that the law granted a certain status to children born out of wedlock.[51] In other words, the law recognized and regulated the existence of concubines and established a precise hierarchy among the different stable relationships that a man might have.

The third woman in the Athenian's life, though not bound to him in a stable relationship, was more than just a casual companion. She was the hetaera. More educated than a woman destined for marriage, and intended "professionally" to accompany men where wives and concubines could not go, the hetaera was a sort of remedy provided by a society of men which, having segregated its women, still considered that the company of some of them could enliven their social activities, meetings among friends, and discussions which their wives, even if they had been allowed to take part, would not have been able to sustain. Enter the hetaera, who was paid for a relationship (including sex) which was neither exclusive nor merely occasional, as indicated by her name, which means "companion." This relationship was meant to be somehow gratifying for the man, even on the intellectual level, and was thus completely different from men's relationships with either wives or prostitutes.

FEMALE PROSTITUTION

Most prostitutes were of servile status, though sometimes freeborn girls who had been exposed as infants were rescued for the purpose of putting them to work as prostitutes. The profession of the prostitute (*porne*) was not forbidden by law but was the object of strong social disapproval. The law of the city concerned itself with prostitutes for only two reasons: to set a ceiling on their prices and to collect a tax on their income.[52]

Very different from that of a common prostitute, however, was the status of the woman who sold herself not in the streets or brothels but in the temples. As in the East, sacred prostitutes (*hierodoulai*) existed in Greece too. After having been consecrated to the divinity, they sold themselves to passers-by, giving the proceeds to the temple to which they were attached.

The legal status of the *hierodoulai* is uncertain. Some maintain that they were slaves of the temple, others that consecration to the goddess made them free, though obliged to live in the temple and serve there as prostitutes.[53] The question is irrelevant. Prostitutes in either case, the *hierodoulai* were privileged, not only for the greater protection and wealth than enjoyed by other prostitutes, but for their "sacredness," which placed them above ordinary *pornai* on the social scale. Pindar wrote of them in his famous *scholion* dedicated to the "sacred girls" of Corinth as "without blame in the lovely bed of tender age to pluck the fruit."[54] Simonides thanks them for having contributed with their prayers to the victory against the Persians.[55]

CONCLUSIONS

The possible social positions of women were as wives, concubines, hetaerae, or prostitutes. Which position a woman held was determined exclusively by her relationship, whether stable or occasional, with a man. And given that this relationship was constructed for the purpose of responding to male needs, the condition of woman could not have been other than it was: personally unsatisfying, nearly nonexistent socially, and regulated by a series of laws that established her inferiority and permanent subordination to a man.

Then, of course, there was women's total exclusion from any form of political participation. The example of Athens is paradigmatic. At Athens only those who were able to defend the city in arms could be citizens (*politai*), with a sole exception. The man who committed a particularly serious crime was considered unworthy to defend the city and was declared *atimos*. Deprived of political rights, the *atimos* became not a second-class citizen but a citizen of the very lowest rank. As such he was called *astos,* to indicate his belonging to the city (*astu*) in the physical sense but his exclusion from the citizen organization. Women were called by the same term—*aste*.[56] Until the age of Pericles, a woman's status as *aste* had no effect on the transmission of citizenship to her children. Her supposed "potential" citizenship, that is, as transmitter of it, was utterly nonexistent for centuries. Until 451–50 B.C., the year in which Pericles established that a mother had to be *aste* for her children to be *politai,* the only way for citizenship to be transmitted *iure sanguinis* was for the father to be Athenian.[57]

They were iron rules, then, that the *polis* imposed on women, shutting them out and depriving them of practically every chance of freedom: rules that both considered them inferior and made them so. This inferiority, already expressed in fact and perceived as traditional by the social conscience, found a theoretical mantle in the Aristotelian classification of a humanity (of freeborn humans, that is) composed of men—"spirit" and "form"—and women—"mothers" and "matter."[58] But it was only with Aristotle that the codification of the female essence and role found a theoretical status destined to last for centuries. Long before Aristotle the Greeks had discussed the "nature" and the "difference" of women. That was to be the subject of a debate that lasted for centuries.

Four

Philosophers and Women

The Reproduction Debate: Does Woman Contribute?

The mystery of birth divided Greek thinkers from the very beginning. Is the child, they asked, born solely from the father or from the mother too? The very terms of the question bespeak a singular attitude. The incontrovertible biological fact that the child is born from the mother (which might have led them to wonder, more logically, if the man made any contribution) was canceled at the outset, sometimes radically. For Hippo and the Stoics in general, the answer was that the child was solely the father's. For Anaxagoras, Alcmaeon, Parmenides, Empedocles, Democritus, Epicurus, and the physician Hippocrates, on the other hand, it was the mother's. Parmenides (born at Elea, ca. 519 B.C.), admitted that the woman too produced a "seed," but claimed that the sex of the child depended on the position of the fetus in the uterus; if it was on the right (the colder side), it would be born male; if on the left (the warmer side), it would be female. The idea was taken up by Empedocles (born in 488), although he maintained that males were born from the warm zone and females from the cold. For Democritus of Abdera (born ca. 470 B.C.), sexual differentiation depended on the relative strength of the father's and mother's seed. If the paternal seed were the stronger and prevailed over the maternal, the child would be male. If the mother's prevailed, it would be female.

Hippocrates (born on Cos in 460 B.C.) said that each sex produced a seed that could be either strong or weak. When a strong male seed meets a strong female seed, a male is born. When a weak male seed meets a weak female seed, a female is born. And, finally, when a weak male seed meets a strong female, or vice versa, the sex depends on the quantitatively more plentiful seed. If the father's seed is more plentiful and strong, the child will be male, but not very virile. If the father's seed is weak, though more plentiful, the child will be a girl, but not very feminine. If the mother's seed is more plentiful, the child will be an effeminate male if the seed is strong, and an unfeminine female if it is weak.[1]

Socrates and Aspasia

The debate had touched the theme of the masculine and feminine "virtues," defined from the beginning in the terms of a search for a "difference." But there were those who had begun to doubt the biological nature of the "difference" or at least of the fact that it was exclusively biological. The first to question it, as far as we know, was Socrates, whom Xenophon cites in the *Symposium* (2.8–9) as saying, referring to the skill of a female juggler, that what the woman was doing was "one of many proofs that the female nature is not naturally inferior to the male, except perhaps she lacks wisdom and physical strength." As it was not nature alone but lack of education that made women inferior, Socrates maintained, it was the duty of husbands to teach their young wives to be good companions, so that they might be able to engage in dialogue and so that they might be allowed, insofar as they were able, to contribute to the good of the family on an equal basis with the men (Xen. *Oec.* 3.12, 14–15).

Socrates was particularly well disposed toward women and did not limit himself to abstract recognition of their capacities; he listened to their advice and even admitted that some of them were wiser than himself. He says this explicity about Aspasia, a unique female figure well worth a closer look.

Daughter of Axiochus, born at Miletus in Asia Minor, we know from Plutarch's *Life of Pericles* (24) that Aspasia lived with Pericles after his divorce from his first wife (by whom he had had two sons) until he died and that she then married a certain Lysicles, a crude and ignorant man who thanks to her influence became the foremost man of Athens. Because she was a foreigner, Pericles could not marry her and she lived with him as his concubine. His love for her was so extraordinary, says Diogenes Laertius (6.16), that he even kissed her every day when he left the house for the agora and again when he returned—most unusual and evidently in contrast with normal conjugal relations, which included neither eroticism nor love.[2] But what is more interesting is Aspasia's relationship with Socrates. It has even been suggested that Socrates learned the so-called Socratic method from Aspasia.[3] And indeed, it seems that Aspasia had rare mastery of the art of conversation.

A disciple of Socrates, Aeschines of Sphettus, wrote a dialogue called *Aspasia* in which he recounted a conversation between Aspasia, Xenophon, and Xenophon's wife. "If your neighbor had gold that was purer than yours," Aspasia asked Xenophon's wife, "would you rather have her gold or yours?" "Hers," was the reply. "And if she had richer jewels and finer clothes?" "I would rather have hers." "And if she had a better husband than yours?" At the woman's embarrassed silence, Aspasia began to question the husband, asking him the same things but substituting horses for gold and land for clothes and asking him finally if he would prefer his neighbor's wife if she were better than his own. At his embarrassed silence, reading their thoughts, she said, "Each of you would like the best husband or wife: and since neither of the two of you has achieved perfection, each of you will always regret this ideal."[4]

Leaving aside the "maieutic" ability attributed to her by the dialogue, it is evident that Aspasia had an idea of marriage that was quite different from the Athenians'. Marriage for her was an encounter between two equals, each of whom should adapt to the needs of the other.[5] Socrates admired her ideas and wisdom to the point that, when he was once asked, "If a man has a good wife, is it he who made her that way?" he deferred to Aspasia, who knew much more than he did on the subject (Xen. *Oec.* 3.14–15).

It is not surprising that many Athenians hated Aspasia. She was not like other women; she was an intellectual. Four of Socrates' pupils mention her in their works: Aeschines, Antisthenes, Xenophon, and Plato. In the *Menexenus,* Plato has Socrates refer to a funeral speech that Aspasia composed for the dead of the Corinthian war (however, both Aspasia and Socrates were dead by the time that war began).[6] Aspasia's ideas on the female role and relations between the sexes were simply not acceptable to the Athenians, and it is no wonder that they slandered her, saying that she was a hetaera or that she encouraged Pericles' sexual escapades by arranging meetings for him with boys and girls.[7] Even if the Athenians' hatred of Aspasia, which culminated in an accusation of "impiety," was really aimed at Pericles (as were the attacks on his close friends the philosopher Anaxagoras and the sculptor Phidias), it still cannot be ruled out that the personality and unpopular ideas of this exceptional woman contributed to this hatred.[8]

Socrates shared Aspasia's ideas on the "female question." Though he never professed total equality between the sexes, Socrates was anything but a misogynist like most of his contemporaries. But what about the others?

The Virtues of Women

Although he echoed certain Socratic themes and thus admitted that nature had granted women "memory and attention" as it had men, Xenophon restated with utter certitude the notion that women are "naturally" destined for domestic work even though Zeus had given the sexes an equal capacity for mastering the passions. This idea is illustrated in the famous conversation in *Oeconomicus,* in which Ischomachos tells Socrates how he has educated his fourteen-year-old wife to be the way he wanted her to be and the way that it was right for her to be.[9] "What can I do to help you? What is my capacity?" his wife had asked him. "By Zeus," Ischomachos answered, "just try to do in the best manner possible what the gods have brought you forth to be capable of and what the law praises." Since in the family both inside and outside work are needed, "the god directly prepared the woman's nature for indoor work and indoor concerns," and men's for outdoor concerns. He gave women a weaker body and more tenderness for infants than men. Accordingly, the woman's duty was, besides reproduction, to control the management of the house and to take care of sick slaves.[10]

Xenophon, then, contains nothing new despite his admission that women share certain abilities with men. Other direct and indirect followers of Socrates continued the teaching of the master, however, carrying it to very different consequences and contributing substantially to making public opinion (solidly oriented toward the traditional) confront new ideas. One of these was Antisthenes, the founder of the Cynic school, who was born and lived in Athens around the turn of the fourth century B.C. For him, men and women had "the same virtues."[11] Cynics did not avoid attempts to put these principles into practice. Believing that men and women should fulfill themselves equally by means of the exercise of their common virtues, the Cynics questioned the centrality of the conjugal relationship and preached sexual liberty as capable of freeing people from the bonds of matrimony. One exponent was Diogenes, a pupil of Antisthenes at Athens, who proposed a community of women.[12] They questioned the idea of female inferiority and formed "alternative" relationships that shocked the Greeks. For example, Crates of Thebes, with his disciple Hipparchia, spent his life traveling, including her in all his experiences and begging with her (according to the teaching of the Cynic school) at the banquets that she attended as though she were a hetaera (Diog. Laert. 6.85 ff.). They shared a relationship altogether outside the rules. Hipparchia, for her part, did not regret her choice: "You don't think that I have arranged my life so badly, do you," she asked a critic, "if I have used the time I would have wasted on weaving for my education?" (6.98). And like Hipparchia, Crates reconfirmed their common choice, giving their daughter for a month to each of his disciples so that she might be free to choose a good companion (6.93).

Other schools besides the Cynics believed in the equality of women. Epicurus, born on Samos in 340 B.C., moved to Athens in 309 and accepted Themistia as a pupil (Diog. Laert. 10.5, 25, 26). Pythagoras, who moved to Magna Graecia around 530, founded a school attended by such important women as Theano. Pythagoreans even posed the problem of the political capacity of women, maintaining their suitability for governing (Stob. 85.19). There is no need to point out how much in contrast this position was not only with normal practice but also with the opinions of other sages. According to Phintys, for example, women had some virtues equal to those of men (courage, justice, and reflection), but they had the capacity neither to wage war nor to govern, although they did have the specific virtue of knowing how to manage a house and take care of a husband (Stob. 84.71). Theophrastus (the peripatetic philosopher whose opinions coincided on this point with the Aristotelian) believed it was necessary that a woman know not "how to administrate a city but rather run a household" (Stob. 85.7). He also maintained, even more drastically, that the education of women was necessary, on condition that it be limited to "what it is necessary to know to run a household; further instruction would just make them lazy, more talkative, and indiscreet" (Stob. 16.30).

But nothing is more edifying than a story told by Plutarch (*Moralia, De mulierum virtutibus* 19) about one of the few men who believed that women could have the same virtues as men. Aretaphila of Cyrene, who freed the city from the tyrant Nicocrates (we shall return to cases of women who led armies in the Hellenistic period). After the victory her fellow citizens invited her to take a role in government, but Aretaphila, "when the city was liberated, retired to her 'gynacaeum' and, refusing all indiscreet activities, spent the rest of her life weaving." This is a perfect example of how women, even though able to behave like men, did so only in case of need and returned afterward to their habitual duties, sacrificing their personal abilities to the harmony of the whole.

As we have seen, there was an alternate tradition of "advanced" thought, which, although it confirmed women's essential domestic role, was not characterized by the misogyny of the major tradition that lasted for the entire history of the *polis* and found ample acceptance in the popular social conscience. Influenced by the teaching of Socrates, some thinkers took their discourse on women far beyond the Socratic point of view. The foremost of these was Plato, whose position on the "female question" has been the subject of heated debate, more than justified by his many ambiguities and contradictions.

Plato: Feminist?

Plato, in fact, departs from positions that could seem and that have been called "feminist."[13] In the *Republic*, envisaging an ideal state, he entrusted the power to a group of "guardians" of the constitution, abolishing the family and private property. The family should not exist because it is there that wealth is accumulated and if the guards had wealth as well as power, they would become "savage masters" (3.416 a–417 b). And "the wives of our guardians are to be common, and their children are to be common, and no parent is to know his own child, nor any child his parent" (5.457 d). The female element of the city, liberated from the family role, must then be incorporated into the community to work together with the men at the management of the political project. Educated with men, after having learned music and gymnastics (as at Crete and Sparta), women must be used exactly like men; they must fulfill identical duties; they can be doctors or "lovers of knowledge," and, like men, they can be guardians. This, then, is Plato's feminism—granting women the same opportunities granted to men in his utopia.[14]

Even more problems emerge from the ideology of the *Laws*. Plato proposes a different political model there, still in part collectivistic, but more practicable, that is, less irreconcilably in contrast with the political and social reality of the time. The city of the *Laws* is divided into 5,040 family groups, each assigned a parcel of land (*kleros*) (5.739 c–741 a). In his discussion of the family, female subordination reappears. In marriage (which all citizens are obliged to contract and to dissolve in case of ten years of sterility), the woman must be under the control of the husband.[15] But family control is not enough; it must be backed up by that of the state.

"By nature more inclined toward hiding and craftiness," women can be a devious element. They can cause the social fabric to break down, as at Sparta, says Plato, where, freed from their family functions and economically powerful, they threatened the solidity of the state.[16] The "difference" (which in the *Republic* was at least partly due to education) returns as an excuse for discrimination and as a justification of a subordination that becomes explicit inferiority in Plato's dialogues.

The man "who lived well his assigned time," we read in the
Timaeus,

> after he travels back into the habitation of his guardian star, will have a
> happy and congenial life; but the man who fails in this, will change in
> his second life into a woman. And if in this condition he continually
> does not cease from evildoing, he will change into the beast who most
> resembles the character of his evil. . . . (42 b–c)[17]

More precisely: "Of the men who came into the world, those who
were cowards or led unrighteous lives may with reason be supposed to have changed into the nature of women in the second
generation" (90 e), according to the plan of "those who made us,"
who "knew that from men would be born women and other
animals" (76 e).

Certainly, the assertion in the *Republic* of women's capacity to
govern had revolutionary potential, as did the abolition of the
family and property. But while the Platonic plan freed women from
the state, in making women equal to men Plato eliminated the
difference, claiming, as Wilamowitz wrote, "that they were men, for
him imperfect men."[18]

As a theorist of the superiority of the relationship between men
over that between a man and a woman (as we shall see in chapter
6),[19] Plato granted women, in the *Republic,* a certain freedom of
action, aimed at the single purpose of rationalizing his political
plan. He expressed in the most radical way the certainty of female
inferiority, an idea later to be theorized without further ambiguity
and contradictions, by the man who definitively locked women in
the circle of their "natural difference"—Aristotle.[20]

Aristotle: Woman-Matter

Addressing himself to an already much-debated theme, Aristotle
explained the female contribution to reproduction. When the
embryo is formed, he said, next to the sperm flows the menstrual
blood, but the role of these two elements is different. The sperm is
blood, like the menses, but more complex. Food that is not expelled
from the organism is converted into blood, and the converting
agent is heat. But the woman, less "warm" than the man, cannot
complete the final conversion, which produces sperm. It is the male

seed that in reproduction "cooks the female residue," converting it into a new being: the seed, in other words, has an active role, while the female blood has a passive role. Though indispensable, the female contribution is one of matter, with which woman is identified. And the contribution of the woman-matter is passive by nature, while the male contribution, man being form and spirit, is active and creative. In essence the male in reproduction, "converts" female matter with his sperm.[21]

Passivity in reproduction is one of the factors that Aristotle uses to justify the social and legal inferiority of women. The *oikos* (a central element of the Aristotelian political plan) is arranged around a head: "Although there may be exceptions to the order of nature, the male is by nature fitter for command than the female."[22] Only this head has the right to participate in the management of the *polis*, and to him too falls command over his wife, slaves, and children, "for the slave has no deliberative faculty at all; the woman has, but it is without authority, and the child has, but it is immature."[23] The difference of the subordinates having been established, the relationships of subordination within the family are different too. The husband–wife relationship is characterized by the fact that the man has "over his wife a constitutional rule."[24] Although constitutional authority (that of the *politikos*) involves an alternation of command among the citizens, in the man–woman relationship, there is no alternation: "The male is by nature superior, and the female inferior, and the one rules, and the other is ruled; this principle of necessity extends to all mankind."[25]

And so we come to the virtues of women, the qualities that allow them best to correspond to the "natural" model. "Silence is a woman's glory," says Aristotle, citing a well-known line of Sophocles, and thus he reconfirms the usual female model.[26] Endowed with a smaller and imperfect reason, incapable of controlling her "lustful" side, the woman, who has no will, must be controlled by either the husband or the state. He uses Sparta as an example:

> The licence of the Lacedaemonian women defeats the intention of the Spartan constitution, and is adverse to the good order of the state. For a husband and a wife, being each a part of every family, the state may be considered as about equally divided into men and women; and,

therefore, in those states in which the condition of women is bad, half the city may be regarded as having no laws. And this is what has actually happened at Sparta; the legislator wanted to make the whole state hardy and temperate, and he has carried out his intention in the case of the men, but he has neglected the women, who live in every sort of intemperance and luxury.[27]

Shut up in the circle of her "materiality," the woman had only negative power: although she guarantees the reproduction of the citizens, she is excluded from the *logos* and if uncontrolled she is dangerous.

Conclusions

We have traced the different traditions in Greek thought regarding the "female question." One trend, departing from the notion that women are radically different—already present in myth—leads to the Aristotelian theory of mother-matter. The other trend, beginning with Socrates, sees women, as, if not truly equal, at least not inferior to men, and believes it possible for women even to achieve personal and intellectual fulfillment not tied exclusively to motherhood.

As reflections of the actual social conscience, the Socratic approach was clearly the minority opinion. For all his teaching, including that on women, Socrates represented to the Athenians an intolerable element of subversion. It is not remarkable that Aristophanes in the *Clouds* (423 B.C.) chose him as the butt of irony, representing Socrates ridiculously installed in his *phrontisterion,* suspended in a basket and intent on measuring the leap of fleas. No one was more dangerous than Socrates as a bringer of new ideas, which Aristophanes—and many other Athenians—blamed for the decline of the *polis.*

Socrates' condemnation in 399 for "impiety" (*graphe asebeias*) of having "speculated about the heaven above, and searched into the earth beneath, and made the worse appear the better cause," and especially of being "a doer of evil who corrupts the youth; and who does not believe in the gods of the State, but has other new divinities of his own,"[28] was, then, a political sentence. It was Athens' response to subversive teaching as an element of corruption and disintegration of traditional values. They did not condemn him only for what he believed on the subject of women, but perhaps also in part for that too. Even his ideas on women endangered the city.

Did the majority of Athenians share what some have termed the popular morality?[29] Obviously, Athenian public opinion has not come down to us directly. We have no documents that tell us what the "average citizen" thought about women. But sources do exist that permit reconstruction of public opinions: the works of the playwrights, poets, or orators whose ideas and views were presented in public forums. The problems of trying to use literature this way are so well known as to make long discussion superfluous.[30] How can one distinguish the opinion of the author from the many contrasting opinions of his characters? Once his opinion has been identified (assuming that is possible)—or at least once the opinion presumably nearest that of the author has been identified, how can one know if it corresponds to popular opinion or if it expresses "advanced" positions that most of the public would not share?

The problem is anything but simple, but we will attempt in the next chapter to discern the attitudes toward women in drama and poetry and the attitudes of the audiences for whom plays and poems were produced.

Five

Women and Literature

Women in Classical Literature

The literature of the classical period, which begins with the tragedies of Aeschylus, gave its public important female characters, images of women of strong character and proud temperament capable of heroic and terrible deeds, women like Antigone and Medea. But the tragedians' attitude toward their heroines and toward the female sex in general has been and continues to be the subject of debate.

THE TRAGEDIES

For some Hellenists, tragedy, and for that matter all the rest of classical literature, reflects a profound disparagement of women mixed with an invincible fear of their negative power. For others (who believe that women enjoyed an elevated social position), such characters as Aeschylus' Clytemnestra or Sophocles' Antigone and Deianeira demonstrate the Greeks' admiration for the female sex.[1] Still others (some of them women) maintain that we should make a sharp distinction between Aeschylus and Sophocles on the one hand, and Euripides on the other. The infamous acts of many Euripidean heroines, says S. B. Pomeroy (who notes in partial support of her position that British suffragists used to recite excerpts from Euripides), reveal the poet's desire to question the moral tradition and to denounce the difficult condition of women in his city.[2]

The problem is far from simple. The complexity of the religious, ethical, and political significance of tragedy, together with the depth of the psychological analysis of the characters (expressions of the contradictions and drama of the human condition), makes it quite easy to fall into excessive simplification and too-rigid schematization. But, in my opinion, it is difficult to ignore the old misogyny and the equally old idea of the necessary subjugation of women in tragedy. Let us look at the women characters who have been called feminist, beginning with the Clytemnestra of Aeschylus.

First performed in 458 B.C., the *Oresteia* (the trilogy consisting of the *Agamemnon,* the *Choephoroi,* and the *Eumenides*) recounts the events following the return of Agamemnon from Troy. His wife, Clytemnestra, who had in his absence become the mistress of Aegisthus, welcomes her husband pretending to love him and swearing that she has been faithful. She then stabs him to death, along with Cassandra, a prisoner he had brought home as his concubine.

Clytemnestra claims not one but two justifications. Before leaving for Troy, Agamemnon had sacrificed their daughter Iphigeneia to the gods in order to obtain favorable winds, killing her "like a sheep." By killing her husband Clytemnestra avenges not only her daughter but also herself.

> Low he lies, he who did outrage against me his wife,
> the darling of each Chryseis beneath Ilium!
> And this woman here, the captive and soothsayer
> and bedfellow for him, the trusty prophetess
> who shared his couch, the public harlot
> of the sailors' benches! They have not failed to get the honor due them.
> For he lies as I have described, and she after singing
> like a swan her last lament in death
> lies beside him, his lover; when he brought in
> a side-dish for his bed, he pandered to my delight!
>
> (Aesch. *Ag.* 1438–47)[3]

That Agamemnon, at Troy, had obtained Chryseis as concubine, and that returning home he had brought Cassandra with him (altogether normal behavior for the Greek man) is perceived by Clytemnestra as an outrage which actually seems to go against the moral tradition. But it is the end of the drama more than this psychological reversal that reveals Aeschylus' real opinion about the female role. Orestes, the son of Agamemnon and Clytemnestra who killed his mother to avenge his father, is defended by Apollo before a court of citizens presided over by Athena. "She who is called the child's mother," says Apollo, "is not its begetter, but the nurse of the newly sown conception. The begetter is the male, and she as a stranger for a stranger preserves the offspring, if no god blights its birth" (*Eumenides* 658–61).

The sentence of the court, which (with Athena casting the deciding vote) acquits Orestes, has a precise significance. What is at issue is the maternal role. Far from demonstrating the historicity of a matriarchal period later replaced by a patriarchal system, the *Oresteia* as a whole and especially in its outcome seems to show the poet's conviction (which in this case seems to be the same as popular opinion) that the woman has a subordinate role in reproduction. This is the poetic expression, then, of the opinion held by many philosophers, and its conclusion is certainly not "feminist."[4]

In the *Suppliants* and the *Aegyptii* Aeschylus represents the rebellion of the fifty daughters of Danaus (the Danaids). After attempting to refuse marriage with their fifty cousins and being forced to go through with it, with one exception (Hypermestra) they all killed their husbands on their wedding night. The Danaids saw marriage as "slavery" and declared that they preferred death. Invoking Zeus to save them from "anguished marriages with unloved men," they describe their suitors as "a swarm of males, hunting us down, furious, crazy, yelling" (*Suppliants* 20–30). But although they seem to insist on the right to a marriage based on love (which would, of course, be highly unusual) the Danaids still do not rebel against their feminine lot and marriage per se. Refusing a particular husband is quite different from refusing marriage as the destiny of women.[5]

This consideration changes the scope of the Danaids' act. Aeschylus' "feminism" (despite certain moments) is highly disputable, as is the "feminism" that some read in the *Antigone* of

Sophocles. Antigone is one of the most important characters in tragedy, the heroine who rebels against the laws of the city that bar her from burying her brother. In the name of the "law of nature," which she declares superior to the laws of the state, she courageously faces death. Aside from the creation of this great female character, the play reveals Sophocles' own opinion on the male–female relationship and the female condition.

Antigone's fiancé Haemon, the son of Creon, the king who has condemned her to death, intercedes on her behalf. But the king accuses him of being the "slave of a woman," and admonishes him "never to squander something for reason of the pleasure of a woman" because "it is better, if it is absolutely necessary to fall, to fall by the hand of a man." Haemon accedes to his father's wish, declaring that he will "consider no marriage more important to attain than being guided by you." The very fact that he eventually takes his life by the side of his beloved's corpse gives the measure of how difficult, if not impossible, it was to have a love relationship independent of family desires, of how much more important in the hierarchy of values was respect for filial duty. Furthermore, Antigone herself, for all her courage and pride, regretted one thing—dying "cursed, without marriage," thereby revealing how absolutely women like Antigone felt destined to marry and how terrible it was to die without having achieved it—to the point that such a fate was considered a curse.[6]

The tragedian whose work, albeit not without contradictions, seems best to express Greek misogyny is Euripides. Indisputably aware of the cultural ferments which, in the Athens of his time, questioned the subordination of women (and because of this considered by some to be the spokesman of the women's rebellion), Euripides confirms with utter certainty the old commonplace of the woman as "scourge, infamous race, unspeakable misfortune" for whoever cannot manage to escape her evil influence. He expresses this with uncommon virulence in the famous invective of Hippolytus:

> O Zeus, why have you settled women in the light of day, to be an evil counterfeit coin among men? For if you wanted to sow the seed of the human race, you needn't have provided it from *women*, but men could

have deposited a sum of bronze or silver or gold in your temples to buy the seed of children for a certain price, each man for the amount appropriate to his estate, and men could live in free houses without women. . . . It is clear that women are a great evil for this reason: the father who begot and raised her pays a dowry to settle her elsewhere in order to relieve himself of trouble. The man who takes the destructive creature home happily puts out adornment for his most evil idol and completely spends all his house's wealth for her clothes. . . . It is easiest for the man who has a nonentity, but a woman sitting at home in silliness is harmful. I hate clever women. There will never be a woman in my house who is cleverer than a woman should be. For Aphrodite brings more evildoing to birth in the clever ones. But the helpless woman is deprived of folly by her small wits. A servant ought never to go near a woman, but mute beasts ought to live with her, so that she has no one to talk to or to take messages back from her. (Eur. *Hipp.* 617–48)

The *topoi* of Greek misogyny in the passage recur with impressive constancy: woman is more dangerous the further away she is from the rule that would keep her silent and ignorant. For Hippolytus the woman should be stupid too, since only stupidity can keep the damage she causes to a minimum. The very bitterness of the attack leads one to assume an identification of Euripides with his character.

But how may one explain the rebellion of another Euripidean character—Medea—from the fate reserved for women?

Of everything that breathes and has intelligence, we women are the most miserable creatures. For first of all we must by a vast expenditure of wealth buy a husband and take a master for our bodies. And this evil is more miserable than the other, and everything depends on whether we get a bad master or a good one. For it is not respectable for women to be divorced or possible to refuse one's husband. A woman must be a seer when she finds herself among new habits and customs, since she will not have learned at home how she can best deal with her husband. And if, after we complete our work well, our husbands live with us bearing the yoke of marriage without constraint, our lives are enviable. If they do not, death is imperative. For a man, when he is miserable living with those inside his home, goes outside and puts an end to his heart's longing. . . . But we must look to one soul alone. They say that we lead a life without danger at home, while the men go to war—but they are wrong: I would rather stand in the hoplite ranks three times than give birth once. (Eur. *Med.* 230–51)

Medea does not lament a personal unhappiness nor does she weep about her individual fate—speaking in the name of all women, for the first time in Greek literature, she rebels against the sufferings of the female condition.

The opposing positions of Hippolytus and Medea are unreconcilable, but the presence in Euripides' plays of two characters so emblematic, each in his or her own way, of extreme positions perhaps has a reason. The Athens of Euripides was the city of Socrates and Aspasia, where the "female question" was the subject of heated debate. As an intellectual quite sensitive to what was being discussed around him, Euripides used Medea to display his awareness of the problem by addressing a fashionable theme. Yet the character he uses to represent the *ideal* woman is very different from Medea. She is Alcestis. King Admetus of Pherae in Thessaly is supposed to die, but he has persuaded Apollo to promise that he can live if someone else will agree to die in his place; no one, however, is willing—not even his mother and father. Only his wife Alcestis is willing to make the sacrifice. She expires in his arms, and he mourns her desperately, because to lose one's wife is the worst of ills. Is this conjugal love on Admetus' part? Certainly, but the point is that his love is bestowed on a woman who, as he himself expressly states, is the best of wives because she sacrificed herself for him (Eur. *Alc.* 341–43).

Another facet of Euripides' opinion of women emerges from the words with which Medea justifies the terrible deed she is preparing to carry out. She is planning to kill her children in order to punish Jason for abandoning her.

> In other matters a woman is filled with fear and is too weak to gaze on battle or on weapons. But when she happens to be wronged in respect to her *bed,* there is no heart more bent on destruction. (Eur. *Med.* 263–66)

"Bed" is therefore the only force capable of provoking rebellion in women, and "bed" is the key word in Euripidean tragedy to express how the poet and his audience conceive the man–woman relationship. This point is clearly confirmed by a play with two female protagonists, the *Andromache.*

Andromache, after the death of Hector and the destruction of Troy, has been assigned as booty to Neoptolemus, who keeps her as a concubine. Hermione, daughter of Menelaus and Helen and wife of Neoptolemus, accuses Andromache of having used witchcraft to make her sterile. Taking advantage of her husband's absence, Hermione decides to kill her rival and the son that Andromache had given Neoptolemus. But the plan fails, and to avoid her husband's wrath Hermione runs away with Orestes, to whom she had been promised before she was given to Neoptolemus.

The most interesting feature of the play, apart from the plot, is the nature of the rivalry between the two women. What is being disputed is not Neoptolemus' love or even affection but rather his "bed." Andromache does not love Neoptolemus; she has always considered Hector her true husband. Hermione, who has planned two homicides out of jealousy, shows no worry or sorrow when Orestes tells her he has overheard a plot to kill Neoptolemus.

The "bed," a word that is repeated about twenty times in the play, is the only object of contention. But what exactly is it? In the first place, it means social security for the wife and economic security for the concubine. Second, it represents women's eternal link between nature and animality.[7] It is what spurs them to the most terrible actions. Medea, who kills her children to defend her rights of the bed, is not very different for Euripides in her intense femininity from Phaedra (the object of Hippolytus' execration), another woman capable of bring misfortune and death. Phaedra and Medea are Hesiod's "evil" with all the characteristics of the "race of women." The tradition that Euripides was a misogynist, albeit because of an unfaithful wife, is perhaps not altogether without basis.[8]

It is interesting to note that in Aristophanes' *Thesmophoriazusae* the Athenian women, who are about to condemn Euripides to death to punish him for calumnies against them, agree to spare him only after he has promised to respect them in future. Produced in 411 B.C., while Euripides was still alive, the *Thesmophoriazusae* is presumably a reflection of what the Athenians thought about him. The English suffragists may have loved Euripides, but his female contemporaries at Athens evidently loved him a good deal less.[9]

THE COMEDIES

The theme of "women's power" returns as a central element of two other comedies of Aristophanes, the *Lysistrata* and the *Ecclesiazusae*. The theme has inspired scholarly debate.[10]

In the first play the Athenian women led by Lysistrata (her name means "she who dissolves armies"), together with the women of the principal cities at war (the year is 411 B.C., after the disastrous Sicilian expedition), decide to have no further sexual relations with their husbands until the war is over. The men, yielding to the women's extortion, finally conclude a peace. In the *Ecclesiazusae*, the women of Athens, tired of government by men, decide to take possession of the state. Under the command of Praxagora, disguised as men with beards and cloaks, they go at dawn to the Assembly to vote in a law that excludes men from governing the city.[11] They formulate a new political plan: lands, money, every sort of property will be held in common; the family will be abolished; a law will prevent injustices against old and ugly women; and children, not knowing who their own parents are, will respect all older people.

At first sight, certainly, both plays contain reasons to believe that women are being appreciated for seeing war as contrary to nature and wanting greater social justice. Actually the message is completely different. To understand what is really occurring we must recognize something essential to the comedy of Aristophanes, namely, the playwright's love for his city.

As a young man Aristophanes saw Athens at the height of its splendor, great, rich, happy, and free. But now Athens was defeated and slipping into an irreversible decline. The decline of the *polis*, then, is the true inspiration of Aristophanes' comedy. The women's victory should be read in this light. Reduced to pure animality, the Athenians forget fatherland and honor. With the victory of the women Athens, the city of reason, disappears from history, and Aristophanes tries to exorcise this tragedy with laughter. In the *Ecclesiazusae*, the women, having taken power, decide that the family should be abolished and that property should be held in common. Although the chronological relationship between the two works is uncertain, it cannot be ruled out that this is a parody of the *Republic*. The bitter reaction of a man who sees all his ideals collapse is to juxtapose communism and gynocracy, that is, a return to primitive conditions and the abdication of men in favor of women. With no means of escape, the playwright uses ridicule and paradox as weapons to destroy the Athens of his time, the Athens of decadence. To him, gynocracy, women's power, simultaneously represents the apex of the ridiculous and the dramatic.[12]

Lettered Women

SAPPHO

That Greek literature is male literature is not surprising in view of the segregation and lack of education of women. What is surprising is that in a rigid social and cultural context like the Greek, some women broke through the wall of silence and expressed their feelings, joys, and sorrows in poetry, and existed despite everything as individuals. It is no accident that this handful of women did not live at Athens, but in environments that were ethically, socially, and culturally different.

The case of Sappho, the only woman on the Olympus of ancient poets, demonstrates that the absence of women "intellectuals" was not due to their inability but was the inevitable result of an exclusion that condemned them to silence.

Sappho, daughter of Scamandronymus and Cleïs, was born at Mytilene on the island of Lesbos around 612 B.C. Of an aristocratic family (we know her brother was cup-bearer to the prytaneum of Mytilene), Sappho married a certain Cercyclas, by whom she had a daughter, Cleïs. At Mytilene, where she spent the greater part of her life (from 604 to 595 she lived in Sicily), Sappho was head of an association (*thiasos*) of young women. The spread of such "clubs" for women in the cities along the coast of Asia Minor (and in mainland Greece, even at Sparta) shows that women's lives in these cities were very different from those at Athens (see chapter 4).

Let us leave aside the problem of Sappho's homosexuality and the more general problem of female homosexuality within the *thiasoi*, as we shall return to this topic in chapter 6. In the *thiasoi*, aristocratic girls received an education that would never have been given Athenian girls. It was "female" education (emphasizing music, singing, and dance), true, but it contributed to forming their personalities and, more important, to giving them the means with which to express those personalities. It is not remarkable that it was at Mytilene and not Athens that Sappho succeeded in saying what she felt in poetry equal to any written by a male poet.[13]

Inspired by the life of the women's *thiasos*, Sappho's poetry sings of rivalry and nostalgia, desperation and sweetness, all the feelings that accompany love. This fragment is an example:

> desire flies about the beautiful girl, and her dress
> makes her shudder as she looks on, and I am happy.[14]

The following lines describe the futility of love when the girl must leave to marry:

> She honored you like a goddess and took pleasure most
> of all in your dancing.
> Now she is preeminent among the women of Lydia,
> as the rosy-fingered moon when the sun has set
> stands out among the stars. Her light shines forth
> upon the salt sea and on the flowery meadows
> and the fair dew is spread about and roses bloom
> and soft chervil and flowery melilot
> and often she walks back and forth and in her desire
> remembers gentle Atthis, and her heart is consumed. . . .[15]

Or again:

> "The truth is, I wish I were dead." She left me whispering often,
> and she said this, "Oh what a cruel fate is ours, Sappho, yes, I
> leave you against my will."
> And I answered her: "Farewell, go and remember me, for you
> know how we cared for you.
> "If you do remember, I want to remind you . . . and were happy
> . . . of violets . . . you sat beside me and with woven garlands
> made of flowers around your soft neck
> "and with perfume, royal, rich . . . you anointed yourself and
> on soft beds you would drive out your passion
> "and then . . . sanctuary . . . was . . . from which we were away. . . ."[16]

These fragments also describe the effects of love:

Love shook my heart like a wind falling on oaks in the
mountains.[17]

Once again love the limb-looser whirls me about,
bitter-sweet, irresistible creature.[18]

Love, again, is the theme of the famous ode recorded by the
anonymous *On the Sublime*. This well-known poem was imitated
countless times (by Catullus among others). Sappho wrote the ode
for a friend as she watches her speak with a man, possibly her future
husband.

The man seems to me strong as a god, the man who sits across
from you and listens to your sweet talk nearby
and your lovely laughter—which, when I hear it, strikes fear in
the heart in my breast. For whenever I glance at you, it seems
that I can say nothing at all
but my tongue is broken in silence, and that instant a light fire
rushes beneath my skin, I can no longer see anything in my
eyes and my ears are thundering,
and a cold sweat pours down me, and shuddering grasps me all
over, and I am greener than grass, and I seem to myself to be
little short of death.[19]

OTHER WOMEN POETS

Sappho is the most famous woman poet, but she was not the only
Greek poetess. In the fifth century B.C. Myrtis of Boeotia (of whose
work nothing remains) was said to have been the teacher of Pindar.
Another Boeotian woman, Corinna of Tanagra (a pupil of Myrtis)
won five poetry victories over Pindar. It would not matter that this
information is probably without foundation except that it contra-
dicts a fragment of Corinna: "I blame clear-voiced Myrtis, because—though a woman—she entered into rivalry with Pindar."[20]

Corinna was certainly a poetess of fame and varied inspiration, as
the surviving titles of her works show: "Boeotos" (hero of Boeotia),
"Seven at Thebes," the "Euonimia" (mother of the Eumenides),
"Iolaus" (Heracles' groom), "The Return" (of Orion to his own
country), "The Daughters of Minyas," possibly a "Tanagra," an
"Orestas" (of which a few lines are preserved on papyrus), and two
"Nomoi" ("The Contest of Cithaeron and Helicon" and "The Daugh-
ters of Asopus," preserved on papyrus).[21]

At Argos in the fifth century B.C. lived Telesilla, poetess and warrior heroine. She is supposed to have organized the women of the city to fight against Cleomenes, king of Sparta. Her fellow citizens erected a statue to her in which she was portrayed, with her books thrown aside, putting on a helmet for battle.[22] Telesilla composed largely religious works, of which nine fragments remain (perhaps parts of hymns to Apollo and Artemis). She is particularly famous for having used a meter (acephalous glyconic) called "Telesilleion" alexandrines.

At Sicyon lived Praxilla, a contemporary of Telesilla and author of a dithyramb called "Achilles" and a composition on Adonis of which three hexameters remain. A well-known personage in her city, Praxilla was honored in the fourth century with a bronze statue. But she was more famous in antiquity for the expression "stupider than Praxilla's Adonis." In her poem on Adonis, the hero, asked by Hades what he considered the most beautiful thing in the world, answered: "The sun, the moon, and some fruits."[23] The reply was considered so stupid that it became proverbial.

In the fourth century, perhaps at Telos, lived Erinna. Of her work remain about sixty lines from the poem "The Distaff," composed on the death of a friend, and three epigrams in the *Palatine Anthology*, one of which was written for Baucis:

> Column and my sirens, and mourning urn, you hold my death, these few ashes. Tell all who pass by my tomb to greet me, be they from this city or another country: "The tomb holds a bride, my father called me Baucis, I came from Tenos," so they will know. And tell them that my friend Erinna inscribed this epigram on my tomb.[24]

Aristophanes mentions a poetess named Cleitagora of Sparta.[25] In the Hellenistic period Anyte of Tegea in Arcadia (to whom her fellow citizens erected a statue), was called by Antipater of Thessalonica a "female Homer."[26] Meleager compared her epigrams to purple lilies. She was the author of most delicate verses, such as these written for the girl Myro:

> For her grasshopper, the meadow nightingale, and
> for her cricket, the tree-sleeper, the girl Myro
> made this common tomb and shed a young girl's tear,

because Hades, who cannot be persuaded, went away
and took her two pets with him.[27]

Anyte wrote these lines for the unknown traveler:

Stranger, rest your tired limbs beneath the rock.
The sweet breeze rustles in the green leaves. Drink
the cool water from the spring. Yes, for travelers,
this is a welcome respite in the burning heat.[28]

Finally, there was Nossis, who lived at the end of the fourth
century at Epizephyrian Locris in Magna Graecia, a city where the
noble families belonging to the Hundred Houses seem to have
transmitted their names through the female line, as some deduce
from the fact that Nossis records the name of her mother Theophilis
but not that of her father.[29] Nossis proudly compares herself to
Sappho.[30] Of her works twelve epigrams remain. Those poems
dedicated to the subject of love Meleager described as "fragrant
irises in full bloom."[31] One of the love epigrams reveals a genuine
and passionate poetic vein:

There is nothing sweeter than love; all other delights are secondary. In
comparison, I'd spit even honey from my mouth. This is what Nossis
says. If Aphrodite doesn't love you, you don't know how sweet roses
are.[32]

In the history of Greek literature, there are no poetesses from
Attica. Not one of the women whose cultural and literary activity we
have outlined so far came from that region, and this is not by
chance. The only female intellectual whose name is linked with the
history of Athens is Aspasia, but she was not Athenian but Ionian.
All the poetesses were active in other regions, where women's lives
were somehow freer.

Even if throughout Greece women's lives were ultimately organized around marriage, in some areas ethnically and culturally
different from Athens, women (at least before they were married)
enjoyed experiences quite different from those of Athenian girls
waiting for marriage. They were permitted a life that granted more
importance to their education and to the formation of their personalities. Not surprisingly, these women spoke of themselves as

members of the intellectual world. They demonstrated attitudes not only equal to male ones but sometimes superior in intelligence, sensitivity, and creativity. It bears repeating that in literature as in other fields the presence or absence of great female personages is determined only by cultural facts.

Six

Homosexuality and Love

Homosexual Love in Myth

The subject of Greek homosexuality has become the subject of ever-deeper interest and investigation. It represents an essential part of the study of women. If homosexuality was more widespread in ancient Greece than it is in present-day Western society, where it is widely considered a "deviant" behavior, its effect on the conception of the male–female relationship, and consequently on the female condition, must have been great. In this chapter we will attempt to gauge the extent of homosexuality among the Greeks and to identify the characteristics of relationships between persons of the same sex. How did the Greeks perceive and experience such relationships and what affective and emotional roles were they assigned? What were the social and cultural functions of homosexuality?

First, we may note the large number of explicit attestations to homosexual relationships and emotions—whether requited or unrequited. Second, we may observe the peculiar attitude of classicists when faced by this evidence, which has been for years either totally ignored or interpreted in such a way as to distort its meaning.

Although nearly eighty years have passed since publication of the famous article in which E. Bethe confronted a reality that was difficult to deny, the resistance to admitting that homosexual love for the Greeks was not only as normal as heterosexual but was socially and ethically more "qualified" and "qualifying" has not been altogether conquered.[1]

It is sometimes said even today that homosexuality was "imported" into Greece by the Dorians in the eleventh century B.C. and unknown to Achaeo-Mycenaean culture,[2] "socially unappreciated and legally reproached,"[3] and of limited diffusion. In other words, it was supposed to be an elite and not a mass phenomenon.[4] This suggestion poses a real problem, to which we will return after showing how difficult it is to prove the "Dorian" theory and how obviously without foundation is the statement that homosexuality was socially disapproved of or forbidden by law.[5]

As for the first problem, it is impossible to draw any sort of material conclusion from the Mycenaean sources, which consist of administrative and financial documents with not the merest glimpse of private life. But other documents exist. There are numerous homosexual couplings in mythology: Poseidon and Pelops; Zeus and Ganymede; Laius and Chrysippus, the son of Pelops; Apollo and Hyacinthus, Cyparissos, Admetus, and so on. These myths, as a whole, show clearly widespread male homosexuality throughout Greece beginning in a much earlier period, and they seriously question the idea of the nonexistence (or the limited spread) of this type of love in the pre-Dorian period.[6]

Second, though the Homeric epics contain no explicit references to homosexuality, they do describe friendships of such emotional intensity between men as to leave at least the impression that they were love relationships. This is illustrated most vividly by the friendship of Achilles and Patroclus, which both Aeschylus and Plato considered homosexual.[7]

Finally, there are two well-known and much-discussed pieces of evidence on ancient Cretan and Spartan practices.

Crete and Sparta:
The Role of Homosexuality in Initiation

Strabo recounts, quoting Ephorus, that on Crete adult men called
"lovers" (*erastai*) used to kidnap adolescent boys whom they loved
(*eromenoi*) and take them outside the city for two months. During
that period, the relationships were minutely regulated by the law,
which established the reciprocal obligations of the partner.[8] At
Sparta, according to Plutarch, boys of twelve were entrusted to
"lovers" chosen from the best adult men, and learned from these
lovers how to be true Spartans.[9]

To understand these practices it might be useful to step back
from ancient Greece for a moment and look at the organization of
societies that ethnologists call "traditional" societies, that is, societies organized into divisions of population based on age. In societies
organized along age divisions, an individual's passage from one
class to another is marked by a series of rites of passage, whose
structure—despite many vocal variations—is the following: to be
received into the next highest age class, the initiate (rites of passage
are initiations similar to "mystery" rites) must pass a period of time
far away from the group, living outside the rule of civilized life, in a
state of nature. In other words, one goes through a period that
ethnologists call "marginal" or "segregated," which is accompanied
by a death symbolism more or less realistically represented. This
sometimes precedes the segregation, sometimes follows it, and
sometimes is symbolized by it. And, finally, one is reborn to a new
life.[10] In other words, the rites of passage have a tripartite mor-
phology (separation–segregation–aggregation), whose importance
is not difficult to grasp. By separating oneself from the age class one
must leave, one dies for that class, and a new and different
individual takes a place in the higher class. The existence of rites of
passage in archaic Greece has been recognized for some time thanks
to such scholars as H. Jeanmaire, L. Gernet, and A. Brelich, and it
has been confirmed recently, despite significant differences in
approach and method, by the research of P. Vidal-Naquet, C. Calame,
and B. Lincoln.[11]

Can we conclude that the homosexual relationship had an

institutional role in the complex of these rites and, in particular, that it was an integral part of the pedagogical relationship between adolescent and adult during the period of segregation? This plausible hypothesis would help to clarify the social and cultural characteristics of the homosexual relationship in the classical period, when this kind of love is more than amply documented.[12]

Homosexuality and Bisexual Divinities

Let us begin with a famous passage from Plato, the account of the love between Socrates and Alcibiades in the *Symposium*. Here is Socrates' version:

> Since I became his admirer I have never been allowed to speak to any other fair one, or so much as to look at them. If I do, he goes wild with envy and jealousy, and not only abuses me but can hardly keep his hands off me, and at this moment he may do me some harm. Please to see to this, and either reconcile me to him, or, if he attempts violence, protect me, as I am in bodily fear of his mad and passionate attempts. (213 c–d)[13]

And here is Alcibiades' version:

> Well, he and I were alone together, and I thought that when there was nobody with us, I should hear him speak the language which lovers use to their loves when they are by themselves, and I was delighted. Nothing of the sort; he conversed as usual, and spent the day with me and then went away. Afterwards I challenged him to the palaestra; and he wrestled and closed with me several times when there was no one present; I fancied that I might succeed in this manner. Not a bit; I made no way with him. . . . So I invited him to sup with me, just as if he were a fair youth, and I a designing lover. . . .
>
> When the lamp was put out and the servants had gone away, . . . I gave him a shake, and I said: "Socrates are you asleep?" "What are you meditating?" he said. "I think," I replied, "that of all the lovers whom I have ever had you are the only one who is worthy of me, and you appear to be too modest to speak. Now I feel that I should be a fool to refuse you this or any other favour, and therefore I come to lay at your feet all that I have and all that my friends have, in the hope that you will assist me in the way of virtue, which I desire above all things, and in which I believe that you can help me better than any one else. . . . And so without waiting to hear more I got up, and throwing my coat about him crept under his threadbare cloak, as the time of year was winter, and there I lay during the whole night having this wonderful monster in my

arms. . . . And yet, notwithstanding all, . . . nothing more happened, but in the morning when I awoke (let all the gods and goddesses be my witnesses) I arose as from the couch of a father or an elder brother. (217 b–219d)

Alcibiades' declaration that he wanted to become Socrates' lover in order to better himself supports the view that even the Athenians ascribed a pedagogic function to sexual love. More important, what emerges clearly from the account is the absolute normality of homosexual relations and the evidence that, as a rule, it was a matter of physical relations: the only abnormal aspect, if there is one, seems to have been Socrates' resistance.

Tales of adventures between men are altogether usual in Aristophanes.[14] Xenophon speaks completely naturally about Hieron, carried off by Daïlochus,[15] to praise the chastity of Agesilaos, Xenophon says that he was capable of resisting a man.[16] Lysias defends a client accused of attempted homicide in a fight with another man over a boy.[17] Theocritus' second *Idyll* tells of a girl who, abandoned by her lover, wonders whether she was left for another woman or for a boy.[18] We could continue listing examples, but let us move on to religion.

Bisexual gods were worshipped in many parts of Greece, and rites were celebrated in which men and women exchanged clothing and roles. Ovid tells the story of Hermaphroditus, a beautiful boy who at the age of fifteen was loved by a nymph who literally could not bear to tear herself away from him. They were permanently joined in a bisexual existence.[19] In Amatos on Cyprus (where a bisexual divinity was worshipped), once a year the boys imitated the pain of childbirth, recalling the legend according to which, in that very place, Ariadne died while bearing the son of the absent Theseus.[20]

Macrobius speaks of a hermaphroditic divinity (Aphroditos), during whose worship the men dress as women and the women as men.[21] Argos, the city that had been saved by the armed intervention of the woman Telesilla, held an annual festival (*Hybristika*) in which women and men exchanged clothing.[22] At Cos, bridegrooms dressed as women to receive their brides.[23] At Sparta wives wore men's clothes and shoes, with their hair cut like men's, to receive theii husbands.[24] The traces of an androgynous vision of life are evident.[25] By exemplifying the Greeks' awareness of the sexual duality of human beings, legend and rites seem further proof that homosexuality was considered a natural fact of life.

The theory that homosexuality was practiced rarely and was largely disapproved of socially is denied by the evidence. Once that point has been established, two further points remain: first, whether homosexuality was viewed positively only if it had a pedagogical function (that is, only if the relationship involved an adult and an adolescent), or if it was considered normal even between adults; second, whether still given its pedagogical role it was practiced only by the upper classes or by those who were excluded from the values of *paideia* as well.

These two related problems are not easy to resolve. Some sources could give the impression that relations between adults were looked on with disfavor. In Aristophanes' *Frogs,* for example, Heracles asks Dionysus if he is in love with ". . . a woman?" "No." "A boy?" "No, no." "A man?" "Ah! ah!"[26] Other sources allude to homosexual loves with admiration and respect. One example is the famous Sacred Band of Thebes, composed of 150 pairs of lovers, unbeaten until the battle of Chaeronea (338 B.C.) where they died heroically, each to demonstrate to his loved one the worthiness of his love.[27]

As for homosexuality among the lower classes, a remark attributed by Plato to Alcibiades (in his account of his love for Socrates) seems to confirm that homosexuality was a practice of the higher classes: "I should certainly have more reason to be ashamed of what wise men would say if I were to refuse a favour to such as you, that of what the world, who are mostly fools, would say of me if I granted it."[28] Unlike the heterosexual relationship (which often occurred between a free man and a slave woman), the homosexual relationship occurred only between free men.[29] But this does not necessarily mean that the "ignorant crowd" (even without the pedagogical aspect) did not practice homoerotic love.

One thing seems certain: at least among the upper classes homosexuality was not only a widespread practice but perhaps even a universal one and one that was certainly considered to have high cultural value.

Plato

The effect of the Greek ideal of homosexuality on the male–female relationship can best be understood through a famous passage of the *Symposium* in which Plato recounts (through Aristophanes) how it happened that the human race, originally composed of three sexes, came one day to be divided into only two:

> Let me treat of the nature of man and what has happened to it. . . . The sexes were not two as they are now, but originally three in number; there was man, woman, and the union of the two, having a name corresponding to this double nature, which had once a real existence, but is now lost, and the word "Androgynous" is only preserved as a term of reproach. . . . Primeval man was round, his back and sides forming a circle; and he had four hands and four feet, one head with two faces, looking opposite ways, set on a round neck and precisely alike; also four ears, two privy members and the remainder to correspond. He could walk upright as men now do, backwards or forwards as he pleased, and he could also roll over and over at a great pace, turning on his four hands and four feet, eight in all, like tumblers going over and over with their legs in the air. . . .
>
> Now, the sexes were three. . . . Terrible was their might and strength, and the thoughts of their hearts were great, and they made an attack upon the gods. . . . Doubt reigned in the celestial councils. Should they kill them and annihilate the race with thunderbolts, as they had done the giants, then there would be an end of the sacrifices and worship which men offered to them; but on the other hand, the gods could not suffer their insolence to be unrestrained. At last, after a good deal of reflection, Zeus discovered a way, he said: "Methinks I have a plan which will humble their pride and improve their manners; men shall continue to exist, but I will cut them in two and then they will be diminished in strength and increased in numbers; this will have the advantage of making them more profitable to us. They shall walk upright on two legs, and if they continue insolent and will not be quiet, I will split them again and they shall hop about on a single leg." He spoke and cut men in two . . . [and] bade Apollo give the face and the half of the neck a turn in order that the man might contemplate the section of himself; he would thus learn a lesson of humility. . . . After the division the parts of man, each desiring his other half, came together, and throwing their arms about one another, entwined in mutual embraces,

longing to grow into one; they were on the point of dying from hunger and self-neglect, because they did not like to do anything apart; and when one of the halves died and the other survived, the survivor sought another mate, man or woman, as we call them—being the section of entire men or women—and clung to that. They were being destroyed, when Zeus in pity of them invented a new plan: he turned the parts of generation round to the front, for this had not been always their position, and they sowed the seed no longer as hitherto like grass-hoppers in the ground, but in one another; and after the transposition the male generated in the female in order that by the mutual embraces of man and woman they might breed, and the race might continue; or if man came to man they might be satisfied and rest, and go their ways to the business of life: so ancient is the desire of one another which is implanted in us, reuniting our original nature, making one of two, and healing the state of man.

Each of us when separated, having one side only, like a flat fish, is but the indenture of a man and he is always looking for his other half. Men who are a section of that double nature which was once called An-drogynous are lovers of women; adulterers are generally of this breed, and also adulterous women who lust after men: the women who are a section of the woman do not care for men but have female attachments; the female companions are of this sort. But they who are a section of the male, follow the male, and while they are young, being slices of the original man, they hang about men and embrace them, and they are themselves the best of boys and youths, because they are shameless, but this is not true; for they do not act thus from any want of shame, but because they are valiant and manly, and have a manly countenance, and they embrace that which is like them. And these when they grow up become our statesmen, and these only, which is a great proof of the truth of what I am saying. When they reach manhood they are lovers of youth, and are not naturally inclined to marry or beget children—if at all, they do so only in obedience to the law; but they are satisfied if they may be allowed to live with one another unwedded. (180e–192e)

The passage is instructive for several reasons. First, it shows that the Greeks considered homosexual relationships neither more nor less natural than the heterosexual. In seeking the other half (of the same sex), whether a person was derived from the male or female sex, he or she was trying to put a previously existing unit back together again, exactly as those who derived from the androgynous sex sought partners of the opposite gender. But the passage implies something even more interesting.

For Plato, homosexuals were "the best" because they were originally all man or all woman, unlike heterosexuals who derived from the androgynes. Heterosexuals are either adulterers, says Plato, or "adulterous women who lust after men." Male homosexuals, on the other hand, have "the most manly nature" and therefore "when they grow up become our statesmen." The consequences of all this for the male–female relationship are obvious: noble, educational, experienced by the best, it was in the homosexual relationship that the Greek man expressed his better side, intelligence, will for self-improvement, and a higher level of emotions. This is confirmed by the fact that female prostitution was legal, whereas male prostitution was punished as a crime. This distinction has often been cited as evidence that homosexuality was socially disapproved, but it actually supports the opposite conclusion.

The reason for the different legal treatment was not that homosexuality was socially frowned upon. It was that the relationship between men could not be sold because it was a privileged interpersonal exchange. Gifts between lovers were permitted because they were considered a legitimate attempt to win and keep love, but payment was quite another thing. It removed the element of free choice from the union of two people made in full consciousness of their own moral and political training. Prostitution degraded the relationship, deprived it of its pedagogical function, and reduced a citizen to an object. It made him unfit for political participation in a city of free men. Consequently, whoever made himself object of a purely sexual pleasure should be excluded from the *polis* as well, if not physically, then by means of a penalty that sanctioned his political death, *atimia,* the most serious punishment after the death penalty.[30]

To conclude, female segregation may have contributed to the spead of homosexuality in Greece, but it was neither the only cause nor the most important one. Based on the notion that the individual belongs to two sexes and given its social and intellectual implications, homosexuality reinforced female segregation. For the Greek man the homosexual relationship was a privileged outlet for exchange of experience, and he found in it an answer to his greatest needs. To relegate women to a purely biological role was perfectly natural.

Female Homosexuality

On love between women, the sources are less eloquent than they are on love between men, but that should not be surprising. Unlike male homosexuality, female homosexuality was not an instrument for the training of citizens. It therefore by definition interested only women. Fortunately one Greek woman has left literary evidence for female homosexuality. Sappho is our only direct source for love between women. First it is necessary to look briefly at female communities (one of which was headed by Sappho), documented not only on Lesbos but also in other parts of Greece, Sparta in particular.

These *thiasoi* were not simple finishing schools, as they have often been called. They were far more complex. Deriving perhaps from even more ancient female communities, they had their own divinities and rites, and unmarried girls shared a complete experience of life in them. Apart from differences due to gender, life in these groups was completely analogous to the communal existence of men in corresponding groups.[31] Obviously this does not mean that the girls did not also receive an education. With particular reference to Lesbos, the *Suda* names three *mathetriai,* pupils, of Sappho and she is called *didaskalos,* "teacher."[32]

Sappho taught her pupils music, singing, and dance: arts that transformed them from uneducated youngsters, one of whom is mourned in these verses:

> When you die, you shall lie there, and no memory of you
> shall survive among men of the future, for you have no
> share in the roses of Pieria. No, unnoticed in Hades
> as you were on earth, you shall wander among the dim
> shades once your soul has flown away from us.[33]

Thus Sappho writes of a rival, who did not learn from her that which would have allowed her to emerge from ignorance and would thereby save her from oblivion. But Sappho was not only mistress of the intellect—her girls learned about the weapons of beauty, seduction, and charm: they learned the grace (*charis*) that made them desirable women. Here the description finishing school is not incorrect, but it is certainly insufficient. The education of girls from Lesbos and elsewhere (among Sappho's pupils were Atthis of Miletus, Gongyla of Colophon, and Eunice of Salamis, and there were such rival *thiasoi* as those of Gorgo and Andromeda, also presumably welcoming girls from distant cities) was given over to a pedagogical instrument, namely homosexual love, which might be the last thing one would expect for "nice" girls.

This means, perhaps, that the role of female homosexuality (at least at Sparta and elsewhere in Greece where associations like the Lesbian *thiasos* could be found) was not very different from male homosexuality. At Sparta, says Plutarch, the best women loved girls, and when it happened that more than one adult fell in love with the same girl, they were rivals with one another but joined forces to educate their beloved.[34] Thus, just as the homosexual relationship with an adult was part of a boy's training for citizenship, it was similarly part of a girl's training for wifehood. But we will return to this after confronting the last problem, whether the homosexual relationship as a stage of normal training for adulthood was simply a cultural model, as has been supposed, or a true individual relationship as well. The poetry of Sappho leaves little doubt. Her love poems were never addressed to a group but always to a single girl, such as Gongyla, Atthis, and Anactoria.

Homosexual relations, then, were personal and real. Perhaps it is possible to suppose that only some of the girls had physical relations with the teacher while they were in the *thiasos,* and that others participated only through the teacher's poetry. Indeed the supposition seems supported by comparison with Cretan initiations, in which the youth was accompanied by friends during his segregation with the lover. These friends helped carry the boy off and participated in the ceremonies that marked the end of the segregation. They too became citizens at the same time even though they themselves had not had relations with the adult.[35] We may be certain, however, that homosexuality whether male or female was a cultural fact of fundamental importance in the life of many Greek communities. And it was not only a pedagogical tool in the sense discussed here. It was also an expression of genuine feeling, an interpersonal relationship of often exceptional emotional intensity. The fragment of Sappho cited in Chapter 5 is unequivocal:

> . . . For whenever I glance at you, it seems that I can say nothing at all

> but as my tongue is broken in silence, and that instant a light fire rushes beneath my skin, I can no longer see anything in my eyes and my ears are thundering,

> and cold sweat pours down me, and shuddering grasps me all over, and I am greener than grass, and I seem to myself to be little short of death.

An interesting example of resistance to the hypothesis of the extent and role of Greek homosexuality is an attempt at Freudian analysis of this fragment by G. Devereux. Sappho, he says, displays the following symptoms, among others: irregular breathing and psychophysiological inhibition of speech; disturbances of vision (probably of vascular origin) and ringing in the ears; trembling and pallor (caused by the restriction of the capillaries and by the flow of blood back to the internal organs). In other words, the symptoms are clinically those of an anxiety attack.[36] But these are also the symptoms of love.

Devereux's conclusions are perplexing. It is true, he says, that the symptoms of anxiety can accompany any crisis of love—but in the Greek sources, as a rule, it is crises of homosexual love, not heterosexual, which provoke attacks of anxiety. It would be the perception of the "abnormality" of one's love, then, that would make the manifestations of homosexuality anxiety-producing, as, for instance, those of Sappho. This, he concludes, "can neither prove nor disprove that she was *also* a schoolmistress or a cult-leader. If she was either (or both), this would prove not more than that in Lesbos, quite as much as in some modern societies, female inverts tended to gravitate into professions which brought them in contact with young girls, whose partial segregation and considerable psycho-sexual immaturity—and therefore incomplete differentiatedness—made them willing participants in lesbian experimentation."[37]

We come to the problem that concerns us most. What role did homosexual love have in the lives of women? Despite the analogies that seem to emerge from Plutarch's observations, female homosexuality does not really seem comparable to the male version. The community experience was also the spiritual, educational, and cultural moment. But how many women, when, and where, had this experience? It should not be forgotten that, beyond what we can deduce about Sappho, we know practically nothing about these communities. Moreover, even within these communities homosexuality seems to have played a different role than it did in the lives of men.

It is perhaps no accident that it is a man (Plutarch) who stresses the pedagogical function of the relationship between women, whereas Sappho—though she insists on the educational and ennobling aspect of the life of the *thiasos*—stresses instead the affective and erotic aspect of the relationship. In some way, then, one senses that female homosexuality was culturally "constructed" on the model of the male and presented—by the few male sources that allude to it—as a copy of this. But what, then, was the meaning of homosexual love in the lives of Greek women? Even if it is difficult to say with certainty, the function identified by K. J. Dover seems plausible. Dover describes it a sort of "counterculture" in which women received from their own sex what segregation and monogamy kept them from receiving from men.[38]

Seven

The Hellenistic Age:
New Images, Old Stereotypes

Legal Status: Toward Equality

Traditionally defined as the period between the death of Alexander the Great (323 B.C.) and the Roman conquest of Egypt (30 B.C.), the Hellenistic age was characterized by profound changes in political, philosophical, and scientific visions, in forms of artistic expression, and in concepts of life.[1] And it was characterized by a notable change in the status of women. In this period, women saw growing respect, broader chances to participate in social life, and a perceptible extension of their legal capacities.

It is difficult to say what caused this change. Perhaps it was the end of the city-state and its replacement by the Macedonian monarchies—the Antigonids in Greece, the Seleucids in Asia, and the Ptolemies in Egypt—and the influence on these monarchies of the earlier political systems, some of which, like Egypt, had for centuries recognized women's capacities and rights. Perhaps it was the "disintegration" of classical values, begun by the Cynics and Stoics. Perhaps it was inevitable that all these elements combined to cause profound upheavals and to contribute to the birth of a new world, as indeed the Hellenistic was. Whatever the causes were, however, we do know that the lives of women changed noticeably.[2]

Of course, women were still excluded from participation in

political life. The cases of female participation in the management of power, in fact, are exceptions and they are recorded as such. For example, Aristodama, a poetess from Smyrna, in 218 B.C. was granted citizenship by the Aetolians of Lamia in Thessaly.[3] Another woman was made "archon" at Histria in the second century.[4] Phyle of Priene, in the first century B.C., was made city "magistrate" and she built an aqueduct.[5] Despite exclusion in principle from political participation, Hellenistic women saw no small increase in their opportunities.

The evidence of the Egyptian papyri, which preserve innumerable private documents, reveals profound innovations.[6] Let us set aside the status of Egyptian women, traditionally freer and thereby capable of legal action without a guardian, and consider Greek women. Despite the continuing requirement of a guardian's consent to assume obligation in the traditional forms of Greek law, Greek women acquired new capacities. For example, they could buy and sell goods and property, mortgage their own goods, give and obtain loans, assume obligations of work, make wills, be named heirs and inherit legacies, and—albeit rarely—personally conclude their own marriage contracts.[7]

Sometimes, the mother appears in the marriage contract along with her husband in giving away the daughter in marriage.[8] If the mother is a widow or not legally married, she can exercise a fairly broad *materna potestas* over her daughter, which allows her (in agreement with the mother-in-law) to expose children born posthumously, to place children in apprenticeships, and to give away daughters in marriage.[9] Mothers still could not be witnesses to contracts concluded by other people or own certain types of lands, but otherwise they had nearly full capacities.[10] With rights came obligations; for example, a mother had to provide for the support of the children after the death of the father.[11]

This does not mean that the law did not still create situations of subordination to male power. The social conscience balked at formulations viewed as anachronistic and unjust, and it was the women themselves who rebelled in these cases, claiming their autonomy. For example, in Hellenistic law, a father still had the power of *apheresis*, that is, he could interrupt the marriage of his daughter. But in the second century at Oxyrhynchus, a certain Dionysia reported her father to the prefect, charging that "no law permits taking daughters away from their husbands against their will."[12]

Exposure of infants was still practiced, with girls still the preferred victims. In 1 B.C. at Oxyrhynchus, an absent husband wrote his pregnant wife explicitly to raise the newborn if it was male but to expose it if it was female.[13] His matter-of-fact tone reveals the normality of his instructions.

Illiteracy was more frequent among women than men, as we can see from the percentage of women who had to seek the help of third parties in order to write letters.[14] This fact makes us reflect on the real scope of their new liberties. Perhaps they were less in actual fact than the law might lead us to believe. But that female education was generally on the increase is indisputable.[15] At Alexandria in particular the advancement of women is undeniable.[16] At Teos we have a report of a coeducational school.[17] And there is no absence of women who, in various situations, held political power.

Women and Political Power

Olympias, the mother of Alexander the Great, had an influential role at the Macedonian court. She was accused of having killed her husband (Philip II) so that her son could accede to the throne (although at the time, 336 B.C., she was in exile). While Alexander was fighting against the Persians, she exercised de facto the power of the government, in opposition to the regent Antipater.[18]

In 315, when the Sicyonians killed her husband, Cratesipolis took power and governed for seven years, crucifying more than thirty citizens who had opposed her.[19] In Egypt, more than one woman was either associated with power or sole holder of it. Arsinoë ruled for five years, till 270 B.C., together with her brother Ptolemy II, who according to Egyptian custom was also her husband.[20] In the second century, Cleopatra II and Cleopatra III ruled. In 51 B.C. Cleopatra VII ascended the throne at the age of ten. After getting rid of her brother-husband, Ptolemy XIII, with the help of Julius Caesar, she ruled first with her younger brother Ptolemy XIV and later with her son by Caesar, Ptolemy XV.[21]

It would be in error, however, to conclude from these examples that women were allowed to govern by dynastic rule. Except for the Egyptian queens (whose succession to the throne was, however, linked to marriage to their brothers), the women who had power in the Hellenistic period achieved it mostly as representatives of a dead sovereign, or thanks to abuses and violence that prevailed over institutional laws.[22] This does not take away the fact that the existence of such female figures has significance. These facts offer a very different picture than that of the classical period.

Women in Literature

Had the old conception of the inferior woman and the old misogyny disappeared in the Hellenistic era? As for the classical period, to answer this question it is necessary to examine the literature. That Hellenistic literature presents different female images from those presented in the literature of the classical period is indisputable.

New Comedy is very important in this regard. No longer mythical heroes, no longer demigods, the characters of New Comedy are common men and women, men and women who express everyday emotions and sentiments. The women among these new characters are no longer per se the cause of misfortune but are persons who (like men) can have both good and bad qualities.

Why this change of theme, this new attention to the daily life, sentiments, and private relationships of average people?[23] Interest in public and political life did not disappear. Athens fought to survive in a world dominated by the successors of Alexander; alongside those who wanted Macedonian protection were those who claimed the right to independence. But Athens was no longer the capital of an empire, and by that time had become a provincial city like so many others. Even its cultural primacy was fading and about to pass to Pergamum and Alexandria. And just as Athens was not as it used to be, so public and political life was no longer what gave the Athenian citizen a sense of life.

Comedy, then, sought new themes, observed the life of the city and its people, and described types rather than characters. Developing a tendency already present in the Doric comedy of Epicharmus, in Megarian farce, and in the caricatures of Attic comedy,

New Comedy presented new types: the greedy and irascible father, the son who squanders his fortune thinking only of fun, the professional soldier, the crafty slave. Pollux describes forty-four comic masks, nine of which are of adult males or old people, eleven of youths, seven of slaves, and seventeen of women.

The interest in female characters is obvious. The character types represent women of every sort and social status, from the madam intent on maximizing her profits to the innocent and passive young bride; from the slave devoted to her master to the hetaera who, claiming the right to live, becomes an increasingly important character. New Comedy presents a vast range of female types, introduces the conditions of life of many women who, in the context of a new freedom, now stroll through the streets of Athens, visiting shops.[24]

In this context, we can gather precious indications of the new way of conceiving the conjugal relationship, which has been at least partly freed, even at Athens, from the family preoccupations that had marked it in the classical period, and which is even viewed as a personal relationship based on a free emotional choice. The portrayal of the *epikleros* (heiress), a favorite subject of New Comedy, offers important insights. The situation of the heiress (obliged to marry her nearest relative, see chapter 3) had not particularly interested the poets of the Old Comedy; Aristophanes alludes to her only twice, and marginally (*Birds* 1652 and *Wasps* 583 ff.). Two Middle Comedy poets (Antiphanes and Heniochus) dedicated comedies to the theme, both called *Epikleros*. In New Comedy, the heiress becomes an extremely popular character.

Menander gave the title *Epikleros* to two of his comedies and placed an heiress at the center of the plot of other plays, in particular the *Aspis*.[25] New Comedy playwrights Diphilus of Sinope, Alexis, and Diodorus wrote comedies on the same theme.[26] The subject lent itself to great exploitation, partly because of the comic potential of the marriage of a young girl and a man of advanced age (often her paternal uncle), who in New Comedy typing is an unpleasant, greedy, and ill-tempered old man. Opposite these old men who claim marriage for purely economic reasons, the comedy features characters who violently criticize their decisions. In the *Aspis* (314–15), speaking of old Smicrines who is determined to marry his niece, Chairestratos expresses his disgust, saying that it is better to die than to witness such a shameful act.

In general, everything that limits freedom of personal choice is now considered with disfavor. As in Egypt, in Athens the right of the father to end a daughter's marriage is contested: "You should have looked for a husband for me when I was little. Then it was up to you to decide. But now that you have given me in marriage, the decision, father, seems to be up to me," says one girl.[27]

Women in New Comedy are not necesssarily negative characters because of the "femininity." There are women of noble sentiments, like Habrotonon the harpist, who in the *Arbitrators (Epitrepontes)* is in love with Charisius. She is capable of sacrificing herself for his good, working to ensure that he is reconciled with his wife. Other women are portrayed whose nobility consists in dedication and sacrifice, whose love is devotion, who want only the man's happiness—these are ideal women from a purely male point of view, but now they are described in compassionate accents. The social situation was different and the old misogyny, if not gone, was weakening.

In Hellenistic poetry, the man–woman relationship is in a way equal. The woman is still a cause of suffering, but not because of her "troublesome" nature. She causes suffering when she does not love in return, but she suffers too when her love is not returned. It is love (always sad in Hellenistic poetry) that is the cause of sorrow for all men and women. In the *Idylls* of Theocritus, the Cyclops Polyphemus suffers for Galatea:

> He loved her not with apples or roses or ringlets,
> but with real madness, and he considered everything
> else unimportant. (11.11)

Simethe too, forgotten by her beloved, weeps because "he doesn't know if I'm dead or alive" (2.5). In the *Shut-out* (a *paraklausithuron*, or song in front of a closed door, a typical Hellenistic motif) a girl begs her beloved to let her in:

Love has taken hold of me, I don't deny it. Beloved
stars and lady Night, my fellow-lover, send me now
to the man to whom Cypris hands me over as hostage, and for whom
great
Passion has conquered me.[28]

Love makes men and women equals—equally able to suffer and to make others suffer. None of this means, however, that in the Hellenistic period the traditional themes had disappeared. Women continued to be characterized (though in terms unlike those used in the classical period) as having few worthy qualities, usually because they lack intelligence. "The intelligent woman is a treasure of virtue, but is a rare case," said Menander.[29] Moreover, the women are endowed with negative qualities, foremost among these a love of wine and sex. Still viewed as pure animality, women are often depicted as overindulgers in alcohol. For example, we read on an irreverent epitaph about a woman named Maronis:

Old Maronis the tippler, an urn of dust, lies here. Her Attic drinking cup—everyone will recognize it—is placed above her tomb. Beneath the earth she weeps not for her children or husband, whom she leaves in poverty, but for this above all: that her cup is empty.[30]

The drunken women are unfaithful liars too:

I know that your oath is empty, since your damp myrrh-scented hair betrays you as a wanton; look, your sleepless, heavy eyes betray you, and the ribbon binding the crowns in your hair, and the ringlet shamelessly torn out, and your limbs shaking from unmixed wine. Go away, common whore, the party-loving lyre and the finger-rattling beat of castanets are calling you.[31]

Continually in search of pleasure and in the absence of men, women use the notorious leather dildos (*olisboi*), which were already alluded to in Aristophanes (*Lys.* 26–28). In *Mime* 6 ("The Shoemaker") of Herodas, Metro and Corinna chat about them enthusiastically. Authoritarian and exacting, they consider men to be sexual objects. Bitinna the protagonist of Herodas' fifth *Mime* ("The Jealous Woman"), suspects the slave Gastron of infidelity. She ill-treats him, convinced not only of her right but of the necessity of exercising it:

Don't keep after me! or I'll leave the house.
You want me to let this seven-timer slave off?
If I did, anyone who ran into me would be justified
in spitting in my face.[32]

When they are rich, women are a true misfortune because their arrogance knows no limits. In a play of Menander called *Plokion*, an heiress forces her husband to sell a young and beautiful slave girl, and she personally arranges her son's marriage to the young daughter of a poor neighbor. Tyrannized in every way by his wife, the husband is a character intended to attract public sympathy. Every coin has two sides: on the one hand marrying an heiress is disapproved of because it is an anachronistic and unjust practice; on the other it is considered a danger for husbands because their male dominance is questioned. "The poor man who marries a rich wife doesn't get a wife but a master," said Anaximandrides.[33]

Conclusions

The Greek woman of the Hellenistic age was certainly more liberated than her ancestresses. Ideologically, she was no longer confined to the ghetto of "nature"—in women the dignity of the individual began to be recognized. Hellenistic literature presents new and different female characters and represents women as more independent, enterprising, and active. In some areas, women received the same education as men. On the political scene, some female personages appear in high relief. Besides the Hellenistic queens there were exceptional women who wielded power as magistrates, and there were poetesses and women of culture.

And yet, the commonplaces of the old misogyny continue to show up in the literature, although perhaps the new status of women lies behind it. As always happens when women break out of their traditional confines to invade what are considered male dominions and appropriate intellectual avenues and the instruments of power, some react with clichés of the most facile sort of antifeminism. Indeed, Hellenistic misogyny is different from the archaic and classical versions. It is no longer the expression of a society that, by excluding women, underscores their materiality, accents their negative power, and theorizes their inferiority. It is the simple misogyny of those who see their own certainties wavering and defend themselves by translating the old prejudices into a sort of popular wisdom. They rely on a series of clichés and precepts of supposed common sense to reassert the now anachronistic commonplaces. This misogyny is the sign and the consequence of an altogether new fact: for the first time in their history, the Greeks had to take account of the presence of women.

ROME

Eight

The Hypothesis of Matriarchy

The Protoagricultural Phase

T he opinion was held in the last century, and is still repeated, that ancient "matriarchal" systems existed even in what is now Italy, particularly in Liguria, Etruria, and some areas of Lombardy. The reasoning is similar to that used to defend the theory of matriarchy in Greece. In the protoagricultural phase, they say, women (having become the principal procurers of food and developers of agricultural and related techniques, such as baking, weaving, and pottery) acquired a determining role in the life of the community, which led to "matrilocality" of marriage, "matrilineality" of descent, and, in the opinion of some, to true matriarchy.[1]

In the first place, the economically determining role acquired by women during the protoagricultural phase is not necessarily linked to leadership, even in consideration of the necessity of defending the group itself, which for physiological reasons could not be entrusted to women. Nor can a dominant female deity be considered proof of women's social and political power. The most that can be assumed is that this is a sign of the dignity that society ascribed to the maternal function. But what would this female figure be?

In the first centuries after the foundation of the city (traditionally

101

753 B.C.), Roman religion honored a female figure, whose image appeared in a series of cults: the Mater Matuta of Satricum, the goddess Feronia of Mount Soractus, the Bona Dea, Fortuna of Praeneste, and finally Tanaquil.[2]

Tanaquil and Etruscan Women

Tanaquil has been identified, ever since Bachofen, as a divinity behind whose cult could be discerned a powerful female image, a wielder—or at least transmitter—of regal power, with characteristics analogous to those of the Mediterranean *potnia*.[3] In the historical period, she was venerated as a domestic goddess, closed in the circle of her familiar attributes, which were destined to serve as model and example to Roman *matronae*. But according to the proponents of the matriarchy, this aspect is the outcome of the transformation imposed on her by patriarchal society at the very moment of her triumph, as her story, told by Livy and Dionysius of Halicarnassus, shows.

Wife of the Etruscan Lucumo, who was to become the king of Rome known as Tarquinius Priscus, Tanaquil was "perita ut volgo etrusci, prodigiorum mulier," that is, she knew how to interpret prodigies. Here are two examples of her abilities. When she and her husband, in their carriage on the way to Rome, reached the Janiculum, Tanaquil saw a prodigy. An eagle dropped down and took Lucumo's cap (*pileum*) from his head. It flew away and then returned, as if on a divine mission, to put the cap back on Lucumo's head. Tanaquil interpreted the prodigy to mean that divine will ordained that Lucumo would be king (Livy 1.34; Dion. 3.47).

Some years later another singular event occurred in the royal palace. While a child (the future king Servius Tullius) of a slave woman was sleeping, his head suddenly caught fire. Alerted by the screams of those present, Tanaquil prevented them from throwing water on the boy to put out the fire. When he awoke, the flames vanished. Again Tanaquil interpreted the omen: the child would be the light and support of the palace in difficult times (Livy 1.39; Dion. 4.2).

Tanaquil did not limit herself to reading prodigies; she did other things that were unusual for a woman. When her husband was killed as the victim of a palace plot, she exhorted Servius to take his place: "The kingdom belongs to you, if you are a man and not to those villains who paid others to commit their foul crime. Get up and follow the gods, who once foretold your fame by surrounding your head with sacred fire." Tanaquil spoke to the people "per fenestras in Novam viam versas," from the windows facing the Nova Via. The king, she said, is not dead: he will recover quickly, but in the meantime they should obey Servius (Livy 1.41). For some days Servius affirmed his authority, and when the news of the king's death got out, he took power and "praesidio firmo munitus primus iniussu populi, voluntate patrum regnavit."

This unusual story, which presents Servius—the "rex popularis" par excellence—as a tyrant, is interesting for many reasons. Here it is important to verify whether the legend can be used to support the two formulations, the matriarchal and matrilineal, of the matricentric hypothesis.

Momigliano's work has made it very difficult to believe in Tanaquil as matriarch. She is not, he points out, a goddess, as the Frankfurt school of the history of religion claimed (one thinks especially of W. Otto and F. Altheim), but a female figure elaborated by legendary tradition. More precisely, she is the figure of an Etruscan queen created by the Roman imagination. This means, obviously, that she cannot be used to reconstruct the status of Etruscan women who, despite their divining abilities, were not matriarchs, even in the Roman mind.[4]

There remains little or no support for the theory of female power in Etruria. In the fourth century B.C. the Greek Theopompus tells of their astonishing liberty, of the care they lavished on their bodies, of their habit of attending banquets with men and drinking wine, and above all of bringing up their children without worrying about who their father was.[5] If true, this last could suggest something other than a patriarchal system, but how much weight should we give the testimony of Theopompus? As the only possible female model he had was the Greek, he inevitably misunderstood what he saw and heard about other women. This is not so different from what happened when an Athenian observer described the customs of the Spartans.

All that can be deduced from his account is that Etruscan women had a noteworthy freedom of movement, which is confirmed by iconography and funerary monuments.[6] In the family, presumably, they were not subject to absolute power like that of the Roman *paterfamilias*. Unlike Roman women, Etruscan women attended banquets and reclined on couches like men rather than sat.

The mirrors found in women's tombs (on which were engraved the names of divinities and mythological figures) attest that Etruscan women were educated and knew how to read and write. Clearly this was a society in which women enjoyed a certain freedom of movement and a certain prestige, but no more than that. On the whole, it is possible to conclude that Etruscan women enjoyed status and respect in a role that was, nevertheless, family-oriented. Though they were the honored companions of men, they were always in some measure subordinate to them. A famous sarcophagus in the Villa Giulia Museum in Rome illustrates this. An Etruscan wife of the sixth century B.C. is depicted reclining at the same height beside her husband. This certainly represents a woman who was not enslaved, but at the same time it is the image of a devoted wife to whom her husband, with his arms around her shoulders, offers protection. This is the other face of power; it is what the dominant partner offers the one who accepts subordination.

The legend of female power in Etruria needs to be seen in perspective. Though if she was not a slave, the Etruscan woman was not a matriarch either. The legend of Tanaquil, after all, does not prove the existence of female power. Nor does it prove that succession to the throne was by the female line—this is a rule that would have been in effect in all of Latium and would also be demonstrated by the legend of Aeneas, who became king of Lavinium by virtue of his marriage with the daughter of the Latin king.

That Latin king, however, had no sons. As Y. Thomas observed, marriage with a foreigner is a strategy to avoid the end of a dynasty. "Let us be careful," says Thomas, "of interpreting these facts in terms of matrilineal filiation; what is at stake here is not filiation . . . but power, which is transmitted only from man to man, in a direct line." The succession of the son-in-law, then, has no systematic character but corresponds rather to the necessity of perpetuating a royal line in danger of dying out.[7]

Traces of Ancient Collective Marriage?

Reference is frequently made in the arguments of the proponents of the "matriarchy" to *couvade,* that is, the practice of many "primitive" peoples (including, supposedly, the ancient peoples of Italy)[8] according to which the father simulates labor pains while his wife gives birth. According to Bachofen, this is a male attempt to expropriate the fundamental lever of power that was motherhood.

Even if couvade was actually practiced by the ancient Italians (leaving aside the difficulty of proving such an assertion), this does not mean per se that female power ever actually existed. Couvade can be interpreted much more simply as the expression of the desire to participate in an event which, though of fundamental importance for the group, is not synonymous with possession and exercise of power by its women. Furthermore, today the practice is considered one of the numerous ritual and magic prescriptions which, in "primitive" societies, mark moments of particular importance.[9]

Traces of a classificatory system in Roman kinship terminology is another frequent but weak argument for group marriage. Kinship systems can be of two types: descriptive or classificatory. In descriptive systems the terms for kinship indicate the relationship existing between two individuals. In classificatory systems the terms link not just two people but an individual to a series of individuals who are one another's brothers. For example, in classificatory systems the term "father" indicates not only the parent but also all his brothers (who would be uncles in the descriptive system), and "mother" means not just the female parent but all her sisters as well.

Classificatory systems, it is said, are not the result of an abstract logic but the mirror of concrete social relationships, particularly marriage. In other words, they are the remains of a system in which, because of collective marriage, all the brothers of a group were the husbands of sisters from a different group.

Roman kinship terminology (although it is descriptive) would contain some traces of this system. Let us take just one example. The Latin language has not one but four terms for uncle/aunt: *patruus, matertera, amita,* and *avunculus. Patruus* and *matertera* are the brother of the father and the sister of the mother, that is, they are the parallel uncle and aunt indicated with two terms that are, respectively, expansions of "father" and "mother." In the classificatory system the father's brother is also called father and the sister of the mother is called mother. *Amita* and *avunculus* are the sister of the father and the brother of the mother, that is, the crossed uncle and aunt. But the terms with which they are indicated are not (as in the case of the parallel uncle and aunt) expansions of *mater* and *pater.* They derive, respectively, from the infantile root *ama* (*amita,* in fact, is the name for infantile speech) and from *awos* (*avus*), which means grandfather. This would have a very precise meaning. In the classificatory system, the brother of the maternal grandmother and the grandfather are indicated with the same terms. Therefore, if the brother of the mother's mother is *avus,* the mother's brother (in the absence of another kinship term) can be called *avunculus.*[10]

It is very much open to question whether this terminology can be used to prove the existence of female power. For quite some time anthropologists have believed that kinship terminology does not always or necessarily reflect social relationships.[11] Taken alone, without other evidence of collective marriage, the linguistic argument is meaningless. And no other evidence exists.

The cult of the Mater Matuta has been considered one of the strongest indications of collective marriage. On the festival days when that goddess was worshipped the women prayed not for their own children but for those of their sisters. From this has been inferred a primitive collective maternity of sisters, none of whom was bound by an individual marriage (which did not exist) and each one of whom was mother of all the children born within the group.[12] But there are more convincing explanations of this ritual. The women who participated in the annual Matralia, at which the Mater Matuta was celebrated, actually performed two distinct rites. In the first, a slave woman was brought in to the place where the cult was celebrated and slapped and beaten with a switch; in the second, the women nursed their sisters' children.

On the basis of comparison with Indian religion and the identification of Mater Matuta with Aurora (note the derivation of the adjective *matutinus* from Matuta), Dumézil has interpreted the two rituals as, respectively, the victory of Aurora over Tenebris, represented by the slave, and as the birth and growth of the sun. Aurora was the sister of Night (belonging to the "good" side of the world, unlike Tenebris) and the sun was her son, who reached maturity thanks to the milk given him by Aurora. It would be possible to read an ancient mythology of Aurora in the cult of Mater Matuta.[13]

Other simple but convincing explanations have been suggested. For example, given the frequency of death in childbirth, newborns were often nursed by a maternal aunt after the death of the mother. The aunt would establish a bond of particular affection with the niece or nephew. And given its nearly institutional diffusion, the ritual of nursing and the prayer to Mater Matuta could be explained, again, without any need for recourse to the hypothesis of collective maternity.[14]

The Ancient Ethnographers

We come finally to the other argument regularly cited by the proponents of group marriage: the testimony of the ancient ethnographers. In describing the matrimonial practices of different peoples, Herodotus speaks of the relations between the sexes among the Massagetae (1.216.1), Nasamones (4.172.2–3), Agathyrsi (4.104), Ausees and Machlyes (4.180), and Gindanes (4.176).

Of the Massagetae he says that even though the men were monogamous, they used others' wives promiscuously. Of the Nasamones, he relates that the women were quite promiscuous and that they made their relationships public by planting a stick in front of the man's house. Equally promiscuous, he says, were the Agathyrsi, Ausees, and Machlyes, who, when a child reached three years of age, decided who the father was on the basis of resemblance. Among the Gindanes, the women wore a leather anklet for every man they had had—and enjoyed prestige in proportion to the number of anklets.

But the testimony of the ancient ethnographers is not really reliable enough to permit us to infer collective marriage. In the first place, the sources are contradictory. Nicholas of Damascus, for example, attributes to the Lyburnii the practices that Herodotus attributes to the Ausees, and to the Galactophagi (whose Homeric name is somewhat suspicious) those that Herodotus attributes to the Agathyrsi.[15] Furthermore, according to Strabo (7.3.3), it was not the Nasamones who planted sticks to announce their affairs but the Massagetae and the Arabians, who elsewhere appear altogether without women.

As has been correctly observed, these sources are so imprecise as to allow neither the identification of the peoples they speak about nor the certainty that they even existed. But there is more. As S. Pembroke has pointed out, the Herodotean description of the peoples of the eastern coasts of the Mediterranean is actually a symbolic representation. It is the antithesis of Greece. By taking relations between the sexes as a parameter of justice, Herodotus describes different couplings among them, which are reducible to two models—promiscuous and polygamous on the one hand, and those made public on the other. The latter, for a Greek, was no less "barbarous" than promiscuity.[16] The practices described by Herodotus, to conclude, do more than correspond to reality; they correspond to the desire for an image of barbarism that is the mirror image of the Greek, an image viewed in what has rightly been termed the "mirror of Herodotus."[17]

In trying to evaluate the evidence of the ancient ethnographers, we must bear in mind that they never speak of Rome, so they are not admissible evidence for the prehistory of that city. Once the nineteenth-century notion of a unilinear development of history has been dismissed, these sources, even if they were reliable, may be used only with reference to the peoples whose customs they describe. But more generally, as Pembroke writes, even if the word "gynocracy" appears in the Greek sources, "There is no single instance in which what the Greeks called the rule of women, in Greece or outside it, can be identified as a matrilineal system."[18]

So much for the prehistory of Rome; let us move on to protohistory. From the moment in which it is possible to follow its vicissitudes, the Roman family organization presents itself as solidly patriarchal, and within it can be found no trace of a female condition other than subjection to a male group head and no trace of a female role other than the domestic. Since its earliest manifestation, Roman law was characterized by absolute power of the head of the family group, to which the women were subordinate (as were sons and slaves) in forms that guaranteed not even the elementary right to survival.

The *pater* had an absolute and unlimited power over slaves, sons, and women, which extended even to the right of life and death—*ius vitae ac necis*. This family power was manifested over a woman in a series of impositions and controls for her entire life, a life rigorously planned for the primary purpose of reproduction of the group. The Roman girl who survived infancy (the right of the father to expose or kill children took more female victims in Rome as well as Greece) was destined for very early marriage and another familial power (*manus*) no less that what her father had held. Some of the oldest religious ceremonies demonstrate how inexorably women were destined to fulfill reproductive functions—the cult of the god Tutunus Mutunus (the Greek god Priapus) is a prime example. The Roman bride had to simulate intercourse with an image of the god, straddling his *fascinus* (reproductive organ). Equally significant was the ceremony of the Lupercalia (still celebrated in the Republican period), in which to combat sterility nude men (*Luperci*) armed with goatskin straps beat the women.[19]

It is the cults of the ancient female divinities that reveal the role of women most clearly. Often depicted in the act of nursing, the goddess was worshipped as representation and symbol of the woman faithful to her domestic duties, as the cult of Tanaquil clearly shows. Her statue was displayed in the temple of Semo Sancus or Dius Fidius with a spindle and wool-winder next to it.

The Roman goddess in her various forms was very different from the Great Mediterranean Mother symbol of sexual liberty and of the power of female reproduction. The Roman goddess was the divinization of an image in which the maternal function, though revered, was still anchored to a role exclusively within the circle of the family group and subject to the unlimited power of a *paterfamilias*.

We will return in the next chapter to the condition of women in early Rome. Here the point is to verify the basics of the recurring discussion of a presumed matriarchal prehistory. Indeed, it does not seem possible to reconstruct any trace of such a history in Italy. And with this the subject could be closed were it not extremely interesting and instructive to go back over some of the stages of the centuries-long polemic on the subject, to bring out the many implications and the different "political uses" of the debate.

The Debate on the Matriarchy

Proving the historicity of the matriarchy has been viewed by certain women's groups as a "political" battle to wage against male historiography and anthropology, which would deny its existence on principle. Male and male chauvinist scholars according to, for example, Evelyn Reed, refuse on principle to admit that the matriarchy really existed. They reconstruct ancient history and the reality of the "primitive" peoples in such a way as never to question the idea of the subjection of women, which as a result is understood to be natural, inevitable, and eternal. One example of this is the case of B. Malinowski (1884–1942). After having found a matrilineal system among the Trobriand islanders, he refused to admit that this system was a residue of a matriarchal society in transition toward the patriarchy. Because he was obliged to suggest that among the Trobriands the paternal role was not assumed by the husband, he advanced the hypothesis that this role did not, however, belong to the mother but to the maternal uncle, that is to say, always to a man. But this thesis, says Reed, is obviously aimed at reaffirming the inevitability and eternity of female oppression, and so must be refuted.[20]

It seems to me that it is absolutely mistaken to think that whoever believes in the historicity of the matriarchy is feminist and whoever does not is "male chauvinist."[21] It will be sufficient to reflect on the fact that among the proponents of the matriarchy have been some true "theorists" of female inferiority, foremost among whom stands Bachofen himself. The basic premise of the *Mutterrecht* is that the time when women had power was not the pinnacle of the social system. Although it was better than the earlier phase of "heterism" (or "aphroditism"), which had been characterized by total sexual freedom, to Bachofen matriarchy is inferior to patriarchy because it favors the "female principle," and does not recognize the superiority of the male principle. The principle of motherhood is common to all animal species. Bound in an immediate way to birth, it is a naturalistic phenomenon. Paternity, however, has a spiritual nature, and asserting itself as such it raises the human spirit.[22]

Later—it is true—there were those who accepted the matriarchal thesis in a completely different light and did not believe that patriarchy was superior to matriarchy.[23] Friedrich Engels in particular saw the loss of power by women as a consequence of the birth of classes and the state, destined to be overcome by communism, at which time women would regain their lost rights and dignity.[24] Some scholars of the psychic structures, notably Wilhelm Reich, identified in the arrival of the patriarchy the moment of passage from a sexually free society to a sexually repressed one.

In addition to these interpretations there have been others, which are very difficult to reconcile with a feminist perspective. For example, according to Ernest Jones societies with maternal law (a survival of a time when the male role in procreation was still unknown) are societies that defended themselves from the Oedipus complex. Denying the paternal role, societies of this type would deflect the hostility of the adolescent toward the father by breaking up the primitive father into a tolerant father and a moralistic and severe uncle, onto whom would be directed the love–hate relationship. Societies with paternal law, on the other hand, would not remove but assimilate the Oedipus complex. The passage to patriarchy, in other words, would represent the most important progression in the history of humanity.[25]

Finally, the matriarchal hypothesis has been accepted by such theorists of ethnic and sexual racism as Julius Evola, according to whom the matriarchy goes back to the pre-Aryan and non-Aryan history of the world, whereas the patriarchy can be traced to the Aryan. According to Evola, Bachofen should be read as a providential warning against the danger of a return to matriarchy. Evola rails against "The new masculinized, athletic, and *garçonne* woman, who dedicates herself to the unilateral development of her own body, who betrays the normal mission that is hers in a manly society, who

111

emancipates herself, makes herself independent, and finally breaks into the field of politics."[26]

The examples could continue, but these will suffice. Obviously, to believe in the historicity of the matriarchy is not necessarily a progressive position nor is it necessarily feminist. The debate on female power has never been "neutral;" it has always had political or ideological connotations. To recognize that historical proof of the existence of a matriarchy in Greece and Rome does not exist certainly is not the same as believing that patriarchal organization is the only possibility. Greek and Roman society, from the moment at which it is possible to reconstruct their outlines, were patriarchal. But the patriarchy was only one of the many possible social organizations—the subjection of women is not inevitable or natural or eternal.

Nine

The Period of the Kings
and the Republic

Legal Status of Women

THE ROMAN FAMILIA

In the first centuries of its history, Roman law reflected a rigidly patriarchal society. The only people with full rights were male citizen heads of family groups. Women, even when not subject to a family head, had no political rights (and this has been deemed so natural as not to be considered in modern treatments of the subject) and could exercise civil rights only with the consent of a "tutor" or guardian.

In Roman law the family was very different from what we call a family today. A *familia* was a group of persons, to paraphrase the jurist Ulpian, subject *natura aut iure* to the power of the *paterfamilias,* for reasons deriving from nature (children and descendants) or from law (wives and slaves).[1] The *pater* was an undisputed and absolute lord, whose power extended to the right of life and death (*ius vitae ac necis*) over all those under him. This paternal power (which apparently was originally a single entity called *mancipium*) had been articulated in several forms since the earliest period. These forms had various designations according to the relationship between the parties. *Manus* was the power of the *pater* over his own wife and those of his descendants; *patria potestas* was power over his descendants, both male and female; and *dominica potestas* was that over male and female slaves, who were considered elements of the family inheritance.

FEMALE SLAVES AND THEIR CHILDREN

Of all the women of Rome, those living the most difficult lives were the slaves. Legally considered (like male slaves) "object" and not "subject" of law, female slaves did the heaviest work, cleaning, grinding grain, cultivating the fields. And they had one more duty—they had to be available to the male members of the *familia* should they, as was often the case, prefer to engage in extramarital sexual relations at home with the slaves rather than outside with prostitutes.

It is almost superfluous to say that female slaves could not marry. Without *conubium,* the capacity to contract *iustum matrimonium,* their relationship with a man, even if of conjugal intent and duration, was only a de facto relationship. And when, as usually happened, the man was also of servile status, their union (called *contubernium,* not *matrimonium*) could be interrupted by the master at any moment, should he decide to sell one of the couple. The inevitable consequence was, of course, that the slave woman had no right over her children, who would fall under the *dominica potestas* of the master.

Symptomatic and, for us, incredible is the question asked many times in this context by the Roman jurists: is the child of the female slave to be considered *fructus?* To understand the sense of the question, it is important to know that legally *fructus* are not just the fruits of a tree but all the autonomous products of a thing, such as wood, milk, wool, and so forth. And *fructus* in Roman law would belong to the owner of the "mother-thing," unless it (she) were given in usufruct, in which case the products belong to the holder of the usufruct. The question then was not merely academic. The slave too, like a thing, could be given in usufruct and her children in this case, as *fructus,* according to the principle of the *ius civile,* would belong to the holder of the usufruct. But these were "fruits" too precious for the master of the slave to lose—that is the true reason for the debate. In the interest of the owners, it was better to establish that the slave was not a fruit-bearing thing, as the jurist Brutus claimed in the second century B.C. (*Digest* 7.1.68 pr.). But this principle was so difficult to assert and the debate that followed was so long that traces can still be seen in the work of Gaius in the second century A.D. (*Digest* 22.1.28.1).

FREE WOMEN AND THE *PATERFAMILIAS*

A free woman was in turn under the authority of a man, the *paterfamilias* who, if not master in the legal sense, was so de facto. To understand fully the scope of the powers that the *pater* could exercise over a woman, a brief digression on the nature of *patria potestas* will be helpful.

As will by now be clear, Roman *patria potestas* was very different from the power parents have today over their children. The difference is only partly because in many countries, power rests with both parents conjointly, not just with the father. (As, for example, in Italy since the 1975 family-law reform, although in cases of grave necessity and urgency, the decision-making power still belongs to the father.[2]) More important is the conception today of the power of parents over their children as a protective institution. In other words, today parental control is viewed as being in the interest of the child, whereas *patria potestas* was in the interest of the father and lasted as long as he lived, even after the child reached the age of majority.

When the father died, only the direct descendants were liberated, that is, children and children's children if their natural father was already dead. All the others passed under the *potestas* of the son, who became the new *paterfamilias*. A man was free of *patria potestas* only if he had no living ascendants.

The earliest power that the father could exercise over a *filius familias* was that of exposure. At birth, in a highly symbolic rite, newborns—male and female—were deposited at the feet of the father. He—without explanation or justification—either recognized the child as his by picking it up (*tollere* or *suscipere liberos*) or withheld his recognition by leaving it where it was. The recognized child became a member of the *familia*; the unrecognized child was abandoned to the river or left to die by starvation. Exposed children were more likely to be girls than boys.[3] According to a law attributed to Romulus, Roman citizens who exposed sons or first-born daughters were punished by confiscation of half their property (Dion. Hal. 2.15). The rationale of the law is that the collective interest of the population should not be decimated. But the limitation of the right to expose girl babies was really very weak, given that the Roman woman in the absence of effective contraception was likely to bear many more children after the first-born daughter.

An exposed infant's chances of being saved depended on someone's coming and rescuing it. But when that happened it was usually not for philanthropic reasons. A foundling, especially a girl, could be an excellent financial investment. Made to do domestic chores from a very young age, the girl later could be sold as a slave or, more likely, put to work as a prostitute.

Children, grandchildren, and other descendants could at any moment be sold by the father, in which case they would enter a condition called *causa mancipii,* formally different from slavery but in actual fact identical. Males and females alike were susceptible to this exercise of *patria potestas,* which was mitigated only slightly by a provision in the Twelve Tables (Table IV), according to which a father who had sold a child three times in a row lost *patria potestas* over the child. The limits fixed by this law left plenty of room for the use and abuse of paternal power.

ENGAGEMENT, MARRIAGE, AND HUSBANDS' POWER

The Roman girl was betrothed when quite young in a solemn ceremony called *sponsalia.* A ring was given to the *sponsa,* or bride, to put on her finger nearest the little finger of the left hand—the Romans believed a nerve ran from this finger to the heart.[4] From that moment she was bound to her betrothed by a bond that, although not yet marital, gave her a precise social status and imposed fidelity, among other things. With engagement, in other words, the girl was assigned a role from which there was no recourse and which would assume its full form after the wedding.

In the earliest times, the woman passed from her own family to that of her husband, where she found herself subject to family *manus* in content and extent not very different from the *patria potestas* from which her marriage had removed her.[5] Far from bringing greater freedom, marriage merely gave a woman a new master. And it is no exaggeration to call the husband a master, in that he acquired power over his wife and ownership of property in much the same way. Only one of the ceremonies by which men acquired power over women was egalitarian in its formal structure. This was *confarreatio,* the most ancient nuptial rite in Roman law, which consisted essentially in the division of a loaf of spelt bread between the bride and groom. But *confarreatio* was not a wide-spread ceremony and fell early into disuse. As Gaius recalls in the *Institutes* (1.112), it was used chiefly for the marriage of the Flamen Dialis, one of the most important priests.

Of greater relevance to the reconstruction of women's lives are the institutions of *coemptio* and *usus. Coemptio* (the most widely used of the ceremonies that transferred a woman to a new family) was an application of the old form of sale and purchase, called *mancipatio,* in the course of which the woman, just as though she were an object, was sold to the buyer in the presence of a person (*libripens*) who held a scale on which the buyer put down the price of the object or woman. Even if this procedure was only symbolic later on, its origin was an actual purchase. Even Gaius, in the second century A.D., describes the ritual of *coemptio* by saying that the husband *emit mulierum,* that is, "buys a woman" (Gaius *Inst.* 1.113).

The most convincing evidence that women were not treated much differently from things lies in that unique institution of matrimonial law called *usus.* In the Roman world (and even today) one of the ways property could be acquired was by *usucapion,* that is, the use of the thing itself over a period of time. According to the law of the Twelve Tables, use for a year in the case of movable goods, and two years in the case of immovable property, conferred ownership. *Usus* was simply *usucapion* of a woman. In cases when *coemptio* was not celebrated, in fact, or if technically unsuccessful, the husband (or his father) acquired *manus* over the woman after she had been "used" for a year, the same time period established for movable goods. The remedy prescribed by the Twelve Tables to prevent the husband from acquiring this power is interesting. If the wife, at the end of each year, had spent three nights away from the conjugal home, the husband would not have acquired *manus* over her (Gaius *Inst.* 1.111). The ingenious solution (called *trinoctium* or *trinoctis usurpatio*) was evidently agreed upon with the woman's father, who had financial reasons for not wanting to lose his control over his daughter. Roman laws may have been severe, but they provided their own loopholes—not in the woman's interest, however, but for the benefit of the family to which she belonged.

PROHIBITION OF WINE

The free woman in Rome's first centuries married and exchanged paternal power for the sphere of power of a new *paterfamilias*. That her status was no better after marriage than it had been while she was a girl can be seen in the extent of the husband's powers to punish certain behaviors considered crimes—and punished as such—only when committed by a woman. The first of these was adultery, considered so grave if committed by a woman that the husband was allowed to put her to death, but we shall return to this in a later section.

The second prohibition may seem odd but was taken quite seriously by the Romans—it forbade the drinking of wine by women.[6] There have been numerous attempts to explain this law. According to some, the Romans believed that wine had abortive capacities, and the ban was thus linked to the prohibition of abortion.[7] According to others, wine could cause women to lose their necessary reserve and therefore induce them to commit adultery.[8] A third hypothesis maintains that, like other peoples, the Romans believed wine contained a life force. The woman who drank wine thereby let in an external life force, exactly as the adulteress did.[9] This hypothesis seems the most convincing, but aside from questions about the theoretical basis of the law, two circumstances are indisputable.

The law was inspired by the need to control in some way the female element of the population. And it was rigorously enforced. Varro recounts (recorded in Val. Max. 6.3.9) that Egnatius Metellus "took a cudgel and beat his wife to death because she had drunk some wine" ("quod vinum bibisset, fusti percussam interemit"). To be sure that a woman was not drinking on the sly, her nearest relatives could exercise the *ius osculi,* or "right to kiss." Rather than a special demonstration of affection for female relatives, this was a legally sanctioned power. Kissing a woman was simply a way of checking that she had not been drinking.[10]

A woman could be punished for taking the keys to the cellar (where wine was kept) even if she did not drink; but in that case (despite the testimony of Pliny the Elder who writes of a woman forced to die of hunger for having committed this crime) it seems that instead of being put to death she would be repudiated, as were women who had abortions without their husbands' consent.[11]

RIGHTS TO INHERIT AND MAKE WILLS

According to most historians of Roman law, women originally had inheritance rights like men's. In the absence of testamentary dispositions (given that in Roman law testamentary succession took precedence over legitimate), daughters succeeded the father on an equal basis with sons, and female descendants were on a par with male descendants of the same grade. Furthermore, in the absence of descendants, when the inheritance passed to the collateral, female agnates (that is, collateral relatives of the male side) would have been equal with male agnates, excluding even male relatives of a further grade.

Yet the facts are not all that certain. The law of the Twelve Tables which established the order of succession spoke of *suus* (a son *in potestate*) and, in his absence, of *adgnatus proximus,* the nearest collateral male relative (Table V.4). According to some, the law referred originally only to the male family members.[12]

A well-known legend often is used to suggest that at the origin of Rome, women were not only holders of matrimonial rights but were even capable of disposing liberally and fully of these rights, even by will. The story is that of Acca Larentia, the wife of the shepherd Faustulus who rescued and took care of the infant Romulus and Remus.[13] Acca Larentia, who according to another version of the legend was a prostitute (the word *lupa* means both prostitute and she-wolf), became very rich because she was loved by Hercules, who compensated her lavishly for her favors. When she died, she made the Roman people her heir.

More interesting for us than the usual difficulties interpreting the myth is a more basic problem represented by the difficulty of placing Acca Larentia ethnically and of establishing whether she can be considered a prototype of the Roman woman. Her image is probably not that of an Etruscan woman, that is, of a woman whose status, even though not "matriarchal," was still such as to render more believable the idea that she had full inheritance rights. But the problem goes beyond Acca Larentia. If we grant that Roman women at the time of the foundation of the city had full inheritance rights, does that mean there was another ethnic component along with the Etruscan to which such rights can be traced?

Some mention should be made of a current tendency in historiography to emphasize the contribution of the Sabine element in the formation of Rome. What do we really know about the Sabine women? Some information comes from Plutarch (*Rom.*). In recounting the agreements between the Romans and the Sabines after the abduction, he lists the privileges the Romans granted to the Sabine women so that their status in Rome would not be inferior to what it had been in their own country. First, they would not be obliged to do any work *plen talasias,* except for wool work (19.7). This rule, acording to Plutarch, would be a possible explanation of the Roman nuptial cry "thalasios," intended to recall the duty of the bride (15.4–5). But the explanation is no more reliable than his explanations of the customs of lifting the bride over the threshold of the couple's new house (a relic of the rape) and parting the bride's hair with the point of a spear (to recall that the first Roman–Sabine marriage was an act of war). In the street, the Sabine women had right-of-way over men, foul language could not be used in their presence, a man who displayed himself nude to a woman was to be punished as for homicide, and the Sabines' sons were allowed to wear a sort of necklace called a *bulla* and a garment with a purple border (20.3).

From these few bits of information on the Sabine women it has been inferred that they lived in conditions of exceptional dignity, protected by custom and law and that in the eighth century they enjoyed "in public the same liberty which figurative art documents for the Etruscan women of the sixth century."[14]

Certain factors, more significant than what we read in Plutarch, cast doubt on this rosy picture. Unlike Roman women, who did not have names of their own, the Sabine women had names, but they could not be said aloud. Individual names were considered, as among many "primitives," to be part of the person like a part of the body. Therefore, to know and speak the name of a woman was an expression of inadmissible familiarity.[15] If this is correct, it is impossible to see the Sabine women as anything other than a female population strictly tied to a domestic role and subject to male control. If their names could not even be spoken aloud, how could they have had not only entitlement but also free right of exercise of inheritance rights?

Even if we grant that when the city was founded, Roman women really had inheritance rights, it is difficult to imagine a Sabine influence. It is more probable that they owed their limited privileges to Etruscan influence.

GUARDIANSHIP FOR LIFE

We have seen that family organization allowed only those who had no living ascendants to be free of *patria potestas* (and therefore to hold rights). The capacity to be holders of rights (legal capacity) is different from the capacity to exercise them (capacity to act). In other words, holders of a right are not necessarily considered (by the same order that granted it to them) capable of disposing of it freely. The capacity to act is recognized only for those who have been judged capable of understanding and free will. And whoever has been deemed incapable or only partially capable of understanding and free will is placed under guardianship, the protection and control of a person who will keep the "incapable" party from prejudicial acts.

In Roman law men were considered able to manage themselves and their own interests upon reaching puberty. If they were free of *patria potestas* they were under guardianship only until age fourteen. Women, however, as established in the Twelve Tables were under guardianship for life (the *tutor* as a rule was a relative, but sometimes a person was designated by the father's will or nominated by a magistrate). The reason for this discrimination (at least in

121

the first centuries of the city's history) was clear: women were not able to take care of themselves *propter levitatem animi* (Table V.1), because of the frivolity of their spirit.

It is no exaggeration to say that guardianship for life effectively nullified the legal capacities of Roman women. They could dispose of their acknowledged rights only with the mediation and assent of a man who originally was their nearest relative of the male line, that is, next in line to inherit their property. In other words, the woman had to seek authorization from a man with a vested interest in her property. Even though changes in guardianship laws occurred, they were not always to women's advantage. During the centuries of the Republic women's position improved in some respects, but they suffered notable limitations on their capaicty to inherit. In 196 B.C., for example, the *lex Voconia* established that women could inherit as *adgnatae* only within the second grade, that is, of lateral relatives only sisters. Moreover, women could not receive more than 200,000 asses.[16] To conclude this brief account of the legal status of women, we must look at the legislation of the end of the Republic aimed at ensuring family morality.

AUGUSTAN FAMILY LEGISLATION

The provisions taken to reconfirm the fundamental importance of marriage and the marital ethic were contained in two laws, the *lex Iulia de maritandis ordinibus* of 18 B.C. and the *lex Papia Poppaea nuptialis* of 9 B.C. They were later merged into a single text (*lex Iulia et Papia*).

Augustus established that men between the ages of twenty-five and sixty and women between twenty-five and fifty were obliged to marry or remarry persons of appropriate age groups. Women could wait for two years after the death of a husband and eighteen months after a divorce to remarry. The marriages, moreover, had to be fertile. This was of course impossible to enforce by law but rewards were given those who produced many progeny and sanctions (limitations on rights of succession and inheritance) were applied to those who had no children. Finally, the *ius liberorum* was established to free from guardianship freeborn women who had

had three children and freedwomen (born slave and later freed) who had had four.[17]

Other measures were taken to ensure that family life followed rigorous ancestral principles. The conjugal fidelity of women had always been at the center of the family organization and ideology. Its central importance for all the centuries of the Republic becomes clear when one thinks of the penalties inflicted upon those adulterers who escaped death. Penalties of extraordinary cruelty are recorded by Catullus (15.18), who alludes to them with absolute naturalness, evidently referring to the well-known practice of punitive sodomy with a radish and a mullet, carried out on a woman's seducer ("quem attractis pedibus . . . percurrunt raphanique mugilesque"—whom, with feet drawn up, radishes and mullets run through).

Augustan legislation confirmed that adultery absolutely could not be tolerated. Until then considered exclusively a family question, adultery became a crime for the first time. It could be punished (by exile) by request not only of the husband but of any citizen. The *ius occidendi* remained too. Although Augustus imposed some limits on it, he affirmed it by providing a highly detailed list of cases to establish the circumstances under which it could be exercised. The husband no longer had the right to kill the adulterous wife, but was obliged to repudiate her under pain of accusation of pandering. He retained the right to kill the lover if he caught him *in flagrante delicto* in the husband's house, or if the adulterer was a slave, an "infamous" person (gladiator, actor, dancer, procurer, or prostitute), or even a freedman.

The powers of the father were more extensive. He could kill his adulterous daughter; he could kill her lover, regardless of his social status; and he could exercise the *ius occidendi* if he surprised the adulterers not only in his own house but also in the house of his son-in-law. One circumstance is particularly interesting: by killing his daughter the father not only exercised his right, he created a condition that made legitimate the killing of the accomplice. If he killed the accomplice and not the daughter, in other words, he did not exercise the *ius occidendi* but committed a normal homicide, which was subject to criminal repression.

Apparently unique, the law has its logic. To the father, says Papinian in his commentary on the law, could be conceded an impunity more extensive than to the husband, in the hope that he would not always take advantage of it. To save his daughter, in fact, he might spare the lover. But the husband, consumed by the insult, would probably not restrain himself and therefore his exemption from the law had to be more restricted.[18]

It is difficult to imagine more explicit provisions. The Augustan laws are clearly indicative of the "appropriation" by the state of a family ethic. The family's survival was evidently fundamental and even the intellectuals apparently shared this belief; they defended and praised the laws.[19]

The Augustan legislation limited the fathers' and husbands' power; nevertheless it sanctioned the principle that respect for the family laws was something more than a private interest. Family life was now a collective interest and all citizens had the right to prosecute whoever violated them.

Social Status of Women

The picture of women's life that emerges from the principal laws seems clear enough. But as law and facts are not necessarily the same, it is helpful to try to identify the real conditions of Roman women's lives. Perhaps the rigor of the law was tempered by a more elastic practice.

SYSTEM OF NOMENCLATURE

Roman citizens had three names: a first name, *praenomen*, which was the individual's name; a second, *nomen*, which was the name of the *gens*; and a third, *cognomen*, which indicated the particular family group. Women, however, had only the gentile name and the family name. They had no individual names.

Cornelia, Caecilia, Tullia—these are gentile, not personal names. When there was more than one woman in a group and confusion might arise, designations such as Maior and Minor (elder and younger) or Prima, Seconda, and Tertia were added. This peculiarity of the naming system prompts us to ask whether Roman women really did not have names or whether they had names that were never used.

In the opinion of some, the absence of names was not original. Female *praenomina* once existed, but disappeared before the historical era.[20] According to others, they never existed at all.[21] Still others maintain that they existed but, as among other peoples (such as the Sabines), they were never said aloud for reasons of good manners.[22] In an attempt to resolve the problem R. I. Menager has reexamined the sources and identified three types of female naming.

The first type, the majority, is a single name: Anicia, Aptronia, Aulia, Plautia, Roscia, Saufeia are some examples documented in the inscriptions from the cemetery of Praeneste. Examples from literary sources are Ocrisia and Pinaria. These are single names and merely the feminine form of the name of the father or of the *gens*. The second type is *gentilicium* plus the father's *praenomen* followed by *filia*. As has been justly observed, this system "expresses in its turn the negation of the identity, and a legal relationship identical with that which emerges from the primitive designation of the slave as Gaipor (slave of Gaius), Marcipor (slave of Marcus), Quintipor," and so on.[23]

The third type, which is quite rare, included the *praenomen*. This means that some female *praenomina* existed. In the *liber singularis incerti auctoris de praenominibus,* epitomized by Julius Paris, we read that among "ancient" women the names Rutilia, Caesella, Rodacilla, Murrula, and Burra were common. These derive from color terms (evidently from the hair or skin of the woman so called). We also find Gaia, Lucia, Publia, Numeria, all deriving from male names.[24] To these should be added Mania, Lucia, and Postuma, recorded by Varro (*Ling.* 9.61), and Caecilia, Taracia, and Titia, recorded by Festus (251.6). In fact, seven of these names together with another three not on this list are documented by the literary and epigraphical sources.[25]

Evidently, although the use of *praenomina* for women is attested, it was extraneous to Roman culture and an absolutely exceptional practice, which seems according to all the indicators to have been adopted from another culture. Again the Etruscans enter the picture, because they, unlike other peoples, regularly called women by their first name.[26]

If, for Pericles, great was "the glory of the woman who is talked about the least, whether in praise or blame" (Thuc. 2.45.2), for the Romans the glory of women required that their names never be pronounced. It was said of the Bona Dea that no man (except her husband) ever heard her name as long as she lived.[27] In the fifth century, Macrobius (*Sat.* 1.12.27) praises the modesty of a woman whose name nobody knew. It is difficult not to share the observation made by Moses Finley. By not indicating women with *praenomina,* he writes, "it is as if the Romans wished to suggest that women were not, and ought not be genuine individuals, but only fractions of a family. Anonymous and passive fractions at that. . . ."[28]

FEMALE DISCONTENT AND BACCHIC CULTS

By our standards at least, the conditions of Roman women's lives were ample reason for discontent. A unique and difficult-to-interpret episode narrated by Livy (8.18.8) reveals a certain tension in relations between the sexes.

A trial for poisoning was held in 331 B.C. at Rome. During the consulship of M. Claudius Marcellus and C. Valerius Potitus, many illustrious persons died mysteriously. Reported by a female slave, certain *matronae* were accused of having poisoned them. *Venena,* poisons, were found in their houses but the women said they were medicines. Challenged to drink them, the *matronae* did so and died. At the end of the trial, 160 women had been condemned.[29] However one interprets this disturbing episode, it and other signs indicate the definite existence of a problem.

Around the second century B.C., the status of women deteriorated. Women who lived in the country deeply resented the loss of privileges involved in the female role in the peasant family. Women of the better-off classes had seen their chances to enjoy the privileges of wealth diminish. A series of sumptuary laws (*leges sumptuariae*) had established rigorous limitations on female luxury.

The *lex Oppia* in 215 B.C. had forbidden women to wear excessive quantities of jewelry or colored clothing. Twenty years later, in 195, demonstrations of discontent brought about the repeal of this law.

But in 169 a new provision, the *lex Voconia* (discussed earlier in this chapter) established that women (with the exceptions of Vestal Virgins and the Flaminica Dialis) could not inherit more than 200,000 asses, which greatly irritated the women of the wealthier classes.[30] Furthermore, women of all social classes had to endure the inconvenience caused by the absence of the men, who were occupied in continual wars.

It is no wonder that in this context Bacchic cults asserted themselves increasingly. Our best information comes from Livy (39.13.9 ff.). At first limited to women, these cults spread thanks to the intervention and innovations of the Campanian priestess Paculla Annia and were opened to men as well. After orgiastic dances in the woods of Stimula (the goddess of madness in whose woods, *lucus Stimulae,* at the foot of the Aventine the Maenads had taken refuge), the participants in the rite ran toward the Tiber, into which they threw lit torches.

Should this ritual be interpreted as an expression of freedom or sexual dissoluteness? "Licentious" behavior did take place. The rituals were accompanied not only by the drinking of wine (which, of course, was forbidden to women) but by both heterosexual and homosexual relations. To deduce from this, however, that the Roman woman enjoyed the slightest bit of this freedom in her daily life would certainly be a mistake.

In the first place, the ritual that allowed otherwise forbidden sexual couplings was justified by the pretext of "possession." Second, as we have already seen with reference to the Greek world, the ritual represented a world turned upside down, an inversion of everyday life, a reversal of roles clearly revealed by the fact that the male participants dressed as women (Livy 39.15.9 ff.).

The Bacchic rites indicate a social reality that was the exact opposite of what one might think at first sight. They actually reveal the sexual repression of the Roman woman. Such repression was, of course, perfectly functional for the purpose of procreation, where there was no room for eroticism and love.[31] Every display of emotion, in the context of family life in general and conjugal life in particular, was vigorously reproved. Very significant in this regard is the story (it does not matter whether it is real or imaginary—what

127

is important is that it was retold for didactic purposes) that the senator Manilius risked being expelled from the Senate for kissing his wife in public (Plut. *Cat. Min.* 7.17).[32]

The enormous spread of the Bacchic cults—celebrated primarily by women and at first only by them—must be placed in this context. The ritual was the only moment in which women could express a part of themselves that had been suppressed—only then could they experience eroticism. It was a moment in which they found compensation for the dissatisfaction of an ungratifying emotional and erotic life.

Altogether understandable, then, are the reasons for the enormous spread of the Bacchanalia. Just as understandable are the reasons for the fierce repression with which they were stopped, in the course of which the accusations were again brought against women for using poisons. In the wake of the Bacchanalian scandal, another trial for poisoning was held that made the trial of 331 B.C. appear negligible. Again there were mysterious deaths and a special investigation. The subsequent trial concluded with more than 2,000 women condemned. One of these was the widow of a consul who wanted to get rid of her husband, so went the accusation, so that her son by her first marriage might have access to the consulship (Livy 40.37.4–5). But despite these, let us say, pathological episodes, new and troubling social phenomena pointed to a crisis at hand.

THE POPULATION CRISIS

The birth rate began to fall during the Republic. It fell in massive proportions in the centuries to follow. One hypothesis posits mass lead poisoning. The conduits of the aqueducts that brought water to Rome were made of lead; Roman women used cosmetics that contained large amounts of lead; vessels for food and drink were often made of lead. The theory is not unreasonable; indeed traces of lead have been found in Roman skeletons. But lead poisoning alone, no matter how widespread, cannot account for all the circumstances that contributed to making a declining birth rate a serious social problem.

Contraception was in use by this time. Apart from utterly

ineffective measures (spells and amulets, such as a cat's liver tied to the left foot or a spider bound in the skin of a stag and held in contact with the body), some methods, although rudimentary, were certainly more effective, such as a piece of soft wool saturated with substances that prevented fertilization. Furthermore, abortion was widely practiced.[33]

Decline in the birth rate was due in part to external causes, but it was certainly also partly due to women's life-choices. For women of the lower classes the motivation to use contraception was economic, for the privileged, it was the desire to enjoy the advantages that their new status allowed. They hoped to find an identity that was not exclusively tied to motherhood.

But this could not be allowed, because it conflicted with the need to reproduce a social body and transmit a family and political ideology. Actions against the worrisome phenomenon were taken as soon as it appeared. The provisions of the *lex Iulia,* examined earlier, can be interpreted as such a response. The legislative provisions, moreover, were accompanied by a massive "ideological campaign" intended to forestall transgression in whatever form it took, and to reconfirm the traditional models yet again. We can see this in anecdotes about certain female figures and in funerary inscriptions about women who, having passed their lives in anonymity, were remembered after death for their "exemplary qualities."

MODELS AND TRANSGRESSIONS

So far what has interested us are the general conditions of Roman women's life. Now we will look at some female figures who managed to emerge from anonymity to become celebrated models and exemplars of behavior. The first observation to make about these women is that, other than their "heroic" moment, usually linked to some political event, we know almost nothing of their lives. Apart from the exemplary deed to which they owe their immortality, all is shadow and silence.

Of the women chosen to be remembered in the history of Rome written by men (again, it is not important whether their recorded actions are real or legendary), we begin with Lucretia and Virginia

Rome

(Livy 1 58–60 and 3.44–48, respectively). Wife of Collatinus, Lucretia killed herself after being raped by Sextus, son of Tarquinius Superbus. The people reacted by rising against the foreign kings and throwing them out of the city. Virginia, object of the desires of the decemvir Appius Claudius, did not kill herself but was killed by her father. In her case too, the popular reaction led to the ouster of the decemvir.[34]

The syntactic structure of the two legends is almost identical. Object of illicit desire, a woman dies to affirm the supreme value of conjugal fidelity (Lucretia) and virginity (Virginia). The people find in the outrage the strength to react against power and reconfirm this value, sanctioning the fundamental importance of a law of family morality, evidently one of the pillars on which the social and political organization was based.

Equally predictable and instructive are the stories of Veturia, Volumnia, and Cornelia. Veturia and Volumnia, respectively mother and wife of Coriolanus, went to his camp as he was leading the Volscians against Rome and obtained from him what ambassadors, magistrates, and priests had been unable to obtain. They convinced Coriolanus to abandon arms (Livy 2.40 and Plut. *Cor.* 33–34).

The hagiography of Cornelia, second daughter of Scipio Africanus, mother of the tribunes Tiberius and Gaius Gracchus is well known. She had twelve children (only three of whom lived to adulthood); her daughter Sempronia married Scipio Aemilianus. After the death of her husband, Cornelia would not remarry and refused even the proposal of Ptolemy VII Physcon. She was the exemplary image of the *univira,* a woman who had only one man in her entire life. Cornelia remained the ideal model of womanly behavior, despite the evident contradiction with a strong population policy. What is more, Cornelia was educated and intellectually polished: even Cicero admired the style of her letters. But Cornelia owes her fame to her reply when asked why she did not wear jewels. "These," she said, pointing to her children, "are my jewels." And on the statue erected in her honor she was remembered with the inscription "Cornelia, mother of the Gracchi."[35]

We come finally to Marcia, who became the wife of Cato after he

130

repudiated Atilia for her moral conduct. Marcia was a perfect wife. The orator Hortensius, by now old and alone, asked Cato to let him have Marcia in order to have children by her. Cato agreed and Marcia, although she loved her husband, accepted his decision without protest. The traditions diverge at this point. According to one version, Cato divorced Marcia, who married Hortensius. In the other version, Cato simply lent her to his friend. In either case, Marcia accepted her husband's decision and returned to Cato when Hortensius died.[36]

The popular reaction to this episode was conflicting. Some accused Cato of greediness.[37] Others invoked ethnological precedents to justify his action (Strabo 11.9.1). In the schools, rhetoricians used to exercise their skills by debating "an Cato recte Marciam Hortensio tradiderit," whether Cato was right to give Marcia to Hortensius, or more generically, "conveniante res talis bono viro," whether such behavior was seemly for a good man (Quint. 3.5.11 and 10.5.15).

Perhaps the Stoic Cato "lent" his wife, following without reservation the precepts of the Stoic school, namely, that one should not claim to possess a woman because, being created for procreation, women ought to be common to all.[38] What is interesting to us, however, is Marcia's reaction. What made her accept what was probably contrary to her desires and also in contrast with the model of the *univira*?

There were also women who refused the role of the model woman. Among these, Clodia is famous. She was loved by Catullus and celebrated by him with the name Lesbia. Clodia was a free woman: we are in the first century B.C., when a new type of woman appears on the scene in Rome. Some Roman women were inspired by actresses or Greek hetaerae, and tried to imitate them. In 61 B.C., at age thirty-three, Clodia met Catullus, then twenty-seven. In 59, at the death of her husband, she left Catullus for the even younger Caelius. Few facts are recorded, but they are more than sufficient to understand that Clodia was far from the example propagandized by the women discussed previously; she was a woman who chose and left her lovers, who refused to be an object of possession. When, later abandoned by Caelius, she accuses him of not having returned money she lent him, of having stolen her jewelry, and, finally, of having tried to poison her, the oration written by Cicero in defense of Caelius does not spare her image: "Clytemnestra," he calls her, and worse, *quandrantaria*—a two-bit Clytemnestra.[39] He dwells not so much on the facts contested by Caelius as on Clodia herself, a woman whose conduct alone makes her accusations unreliable.

As soon as she was widowed, said Cicero (not missing the chance to insinuate that Clodia had poisoned her husband), she gave herself to a dissolute life of orgiastic parties both in Rome and at her villa at Baiae on the Bay of Naples. The slaves who testified in her favor had no credibility: they too participated in their mistress's debauchery, and she had not hesitated to free them in order to obtain their complicity. As if that were not enough, Clodia was the incestuous lover of Clodius, her brother, the bitter enemy of Cicero.

That was essentially Caelius' defense, and he was acquitted. The case is symptomatic; Clodia's accusations could not have any grounds. She was "different," and as such could not possibly be telling the truth.

Despite the clear signs of malcontent and rebellion that spread in the second century, despite the attempt at "liberation" sought in the Bacchanalia, despite the "Lesbias" (there must have been others, not loved by Catullus and thus not known), the average Roman woman, the anonymous woman, the woman not talked about, was probably not very different from Lucretia or Cornelia.

The funerary inscriptions prove this. The eulogies for women who have died highlight their qualities: *lanifica, pia, pudica, casta, domiseda* (wool worker, faithful, modest, chaste, stay-at-home) are the adjectives that appear with greatest frequency—stylized praises that underscore the persistence of the model.[40]

FUNERARY INSCRIPTIONS

Among the funeral eulogies of Roman women, two are particularly illuminating: the eulogy of a certain Claudia and the famous inscription known as the *laudatio Turiae*.

On the tomb of Claudia, who died in the second century B.C., an inscription invites the passerby to stop:

Friend, I have not much to say; stop and read it. This tomb, which is not fair, is for a fair woman. Her parents gave her the name Claudia. She loved her husband in her heart. She bore two sons, one of whom she left on earth, the other beneath it. She was pleasant to talk with, and she walked with grace. She kept the house and worked in wool. That is all. You may go.[41]

According to the unknown husband, all that Claudia would have wanted to be remembered about her were her conjugal devotion, motherhood, and pleasant demeanor. All she ever did in her life could be summed up in two phrases: "lanam fecit, domum servit." That was all a woman should do if she wanted to be remembered with admiration. And at the end of the Republic, things had not changed very much. The eulogy of Turia, who died between 8 and 2 B.C., demonstrates this.

Rare, says Turia's husband, are marriages like theirs, which lasted forty-one years and during which the wife was always perfect. To save her husband from political persecution, Turia sold her jewels. Not having children and not wanting to deprive her husband of fatherhood, she offered him a divorce so that he could have children with another woman, promising to consider those children as though they were her own. But the husband refused, so as not to exchange "certa dubiis" (a good wife for an unknown quantity). Turia remained with her husband.[42]

It is not easy to find examples like this of total dedication to the ideal role. Even with a husband who (exceptionally, it would seem) is disposed for affection's sake (but also, as he himself says, so as not to run too many risks!) to accept a wife who has not done her fundamental duty, the wife felt this duty as absolute. She experienced her inability to fulfill it as an unpardonable inadequacy—an extraordinary example of guilt transfer and an irrefutable demonstration of the efficacy of a system of "conditioning."

If not all women were like Claudia and Turia, if some of them dedicated themselves to arts and literature and proposed some other female image, these women made an individual choice that the social conscience did not accept. The "different" women represented degeneration, corruption, danger. The model was always that of the *matrona,* the wife and mother who, in the fulfillment of her family duties, forgot herself. Or rather, like Cornelia, they fulfilled themselves vicariously and asked for nothing in return except the awareness of having contributed to the greatness of Rome.

At this point the outlines of the difference between the Greek and the Roman concepts of the female role begin to emerge. The Roman woman was not segregated as was the Greek woman. As Cornelius Nepos points out in the introduction to his *Lives of Illustrious Men*, the Romans considered behavior honorable for a woman that the Greeks would never have allowed. The Romans did not believe that women should be shut up in a special part of the house or that they should be forbidden to dine with men or go out in the street.

In other words the Roman woman was not tied, like the Greek woman, to a purely biological function. It cannot honestly be said that the Romans considered women—as did the Greeks—simple tools of reproduction. Roman women were also a fundamental instrument of the transmission of a culture, a large measure of whose perpetuation was entrusted to them. Unlike Greek women, they personally brought up their children. It was their job to prepare them to become *cives romani*, with all the pride that this involved. And if they did it well they were repaid with honors that Greek women would never have received.[43]

Perhaps the liberality of the Romans toward their women is not altogether accidental. Given their duties, women had to participate in some way in men's lives in order to assimilate their values and become more faithful transmitters of them.

Ten

The Principate and the Empire: The Emancipation of Women?

The Centuries of Expansion

PATRIA POTESTAS

At the end of the Republic, the women of Rome were freer and more aware. The law had taken note of and in part supported these facts, conceding rights that had hitherto been denied. The surpassing of the old gentile law (which in the second century, as Gaius says, had fallen into disuse) and the consequent breaking up of the *patria potestas* had played a significant role in this process, granting new liberties to women.[1]

This does not mean, however, that the powers of the *pater* did not remain strong. Evidence enough of this is the continuance of the father's right to expose newborns. Two letters of Pliny the Younger (10.65 and 10.66) testify to the spread of the practice. Pliny submitted a problem to Trajan which had already been confronted by Augustus, Vespasian, Titus, and Domitian (as he recalls), but had not yet been resolved: was the father who exposed a child and later claimed it obliged to reimburse the person who had rescued it for his expenditures on the child's food?[2] Evidently still practiced on a large scale, exposure, as always, continued to claim more female victims than male: an inscription of the Trajanic period, from which it appears that of 179 beneficiaries of alimentary assistance 145 were male and 34 female, is hard to explain otherwise. As in previous centuries, females were decimated at birth. And in later centuries, the continuation of imperial provisions on the subject shows that the practice continued to be widespread.

In 329, Constantine affirmed the right to claim the liberty of an exposed child held in de facto slavery, with the obligation to give the person who had rescued the infant the equivalent of the foundling's value or a slave (*Cod. Theod.* 5.10.1). In 331 he established that whoever had brought up an exposed child could at his pleasure give him either slave or free status (5.9.2).[3] Only in 374 did a constitution of Valentinian, Valens, and Gratian preserved in the *Codex* of Justinian actually forbid exposure. But evidently the prohibition did not eliminate the practice, because in 529 Justinian was forced to make a new law to the effect that whoever had brought up a rescued infant could give the child slave or free status (*Cod. Iust.* 8.51[52].3).

Yet *patria potestas* had undergone serious limitations in comparison with previous centuries. The father who had not exposed his children could no longer get rid of them by selling them into de facto slavery (as he once could) or putting them to death. In the second century, Trajan stripped a father who had mistreated his son of *patria potestas* and hereditary expectations (*Digesta* 37.12.5). Hadrian exiled to an island a father who had killed a son who had committed adultery with his stepmother (*Digesta* 48.9.5). Finally, Justinian made punishment for the killing of a child the same as for any other homicide (*Institutes* 4.18.6).

MARRIAGE AND DIVORCE

The institution that underwent the greatest transformation was marriage. Under the kings and at the beginning of the Republic, marriage involved the transfer of the wife into the *familia* of the husband. Over time, this practice was viewed with increasing disfavor, and marriage was progressively released from *manus* and transformed, at least in principle, into an equal personal relationship based on the will of two people to be one another's husband or wife.

As long as they possessed *conubium*—the legal state of being marriageable based on having reached puberty and being a citizen—in the classical period two persons were considered bound by marriage if they lived together with what the jurists called *affectio maritalis,* that is, the intent of being husband and wife. The ceremonies that accompanied the beginning of conjugal life had no constitutional value. They were not necessary to begin the relationship but they did have a function; namely, to confer solemnity on the marriage. The ceremonies also served to furnish indisputable proof of the existence of *affectio maritalis* should the legitimacy of the union later be contested. Intent could be inferred in other ways, however, for example, in the so-called *honor matrimonii,* in which a woman wore certain clothes and participated in ceremonies reserved for *matronae.*[4]

It is logical that there were no legal acts to end marriage. Given that the intention of being husband and wife had to be continuous, it was sufficient that, failing this intention, the couple should cease to live together: divorce, on the basis of these circumstances, was automatic. As a rule, divorce was accompanied by such declarations as the famous phrase "tuas res tibi habeto"—Take your things—which the husband (he usually took the initiative) said to the wife. As in the ceremony with which the cohabitation had begun, these declarations had the sole function of making public the intent, should proof later be required.[5]

Very rarely in history has there been a conception of such great freedom to divorce, at least at the legal level. Equally remarkable, especially compared with the preceding centuries, is the fact that both men and women had the same rights of divorce. We will return to the very different matter of how society viewed the choice to end a union when it was made by a woman. The point here is that despite the undeniable double standard there was progress represented by the new configuration of marriage and the granting of new freedoms to women. In this light, it is very interesting to follow the evolution of the laws on the dowry.

THE DOWRY

The time when women were bought and sold was gone. With marriage *cum manu* arose the practice of giving women who married a dowry (*dos*). This was a certain quantity of goods that both compensated her for the loss of her expectations to inherit within the group of origin (an automatic consequence of her passing to a new *familia*) and represented a contribution to her maintenance in the new family.

In marriage *sine manu*, the dowry remained as a contribution to the wife *ad onera matrimonii ferenda*. As an instrument of economic cooperation in the conjugal life, it was practiced without exception. Even if it was not legally necessary in order for union to be a marriage, it was (besides being a mark of social status) one of the elements of proof that allowed a marriage to be distinguished from concubinage.[6]

According to the laws of the *ius civile*, the goods of the dowry were the property of the husband (or, if he was a *filius familias*, of whoever held power over him). But beginning in the Augustan period, a series of provisions established increasingly strong limits on his power of disposing of the dowry and attributed to the woman the right to control the goods that constituted it.

In 18 B.C. the *lex Iulia de fundo dotali* (actually a chapter of the *lex Iulia de adulteriis*) forbade the husband to alienate dotal funds located on Italian soil. In postclassical law, the prohibition was extended to any unmovable goods. Justinian established that agreement of the wife to the alienation had no effect, a protective measure that points up the psychological dependence of women but intervenes decisively to protect their interests.

Other laws added to these in the course of the centuries were intended to allow the wife to recover the dowry in case of dissolution of the marriage. Originally subject to special agreement between the spouses, in the last centuries of the Republic the right to restitution had become automatic. In other words, the husband could always be obliged through a special action called *actio rei uxoriae* to restore the dowry to the wife, although he retained the right to withhold a part for "immorality" on her part and, of course, for adultery.

The principle that the dowry should revert to the wife when the marriage ended became further entrenched when it was established that the restitution was an obligation not only of the divorcing husband but of his heirs in case he predeceased his wife. The law that the husband was the owner of the dotal property, though it continued to exist on the theoretical level, had been surpassed.[7]

GUARDIANSHIP

In the last centuries of the Republic, the laws that kept women under lifetime guardianship (*tutela*) began to undergo substantial modification. By means of a complex mechanism called *coemptio fiduciae causa*, women could replace the legitimate tutor (a relative) with a person they trusted. This person would not interfere in their decisions and left them free to do as they wished. Fairly frequently, a husband (thus empowered by marriage *in manu*), rather than naming a tutor in his will, allowed his widow to choose one of her own liking (*tutoris optio*), with the further option of replacing him later. Beginning under the Principate, a woman whose guardian had denied her authorization to do something could take action against him.

Under Claudius, legitimate guardianship of freeborn (*ingenua*) women was abolished, and only libertine women were subject to it, their guardian being their former master. Beginning in the reign of Constantine, guardianship of women disappeared.[8] In the centuries of the Empire, even the old principle that *tutela*, being *virile officium*, could not be exercised by a woman was undermined (*Digesta* 26.1.16). In the first half of the second century, the jurist Neratius admitted that women who had made a *postulatio* to the emperor could exercise this *manus masculorum* (*Digesta* 26.1.18).

To admit female capacity as a general rule (despite the example of Greco-Egyptian usage, which had long recognized women guardians) was still difficult. In A.D. 224, the ancient law forbidding women from being guardians was confirmed by Alexander Severus (*Cod. Theod.* 5.35.1). But in 390 widows were allowed to be guardians of their children and grandchildren, though only in the absence of legitimate and testamentary guardians and on condition that they solemnly declared that they would not remarry (*Cod. Theod.* 5.35.2). In 530, finally, Justinian extended the right of guardianship to the natural mother.[9]

KINSHIP IN THE FEMALE LINE

Another important modification of the legal system contributed to improving the status of women. Earlier the only kinship recognized by law had been that of the male line (*adgnatio*). Not even the relationship between mother and son was recognized and safeguarded by law. At the end of the Republic, a series of provisions set in motion a revision of these principles. In the case of shameful conduct on the part of the husband and with the intervention of the praetor, a woman would obtain custody of her children. It was formally established that the children were obliged to respect father and mother equally (*Digesta* 37.15.1). Under Hadrian, the *senatusconsultum Tertullianum* established that a mother who had three children (thus, thanks to the *ius liberorum,* not subject to *tutela* herself), could inherit from them, albeit only after the children's children, their father, and certain agnates (*Digesta* 38.17). In A.D. 178, the *senatusconsultum Orfitianum* established that children could inherit from a mother ahead of her brothers and other agnates (*Digesta* 37.17; *Cod. Iust.* 6.57; *Inst. Iust.* 3.4). Finally, under Justinian, a mother could inherit from her children even without the *ius liberorum* (*Inst. Iust.* 3.3; *Cod. Iust.* 6.56).

These, then, were the innovations (determined in part by internal factors and in part by the influence of Hellenistic law) that altered the old laws of the *ius civile* in women's favor. The change was due to profound changes in Roman society and particularly happy economic and cultural situations, from which even the female population derived advantage. We will now look beyond the abstract assertions of the laws to see the real conditions of the lives of women and the male response to these changes.

EMANCIPATION: MASS OR ELITE PHENOMENON?

The centuries between the Principate and the Empire saw the "emancipation" of Roman women. The new rights (except of course political rights, which in Rome as in Greece were reserved for men) allowed women, it has been said, to instruct themselves and cultivate their intellectual interests, to attempt many activities that had been for men only, and to make full use of the law to end unhappy marriages and contract new ones. They practiced birth control and abortion, formed freely chosen amorous bonds, lived outside of matrimony, and enjoyed a new liberty that had been absolutely unthinkable—sexual freedom.

At least this is the picture that is usually drawn. And according to the point of view of the observer, the interpretations are diverse and contradictory. Some point to the affirmation and victory of women, who in that period won liberty in some ways comparable to modern ones.[10] There was deplorable laxity of morals, say others, immorality without restraint, carelessness of the fate of the state; and, consequently, the new freedom was a contributor—if not the principal cause of—the fall of the Empire.

But is the image of a Rome populated by emancipated women intellectually fulfilled and free of the traditional subjugation to men accurate? The literature presents figures of women quite different from the ancient *matronae*: women who show off their education by speaking Greek in public (Juv. 1.185–91), who go to public baths (6.419 ff.), who train to fight (1.23) or hunt (1.247), who drink wine (Mart. 7.67), wear cosmetics (Juv. 6.464–74), who divorce as often as they wish—one woman had eight husbands in five years (Juv. 6.229–391)! Despite the prohibition on women *postulare pro aliis*—to plead on others' behalf—we have mention of a woman lawyer, a certain Afrania (or Carfania), wife of the senator Licinius Buccio.[11] Another woman, Hortensia, daughter of the famous orator Q. Hortensius Hortalus, in 42 B.C. delivered an oration before the triumvirs.[12]

In the Augustan period, Sulpicia wrote elegies inspired by her love for a certain Cerinthus.[13] Another Sulpicia, a contemporary of Martial, wrote love poetry (Mart. 10.35 and 38). In the Imperial age, the poetess Melinno wrote a poem on the greatness of Rome (Stob. 3.7). Many women took part in cults of oriental origin, particularly that of Isis, the goddess who in a papyrus from the second century B.C. (*POxy.* 1380.11.214–16) is thanked for having given women strength equal to that of men. Under Isis' influence, according to Diodorus, Egyptian queens had more prestige than the kings and wives gave orders to husbands, who at marriage agreed by contract to obey them (Diod. Sic. 1.27). In other words, the cult of this goddess (discussed later) had contributed substantially to raising women's status in Egypt.

Rejecting the notion of their own inferiority and thus of their necessary subjugation, at least some women claimed greater freedom. They began to rebel against the practice of arranging marriages for family reasons, which they had been accustomed to accepting without argument. In the reign of Marcus Aurelius, the number of women of senatorial rank who wished to marry freedmen was so great that the emperor established that marriages of that type would not be considered valid. In the third century (214–218), Callixtus, a former slave who became pope, authorized senatorial women who did not wish to lose their privileges to live in concubinage with plebeians and freedmen. At the same time, Soemias, the Syrian mother of the then quite young emperor Elagabalus founded a *senaculum* ("mini-senate") of women with headquarters on the Quirinal Hill. Its purpose was to prevent senatorial women from losing their privileges if they married nonsenatorial men.[14] From inscriptions of the third century we learn that Hydria Tertulla and Cassia Faretria kept their rank although they married plebeians.[15]

That beginning at the end of the Republic there were "emancipated" women at Rome and that the number of these women greatly increased between the first and second centuries is beyond dispute. But can we speak of emancipation as a general fact? The women who enjoyed new privileges and fought for others all belonged to a single social class—the aristocracy. We know very little about women of other classes. We do know of a woman named Asellina of Pompeii who sold hot drinks.[16] We know of Roman women who worked in shops, who were copyists (*amanuenses*), or dressmakers (*vestificae*). Some women were teachers or physicians.[17] But the fact that women worked outside the home does not necessarily indicate emancipation. For the Romans, when work served to make money it was beneath the dignity of a free man. Accordingly, female presence or absence in the work sphere cannot considered an indicator of freedom.[18] The right to work was not among women's claims; it was a necessity for some women. Even if work meant a greater freedom of movement, it would be mistaken to interpret it by present-day standards as an opportunity for personal fulfillment.

In discussing emancipation, we can speak about only certain women, those who already enjoyed other privileges. Even within these limits emancipation was a difficult process, partly supported by legislation but accepted with enormous difficulty by the social conscience, as can be seen clearly in the image men had of the "emancipated" woman.

MALE VIEWS OF EMANCIPATED WOMEN

What was the male attitude toward women who used their new liberties? How did men view the relationship between the sexes? What did they expect from women? Though they never scaled the heights of Greek misogyny, the Romans always had a very precise idea of the role of women and a fairly bleak vision of the conjugal relationship. Like the Greeks, the Romans wanted their women under their thumbs.

Paraphrasing Plato, Scipio (in Cicero *Res Publica* 1.43) says that it is anarchy when slaves and women do not obey. In recommending that the Romans observe the laws of their fathers, Livy did not miss the occasion to put them on guard against the dangers of the new trends. Women were already difficult to control when they were held by the chains of the old laws, he said. But if we give them freedom, if we give them rights like our own, what will happen? When they are equal, they will have become superior (34.3).

But even submissive women (perhaps they were not sufficiently so) caused no small amount of trouble. In 131 B.C., the censor Metellus Numidicus had said, "If, fellow citizens, we could live without wives, we all would do without that annoyance of matrimony. But since nature has ordained that we cannot live happily with them, neither is it possible to live without them, we should think about our long-term well-being rather than our short-term pleasure" (Aul. Gell. *NA* 1.6.2).

One hundred years later, to induce the Romans to marry, Augustus read this speech in the Senate and had it posted so that all could learn its content. And two hundred years later, the orator Titus Castricius wondered if Metellus had not been mistaken to appeal to the necessity of nature instead of having illustrated the joys of matrimony, yet he concluded that Metellus was right. Orators, he said, can make false, tendentious, captious, and tricky statements, but only if they are realistic. As the tribulations of marriages are well known to all, Metellus was correct not to try to hide them—the need of the state was the only argument that could convince men to marry (*NA* 1.6.4–6).

The new fact of the "emancipation" of women needs to be placed in this context in order to understand its scope. How would the Romans react to the assumption by women of behaviors which went against the old rule of subjugation, which questioned the idea of marriage as "necessary evil" for the good of the state? The poems of Martial and Juvenal suggest that male reactions were not altogether positive.

In the second half of the first century A.D., Martial had before him a great many women whose behavior and ideology were at odds with the old models. The "chaste" Laevina bathes in the waters of Lake Avernus or at Baiae and then "falls into flames, leaves her husband, and follows a youngster" (1.62). The wife of Gallus, accused of greediness, in fact is very generous. She does not accept, she gives (2.56). Polla has her husband under the surveillance of her slaves, but she does not want to be under surveillance herself: Martial writes, "This is the equivalent, Polla, of changing the husband into the wife" (10.69). The wife of Alauda complains because her husband makes love with slave women; but she does it with litter-bearers: they are "two of a kind" (12.58). The wife of Caridemus has an affair with her doctor (6.31), and another wife asks her husband's consent to have a lover (3.92). The wife of Pannychus surrounds herself with eunuchs. Why? "Volt futui Caelia nec parere"—Caelia wants to make love not babies (6.67). Proculeia abandons her husband, now old, because he is no longer rich enough, and dismisses him with the phrase that once was the husband's to use: "tuas res tibi habeto" (10.41).

Like the women described in Hellenistic literature, Roman women got drunk (1.87), and when they were rich, they were tyrannical: "Are you asking why I don't want to take a rich wife? I don't want a husband for a wife. Let the matron, Priscus, stay beneath the husband: otherwise women and men can't be equals" (8.12).

If this was the situation, no wonder husbands longed for widowhood: "Lycoris, Fabianus, has buried all the friends she had. May she become a friend of my wife!" (4.24). The hope for widowhood as liberation from the oppression of wives appears not only in satire but also in other genres of literature. In the *Cistellaria* (175), Plautus says that a woman who died had "obliged her husband for the first time." An easy laugh, yes, and significant for that very reason.

In the writings of Juvenal, the greatest Roman satiric poet, the denunciation of female wickedness becomes ferocious. Juvenal was merciless to men too, accusing them of forgetting the moral virtue of their fathers, corrupted as they were by comforts and riches. But his invectives against women (whom he attacked both as individuals and as a sex in general) are certainly the harshest. The sixth *Satire,* perhaps the most famous, is ruthless.[19] Postumus intends to take a wife:

> . . . And here you are in *this*
> Day and age, man, getting yourself engaged,
> Fixing up marriage-covenant, dowry, betrothal-party;
> . . . Postumus, are you *really*
> Taking a wife? You used to be sane enough—what
> Fury's got into you, what snake has stung you up?
> Why endure such bitch-tyranny when rope's available
> By the fathom, when all those dizzying top-floor windows
> Are open for you, when there are bridges handy
> To jump from?
>
> (6.25–32)

Ursidius wants a child and therefore seeks a wife like the women of olden times, but now "the women worthy to touch the sacred fillets of Ceres, the women whose own fathers don't shrink from their kisses, are few" (50–51). To marry is a risk: "You take a wife and the harpists Echion or Glaphyrus or Ambrosius, the flutist, have become fathers" (76–77).

Juvenal makes no distinctions. Women are all the same from the wives of the emperors to the lowliest.

Hear what the emperor Claudius had to put up with. As soon as his wife thought that he was asleep, this imperial whore put on the hood she wore at night, determined to prefer a cheap pad to the royal bed, and left the house with one female slave only. No, hiding her black hair in a yellow wig, she entered the brothel, warm with its old patchwork quilts and her empty cell, her very own. Then she took her stand, naked, her nipples gilded, assuming the name of Lycisca, and displayed the stomach you came from, noble Britannicus. She obligingly received customers and asked for her money, and lay there through the night taking in the thrusts of all comers. Then when the pimp sent the girls home, at last she went away sadly, and (it was all she could do) was the last to close up her cell—yet she was still burning, her vagina stiff and erected, tired by men, but not yet satisfied, she left, her face dirty and bruised, grimy with lampsmoke, she brought back to her pillow the smell of the brothel. (115–35)

The contagion of corruption affected even the lowliest: "By now luxury is the equal vice of all women, both mistress and slave: the one who wears out the rough cobblestone barefoot is no better than the one who has herself carried around in a litter borne by Syrian giants" (347–49). The very poorest, however, have a point in their favor: "Pauper women endure the trials of childbirth and endure the burdens of nursing, when fortune demands it. But virtually no gilded bed is laid out for childbirth" (588–90). Roman ladies amuse themselves with eunuchs:

> So beardless to kiss, and no worry about abortions!
> But the biggest thrill is one who was fully-grown,
> A lusty black-quilled male, before the surgeons
> Went to work on his groin. . . .
> Everyone knows him—displaying his well-endowed person
> At the baths: Priapus might well be jealous. And yet
> He's a eunuch. His mistress arranged it. So let them sleep together. . . .
> (364–74)

That is not all. Especially if they are wealthy, women give the orders at home, impose their lovers on their husbands, buy and sell as they wish, and are absolute and despotic mistresses (136, 141, and 205–12). They have other minor defects, equally intolerable. They are affected; they try to imitate Greek women, even in bed (183–90). There is one "who, as soon as she sits down to dinner, praises Vergil and excuses Dido's suicide; matches and compares poets, weighing Vergil on one side of the scale and Homer on the other. Schoolmasters yield; professors are vanquished, everyone in the party is silenced" (432–37). To conclude, they are able, for love of money, to kill their own children, but they are even worse than Medea:

> Whatever the tragic poets
> Tell us about Medea and Procne may well have happened:
> I won't dispute that. Such women were monsters of daring
> In their own day—but not from the lust for cash.
> We find it less freakish when wrath provides the incentive
> For a woman's crimes, when whitehot passion whirls her
> Headlong, like some boulder that's carried away by a landslide,
> What I can't stand is the calculating woman
> Who plans her crimes in cold blood. Our wives sit and watch
> Alcestis undertaking to die in her husband's stead:
> If they had a similar chance, *they'd* gladly sacrifice
> Their husband's life for their lapdogs'.
>
> (642–50)

One could object at this point that Juvenal's hatred for women bears the hallmarks of an individual misogynist and that one ought not to generalize from it. But that would be only partly correct. Certainly Juvenal expresses an aversion to the female sex which borders on the pathological. For him no woman is any good; every marriage is a despicable union. Martial was different; he believed that there were successful marriages and he respected some women. Nigrina, he says, was dearly loved by her husband (4.75; 9.30); Claudia Rufina and Aulus Prudens were happy (11.53); Theophila, an educated woman and a poetess, was a devoted wife (7.69). The poetess Sulpicia was not only faithful to her husband, but in her work she exhorted girls to conjugal fidelity (10.35). Martial respected some of the *doctae puellae*, the intellectuals whom Juvenal mocks.

Despite this difference in individual attitudes, the same themes and the same accusations return in the two poets—and evidently they echo the commonplaces of the era. Nor would it be correct to object that satire is by definition malevolent. Other sources reflect an attitude that is anything but favorable to women. This becomes obvious when we examine the way they talk about a female behavior that, according to the evidence of the period, had become widespread; namely, the voluntary interruption of pregnancy.

ABORTION

Beginning in the first century A.D., references to abortion become increasingly numerous. In A.D. 62, Nero decided to get rid of his wife, Octavia, in order to marry Poppaea. Forgetting that he had already accused her of being sterile, he accused Octavia of having aborted to eliminate the product of an adulterous relationship with Anicetus. The choice of this grave and defaming accusation was not casual; it made it easier to justify the drastic punishment the emperor inflicted on his wife. She was exiled to the island of Pandateria where she was subsequently killed (Tac. *Ann.* 14.63.1).

Plutarch denounced "dissolute women who use expulsives and abortives only to be impregnated anew and find pleasure" (*Mor.* 134 f). Toward the middle of the first century, the philosopher Favorinus, taking up an accusation already made against women by Ovid and Seneca, speaks of the madness of women who not only do not nurse their children but who abort them in order not to disfigure their bellies.[20]

The practice of voluntarily interrupting pregnancy was evidently common. This is demonstrated by the interest in the problem on the part of physicians, such as Soranus of Ephesus (who practiced in Rome in the first decades of the second century), and astrologers, such as Maximus (also in the second century) who noted the influence of the moon on abortion and identified favorable and unfavorable periods.[21]

Particularly interesting is the reproach the practice inspired. To identify the reasons for such disapproval it is useful to examine the response by the jurist Julian (ca. A.D. 120) to the following question. If the slave Arethusa has been given her freedom on condition that she bear three children, and if Arethusa does not bear them because she is forced by the heir to use contraceptives or to abort, can she be considered free? Julian's reply was positive: Arethusa had to be considered free (*Digesta* 40.7.16, Ulpian). Evidently, it was perfectly normal and acceptable to make slaves abort. Abortion was not disapproved of because it was a taking of human life. If decided by the master or husband, it was within the law, just as earlier the killing of a son or daughter by a father had been within the law.

The Romans were against the interruption of pregnancy for different reasons than were the Christians, for whom the fetus was a human being. "For us, once homicide has been forbidden," writes Tertullian, "it is forbidden too to kill the embryo in the uterus; where there is blood, it flows in man, it is not lawful to destroy it. To impede birth is to hasten homicide; and it is no different to tear away the soul already born or destroy it while it is being born. He who will be a man is already a man, just as all fruit is already in the seed" (*Apol.* 9.8). For the Romans, however, as the jurist Papinian says, the unborn child "homo non recte dicitur," the unborn child is not a man. For them (as for the Stoics) the fetus was only *spes animantis,* the hope of a living being (*Digesta* 35 pr; 9; 11.8.2).

Why, then, were they so against abortion and why did they assume that women who practiced it did so for immoral reasons? They accused them of trying to hide the fruit of illicit relations, indulging in unbridled sexual activity, or not wanting to lose their figures. It was because the right to decide was the man's and the man's only. And now in the second century a new juridical institution makes its appearance: the custody of the womb in the interest of the husband.

During the reign of Marcus Aurelius and Lucius Verus, one Rutilius Severus, whose divorced wife denied being pregnant while he maintained that she was, asked the emperors to resolve the problem. The *divi fratres* decided that the woman should be examined by three midwives and if she was found to be pregnant, a guard should be set over her to make sure she did not abort (*Digesta* 25.4.1).[22]

To conclude: the law was changed, and with it women's morals—or those of some women. But the attitude of observers of this phenomenon was all but favorable. Novelties in this area were regarded with suspicion: emancipated women were not trusted. Probably some women (among whom the privileged classes who could take advantage of the liberties granted) abused, so to speak, these liberties. But from these cases, the common sense drew general rules: every liberty was viewed as a sign of license, dissoluteness, lack of self-control, selfishness, and luxury.

EXEMPLARY WIVES

Men found it hard to accept the idea that their daughters, wives, and mothers were different from Virginia and Lucretia. The models they proposed to oppose the widespread degeneration were not very different from the old ones. Martial recalls a woman worthy of every elegy: "When chaste Arria handed to Paetus the sword which she had drawn from her own breast, she said, 'If you believe me, the wound that I have made does not hurt, but the wound that you are going to make, that one, Paetus, hurts me'" (1.13).

Both Tacitus (*Ann.* 6.29 and 16.10) and Pliny (*Letters* 3.16, where he speaks of praiseworthy women) mention this woman. Arria had proved herself on several occasions. She had kept the death of her son a secret from her husband in order not to grieve him while he was recovering from an illness. She entered the sickroom smiling to reassure him and left it to weep, returning only when she was able to smile again. In A.D. 42, Caecina Paetus, her husband, was condemned to death for having taken part in the conspiracy of Scribonianus against Claudius. When Scribonianus was sentenced, Arria wrote to his widow, reproaching her for not having killed herself along with her husband, as she herself intended to do—and did. Her son-in-law tried to dissuade her, asking her if she would be happy if her daughter were to commit suicide knowing that he had to die. But his question was no no avail. "Yes," she replied, "if she was as happy with you as I have been with Paetus." When the moment came, Arria did not hesitate. Before her husband's eyes, encouraging him to do the same, she thrust the dagger into her breast, withdrew it, and handed it to him saying "Paete, non dolet"—Paetus, it does not hurt.[23]

These, then, were the women to respect: those like Arria or the wife (Pliny 6.24) who threw herself into Lake Como with her husband, who was incurably ill.

FEMALE DIVINITIES AND CULTS

In our discussion of the earliest period of Rome's history we alluded to the female divinities worshipped at Rome. We noted the analogy between the divine images and the female condition; now we may examine the ways the cults of these divinities changed along with the changes in morals and laws.

At Rome, as in Greece, female cults had existed since earliest antiquity, articulated according to the status of the women who could take part in them. The first distinction within the female population in this respect was that between virgins and married women (*matronae*), marked by the division between the cult of Fortuna Virginalis (at puberty girls dedicated the togas they wore as children) and that of Fortuna Primigenia of Praeneste, protectress of *matronae*.

Within the category of married women, there was a subcategory represented by the *univirae,* women who had only one man, to whom were reserved exclusive cults such as Fortuna Muliebris, whose birth was linked to the legend of Coriolanus; Pudicitia (Chastity), reserved for patrician *univirae;* and the Bona Dea, which was celebrated every year at the house of the wife of the consul, who removed himself from the house for the occasion.

Along with the distinction between virgins and matrons, other classifications separated women according to whether they were free or slave, patrician or plebeian, "honest" women or prostitutes. And according to which category or categories they belonged, they participated in the special and reserved cults. Slaves celebrated the Nonae Caprotinae (called *feriae ancillarum*), a sort of caricature of the festivals reserved for *matronae,* probably originally a parallel of the matronal festivals. Plebeian women celebrated Plebeian Chastity, analogous to the patrician cult and begun, according to legend, after Virginia (in 256 B.C.) had been expelled from the cult of her equals for having maried a plebeian. Prostitutes, finally, participated in the cult of Fortuna Virilis (parallel to that of Fortuna Muliebris), which took place in the men's baths.[24]

The separation of the cults, in other words, marked a number of basic distinctions intended to reproduce an insurmountable social

151

and legal order and to codify a model of life characterized, as in Greece, by the identification of marriage as the central moment in women's life and by the indication of an ideal code of behavior represented by the *univira*. Nor did the situation change with the gradual spread of divorce (usually initiated by the man) and with the Augustan population policy, which obliged the widowed and divorced to remarry. Even if a woman had more than one husband for reasons having nothing to do with her own wishes (because she had been widowed or repudiated), the woman who remarried lost the privileges linked to the status of *univira;* she was in a certain way penalized for not adhering to a model that social practice had made obsolete.[25]

The articulation of the cults corresponds, therefore, to a very significant classification of women. It indicates clearly the role assigned to them in society and the behavior that was expected of them. Furthermore, the symmetry between patrician and plebeian rites (as with Pudicitia) shows beyond a doubt that the ideology of the lower classes was no different from that of the aristocracy. Despite the social separation that cults and rites marked, the model of behavior proposed was the same.

Beginning in the second century B.C., prodigies had been interpreted to denounce the licentious behavior of certain matrons. Because the Romans believed that the prosperity and greatness of the state depended in large part on the behavior of its women, the guilty parties were punished and a temple was erected to Venus Obsequens, the goddess who reminded women of their duty.

In 114 B.C., a particularly worrying *prodigium* occurred to warn anew against female immorality. An aristocratic girl, Helvia, was struck by lightning, which undid her clothing as it killed her. This was taken as a sign not only of her own dissoluteness but of all women, in particular of those of the equestrian class. Helvia was the daughter of a knight. She was struck after her father had made her mount a horse to protect her from a violent storm during a trip. The state reacted firmly: a new temple was erected and dedicated to Venus Verticordia, literally the goddess who "turned the hearts" of women to virtue.[26] Three Vestal Virgins accused of having violated their thirty-year vow of chastity were buried alive.[27]

The situation did not improve. In 63 B.C., the cult of the Bona Dea was desecrated by P. Clodius Pulcher, who sneaked, dressed in women's clothing, into the house of Julius Caesar, whose wife was hostess to the rites of that year. Caesar repudiated Pompeia because he wished his wife to be "not so much as suspected." The story is told in Plutarch's *Life of Caesar* (10). In the time of Juvenal, if we give credence to his stories, the altars of Pudicitia and the Bona Dea were desecrated by women who chose sacred places to exhibit their luxury.

Why, you may ask yourself, does the notorious Maura
Sniff at the air in that knowing, derisive way
As she and her dear friend Tullia pass by the ancient altar
Of Chastity? and what is Tullia whispering to her?
Here, at night, they stagger out of their litters
And relieve themselves, pissing in long hard bursts
All over the Goddess's statue. Thus, while the Moon
Looks down on their motions, they take turns to ride each other,
And finally go home. So you, next morning
On your way to some great house, will splash through your wife's
  piddle.
    Notorious, too, are the ritual mysteries
Of the Good Goddess, when flute-music stirs the loins,
And frenzied women, devotees of Priapus,
Sweep along in procession, howling, tossing their hair,
Wine-flown, horn-crazy, burning with the desire
To get themselves laid. Hark at the way they whinny
In mounting lust, see that copious flow, the pure
And vintage wine of passion, that splashes their thighs!
Off goes Saufeia's wreath, she challenges the call-girls
To a contest of bumps and grinds, emerges victorious,
But herself is eclipsed in turn—an admiring loser—
By the liquid movements of Medullina's buttocks:
So the ladies, with a display of talent to match their birth,
Win all the prizes. No make-belief here, no pretence,
Each act is performed in earnest, and guaranteed
To warm the age-chilled balls of a Nestor or a Priam.
Delay breeds itching impatience, boosts the pure female
Urge, and from every side of the grotto a clamorous
Cry goes up, 'It's time! Let in the men!'

(Juv. 6.305–27)[28]

Juvenal's description must of course be accepted with caution. After what we have seen of his personality, the suspicion that he exaggerates is more than legitimate. Nevertheless, there is no doubt that female cults changed—or rather the cults were the same, but the women now behaved in such a way as to be unworthy to participate in them. The discrepancy between ideology and practice became ever stronger and more dangerous: on one side were the old principles, unchanged by time and still of fundamental importance for the state; on the other was the attitude of the women. The profound changes in female behavior were not accompanied by changes in the ideology and the models of the ancient religion and cults. It was the women who questioned the principles that the *civitas* continued to embrace.

Only one cult (of those properly Roman) seems different at first sight. For this reason it has been identified as one of the factors contributing to the emancipation of women. In the cult of Vesta, the priestesses were in some ways "emancipated" women.

According to Plutarch's *Life of Numa Pompilius* 10, there were at first two Vestal Virgins, then four, and finally six. According to Dionysius of Halicarnassus (1.76.3), originally they served the goddess for five years; later they were consecrated to the goddess for thirty years. During this period they maintained a vow of chastity and were freed from *patria potestas* and guardianship. They alone among women (and many centuries ahead of other women) could make wills without male authorization. The figure of the priestess of Vesta has been viewed as a woman who was different and freer, whose existence would have contributed to emancipation.[29]

Yet in considering the emancipation of the Vestal Virgins there is much to discuss. In the first place, while under vow of chastity the Vestal Virgin was (like the goddess whose image she represented) at the same time *virgo* and *mater*, fertile like the earth. For this reason she was called Tellus Mater (Mother Earth). Second, her dress and hair (divided into six locks with the aid of curved pins and held by a wool fillet worked with red and white threads) were those of an *uxor* and her status was that of a matron. Furthermore, she performed rites that reproduced certain typical women's functions which were stylized in the *stercoratio* (cleaning) and preparation of certain foods. Finally, the Vestals celebrated the *fascinus,* the male reproductive organ. This is the same Tutunus Mutunus that brides honored in a solemn ceremony before their weddings to ward off sterility. In sum, although legally emancipated from the father and free of guardianship, Vestal Virgins, like all other Roman women, were under the authority of a man. They were chosen between six and ten years of age by the Pontifex Maximus. He selected them from among the other candidates by intoning a solemn formula (*Te, Amata, capio*). The girl was liberated from subordination within the family but now fell under the rule of the Pontifex, whose power extended to life and death. A Vestal Virgin who violated her vow of chastity would be buried alive in a public ceremony, which served to instruct not only Vestal Virgins but all women tempted to shirk their duties.

Despite her sacred office and virginity, then, the image of Vestal Virgin reproduced the model of the *matrona.* It is not in the figure of the Vestal that we can identify the elements of women's emancipation. And more generally, it is not in the traditional cults of Roman religion, which defended themselves against any force that threatened change or permitted new attitudes about women. The decisiveness with which they did so shows strongly how the "official" ideology opposed emancipation. Finding ample response in the social conscience, the state intended to maintain whole and unchanged the principles and models of early Rome. But this does not mean that other religions did not contribute significantly to women's emancipation.

ORIENTAL CULTS: ISIS

In the third century B.C., a series of cults of other regions of the Empire became juxtaposed with the traditional Roman ones. They helped women escape the restricting conditions that the ancient cults told them were inevitable. In the Republican period, the Bacchanalia episode had already signaled the women's malaise, and had endangered the principles on which the family and legal organization was founded.

From the third century on, the Greek cult of Aphrodite had been grafted on to that of the Roman Fortuna. The cult was celebrated in the festivals known as Veneralia. In 205 B.C., the cult of the Great Goddess was introduced from Phrygia. The Great Goddess had been indicated by the Sybilline Books as the only divinity able to save Rome from Hannibal. She was venerated in the West with the name Magna Mater Idaea. The cult of Venus Ericina (worshipped at Eryx in Sicily) was celebrated in the Vinalia. Gradually, the Roman Venus was identified with the Syrian Astarte and the Egyptian Isis.[30] The cult of Isis, in particular, contributed perceptibly to changing women.

Isis consoled human suffering and inspired hope in a life beyond death. To her all human beings were equal, whether slaves or free. All had an immortal soul, despite social status or sex. Her priests could be either men or women, and all women could participate in her worship. Besides being a wife and mother, Isis had been a prostitute for ten years; even women who sold themselves were accepted in the cult. The cult of Isis permitted the mingling of persons who would never have had contacts in most social situations.

What is more, the ritual of mystical contact with the goddess was of a mysterious sexual nature. It followed that those who attended the temples of the goddess, which began to appear in Rome around 50 B.C., were accused of prostitution in popular gossip and by the authorities. The attempts to stop the spread of the cult were numerous. Augustus ordered the demolition of the temple of Isis and Serapis, which had been built after the death of Caesar. No one would accept the job of executing the sacrilegious order, so the consul had to knock down the door himself with an ax (Dio Cass. 47.15 and 53.2; Val. Max. 1.3.3).

In 19 B.C., a singular episode furnished the pretext for more repression. Decius Mundus, to obtain the favors of Paullina, had convinced the priests of the goddess with a handsome bribe to tell the woman that the god Anubis wanted to meet her in the temple at night. Decius Mundus appeared disguised as the god and satisfied his desire, but the emperor Tiberius found out about the incident and reacted severely. He had the priests crucified, the temple demolished, and the statue of the goddess thrown into the Tiber.[31]

The spread of the new cults disturbed the established order and threw into confusion the homes of the Romans. The cults were viewed as the cause of inadmissible licentiousness. If Juvenal described two women who practiced homosexual love at the altar of Pudicitia (6.522–30), Minucius Felix and Tertullian believed that the new temples were places of adultery and prostitution. True or false, the rumors were not casual. In the name of the new cults, too many things were changing, too many principles were being shaken, too many liberties were being claimed by persons who, earlier, could never have questioned their inferior status. Slaves and women now believed themselves "persons" equal to freeborn persons and men, respectively. And yet another cult arose to help spread the new and subversive ideas—Christianity.

CHRISTIANITY

The preaching of Christ brought profound and radical innovations to the relationship between the sexes. It questioned both Jewish and Roman ideas. For the Jews, marriage was sacred, but the organization and ideology of the family was anything but favorable to women. Viewed solely as instrument of procreation, the woman was totally under male power, particularly that of her husband, who could have more than one wife and repudiate them at will.[32] For Jesus, however, marriage was monogamic and indissoluble. When the Pharisees, to provoke him, asked Jesus if repudiation was allowed, he explained that at marriage a man left his father and mother by divine will so as to be "a single flesh" with his wife. No one, therefore, could separate what God had joined (Matt. 19:3–9; Mark 10:2–9).

For the Romans (who, unlike the Jews, were monogamous) the preachings of Christ were revolutionary too. Divorce was common and had been allowed since earliest antiquity. Another principle preached by the Christians disturbed the Romans. According to Jesus and his followers, men and women had equal dignity in marriage. The husband, wrote Paul in 1 Cor. 7:3–5,

> must give the wife what is due to her, and the wife equally must give the husband his due. The wife cannot claim her body as her own; it is her husband's. Equally, the husband cannot claim his body as his own; it is his wife's. Do not deny yourselves to one another, except when you

157

agree upon a temporary abstinence in order to devote yourselves to prayer; afterwards you may come together again; otherwise, for lack of self-control, you may be tempted by Satan.

Elsewhere (Gal. 3:28), Paul asserted more generally that there should be "neither Jew nor Greek nor slave nor free man nor woman nor man."

That the assertion of such principles contributed no small amount to giving women a new consciousness and to teaching men greater respect for women is beyond dispute. But another aspect of early Christianity should be taken into consideration. The teachings contained explicit references to the preeminent position of the man in the family and to male superiority. "Woman's head is man," wrote Paul, after describing marriage as an equal partnership, "man is the image of God, and the mirror of his glory, whereas woman reflects the glory of man" (1 Cor. 11:3, 11:7).

The theme of subordination returns, accompanied by another theme that had important consequences; namely, one who lives in a state of chastity is nearer to God than one who lives in matrimony. "To the unmarried and to widows I say this: it is a good thing if they stay as I am myself; but if they cannot control themselves, they should marry. Better be married than burn with vain desire," says Paul (1 Cor. 7:8–9). Marriage serves to avoid the temptations of the flesh, but whoever lives in chastity is nearer the kingdom of heaven.[33] This principle was to be developed in subsequent centuries with increasing gynecophobia.

Christ's preaching introduced new and upsetting principles: women, whom he baptized equally with men, were for him persons despite their sexual identity. Both the Jewish tradition and the Roman view of the female sex were surpassed by this new view of the relationship between the sexes. Furthermore, Jesus was disposed to understand and pardon even the most serious offense of women, namely, adultery. It was Jesus himself who, in the Gospel according to John, saved the adulteress the scribes and Pharisees were about to stone (John 7:53 and 8:11).[34]

Two religions, then, in very different ways, contributed to changing women's lives and helped them overcome the negative image they had carried for centuries.

The women who lived in the centuries of their diffusion and activity (the centuries of the maximum greatness of Rome) benefited from, besides particularly happy political, economic, and social conditions, transformations of ideas of no slight importance. But in the centuries that followed, that is, the the late Empire, things changed again. The tendency toward emancipation, realized at least legally, and, even if opposed by the social conscience, enjoyed by at least one level of the female population, underwent not only an arrest but an inversion. Women were again pushed into conditions of subordination from which they had almost escaped.

The Fall of the Empire

WAS IT WOMEN'S FAULT?

This is clearly not the place to examine the causes of the decline and fall of the Roman Empire, but neither is it possible for investigators of the female condition to forget that in the opinion of some, women played a central role in bringing the fall about.

One of the fundamental causes of the fall of Rome was, in fact, the drop in the birth rate, which began in the last centuries of the Republic and reached its peak in the second century A.D., with politically disastrous consequences. The Roman ruling class was decimated. Before an ever-greater mass of new citizens (many of whom were enfranchised former slaves), the aristocracy was no longer able to ensure its own replacement. The gradual disappearance of the "best" had the fatal consequence of the disappearance of the ideals and virtues that had made Rome great.[35] The refusal of women to assume the burdens and consequences of motherhood, the first of their responsibilities, was identified as a cause for the drop in births. Always greedier for pleasures and luxury, women were seen as the cause of irreparable imbalance of payments. Silks had to be imported from China; perfumes came from Arabia; jewels from the Orient. Tiberius had already claimed that the extravagance of women had enriched Rome's enemies while impoverishing the Romans (Tac. *Ann.* 3.53.5).

But the faults imputed to women were insufficient to explain a collapse due to much more complex economic, financial, and military reasons; the theory does not merit much space, except for one significant fact. The falling birth rate, which certainly was one cause of the entry of new classes to the different levels of power, was in part due to a female choice. But to what extent?

The population crisis struck not only the cities but also the rural areas where the peasants were no longer able to sustain the burden of tribute. Among the upper classes, moreover, the drop in births was desired by only some. Many women who wanted children did not have them; for example, the wives of Augustus, Tiberius, Caligula, Claudius, and Nero. These emperors died without leaving descendants; and Nerva, Trajan, Hadrian, and Antoninus were obliged to adopt sons in order to ensure dynastic continuity. For all the emancipated women who refused motherhood as a life choice, there were others obliged to give it up for economic reasons or because they were sterile. And as for love of luxury, how many men loved comforts and riches no less than their women?

If we have dwelt on the subject, it has not been to take it into serious consideration, but to highlight a significant circumstance; that is, the notion that the crisis of a political and economic system created by men could now be partially blamed on women.

FAMILY POLICY

With the changing of political, economic, and social conditions, and the bureaucratization of power and the militarization of the state, the conditions that had allowed and favored emancipation no longer existed. The sector where the most important interventions now occurred was the family, which the Christian concept of marriage strongly influenced.

The Christians believed that marriage should be a free choice of the parties involved. Although arranged marriages continued, more and more marriages came to be decided by the contracting parties themselves and not by their parents. This gave marriage a new and higher ethical significance, but Christianity also acted to under-value the role of consent of the spouses. It transformed—with partial success—the ancient concept of *affectio maritalis*.

We have seen that for classical law the intention of being married had to be continuous, that is, it had to sustain the union for the whole course of matrimonial life. Intention could be inferred from a series of factors, none of which had constitutive value. For the Christian, on the other hand, in order for a union to be a marriage, the will to contract it had to be displayed in preestablished forms in the presence of the Church. And to this will they attributed an irrevocable constitutive value. The Christians, in other words, took into consideration only the initial will, fixing it, as it were, in time; and only it had determining validity. The Christian emperors sought in many ways to modify the old system of marriage to make it correspond to the new state religion.

In the classical period, the simple lapse of *affectio maritalis* in only one of the spouses automatically involved divorce; in postclassical law it became customary to document the dissolution of marriage with a written act called *libellus repudii,* which the emperor Justinian made obligatory. The imperial interventions, from Constantine to Justinian, also put into practice a policy intended to impede or at least limit divorce by establishing for the first time a list of justifiable circumstances. The dissolution of marriage, they established, could occur *bona gratia* and *ex iusta causa. Bona gratia* divorces were determined by circumstances that made cohabitation impossible, even if not one of the parties' fault, such as a vow of chastity or impotence. *Ex iusta causa,* however, were divorces attributable to the fault of one of the partners. The faults, obviously, were different for men and women.

Besides any actions that justified the request for divorce by either the husband or the wife (such as an attempt on the life of the spouse), only the most serious acts on the part of the husband were considered "faults," such as attempting to prostitute the wife. The wife, on the other hand, was considered guilty not only for committing adultery (which was not a "fault" if committed by the husband unless he had a concubine) but also for attending banquets or baths with nonrelatives or attending shows without her husband's permission.

The other divorces, the *repudii sine ulla causa* (that is, on the initiative of one of the partners not having to do with one of the circumstances just listed) and divorces *communi consensu* (by common consent of the spouses, simply on the basis of a desire to dissolve a marriage) were thwarted by the imposition of a fine.[36]

It should be said that these provisions met such strong resistance that in 566 Justin II, successor to Justinian, was obliged to abolish the fine for divorce *communi consensu*. Nevertheless, the basis of marriage had been transformed. The principle that it was founded on the free will of the contracting parties had been consolidated, but the second principle, by which free will could also dissolve it, had been in part annulled.

REPRESSION OF ADULTERY

Another aspect of imperial policy with regard to family morality is particularly indicative of the tendencies of the period. Attempting to recover ancient values, the emperors intervened assiduously, dictating numerous laws on the repression of adultery. As in the earlier period, infidelity in a betrothed couple was considered adultery, too, and female adultery was repressed with ever more severity in the late Empire.

At this point we must take a step backward and return to the centuries of emancipation. During these centuries, along with the new laws and unflagging efforts of legislation and jurisprudence to adapt the rigid ancient laws to the exigencies of a more open society, there remained the framework of a society whose ideology showed no sign of abating on at least one fundamental point. On what was considered the pillar of the stability, security, and very fabric of society, political power could not and would not bend. Female emancipation, the greater participation of women in cultural and social life, had been tolerated on condition that the family morality remained unquestioned. And the laws protecting family morality were unchanged for hundreds of years.

The chain of provisions during the Principate and Empire had not mitigated the ancient severity with which violations had always been punished. Although the provision of a *senatusconsultum Claudianum* (52 B.C.) might seem to do so, its true rationale was economic. According to this law, a free woman who had relations with a slave became the master's slave along with any children she might have if she did not end the relationship after three warnings by the master (*Inst. Iust.* 3.12). In this fundamental economic principle the slave represented labor-power, and his children had to belong to the master. The *senatusconsultum Claudianum* was important in the context of the period, but its reasoning is not surprising. Other provisions clearly reveal the attitude of the state toward the freedom that women were assuming with ever-greater frequency.

The *lex Iulia,* as we have seen, established that female adultery represented a danger for society as a whole and could be punished on request of any citizen. Subsequent legislation, far from reducing the penalties with which they were punished, made them even more severe. Juvenal had portrayed as a grave danger the fact that the *lex Iulia* was not sufficiently applied. "Ubi nunc lex Iulia? Dormis?"—Where are you now, *lex Iulia?* Are you asleep? (2.37). If the *lex Iulia* was dormant and the citizens were lax in their demands for its application, the Christian emperors certainly were not. They were diligent in their regulation of the burning problem.[37]

Constantine and Constans, in A.D. 339, established that an adulteress and her lover should be condemned to death and burned at the stake or sentenced to the terrible *poena cullei,* the ancient penalty for parricide. This entailed closing the condemned in a bag together with a dog, a monkey, a rooster, or a viper and throwing them into a river (*Cod. Theod.* 11.36.4). Moreover, the *lex Iulia,* while affirming the right also limited the *ius occidendi* of the father and husband. Under the Empire this power was extended anew. According to the *lex Iulia,* the husband could kill with impunity only certain lovers of the adulterous wife: if he killed the wife, he was subject to punishment for homicide. In later centuries, a series of laws modified the situation.

Antoninus Pius established that the man who killed his adulterous wife should be punished not as for homicide but less severely, depending on his social class. If he was *humilis loci,* he was sentenced to forced labor for life; if *honestior,* to *relegatio in insulam,* exile to an island. Marcus Aurelius and Commodus confirmed that law and established less severe penalties for the husband who had killed his wife outside the conditions of time and place that under the *lex Iulia* justified the killing of the lover (*Digesta* 48.5.39[38].8). Alexander Severus established that this penalty should be exile

(*Cod. Iust.* 9.9.4). Finally, the situation reverted to what had existed before the *lex Iulia,* that is, a husband could kill his wife with impunity.

In 506, the *lex Romana Visigothorum,* aimed at Romans who lived under the Visigoths, established that the husband should not be punished for killing either the lover or the wife.[38] The several epitomes of the law, particularly that of Egidius, confirmed this law, perhaps inspired by Visigoth law, which was very severe toward women, or perhaps influenced by the so-called vulgar law, that is the law in use in the provinces.[39]

Only under Justinian were the limits of the impunity again tightened. In *Novella* 117.15, the emperor recalled that the impunity granted to the husband covered killing only the lover, not the wife. He established further that to kill the lover with impunity, the husband had to send the lover three written warnings signed by trustworthy witnesses. In other words, the husband enjoyed the traditional impunity only if he killed his wife's steady lover, and not a man who had a casual affair with her. The new law did not please the "doctors," who, to ridicule it, invented a formula whereby the husband, ironically named Martinus Cornilianus, served notice to the lover, called Tristanus Bravus, to stop seeing his wife.[40]

Again thanks to Justinian, an adulteress could avoid the death penalty. The emperor established in 556 that a guilty wife could be shut up in a convent. She could leave only if the husband pardoned her within two years. If he did not or if he died within this period, she had to spend the rest of her life there (*Nov.* 134.10). The Justinianian provision is interesting: moved by opposition in principle to the death penalty, Justinian still considered adultery a crime so unpardonable that he established detention as a penalty for the first time in Roman history. Earlier it had been only a preventive measure before a trial; punishments, though harsh, had never involved limitation of personal liberty. Adultery was the first crime punished by this type of sanction. As at the dawn of Roman history, women's faithfulness to wifely responsibilites was perceived as her fundamental and absolute duty.

ABORTION: FROM PRIVATE PROBLEM TO CRIME

It cannot be surprising at this point that under the Empire, for the first time in the history of Rome, abortion was considered a crime and punished as such. Although considered a serious offense if performed on the woman's initiative alone, the interruption of pregnancy had always been a private affair (and as such not subject to intervention by the state). It was up to fathers or husbands to react by punishing their guilty wives and daughters themselves. But the situation changed with a rescript of the emperors Septimius Severus and Caracalla (who ruled between A.D. 198 and 211). The occasion was furnished by the case of a woman who had an abortion after she was divorced. The first public sanction for abortion was exile.[41]

The rationale of the law is obvious: for the Romans, the unborn child was not a person, and the interruption of pregnancy therefore was not opposed on grounds that it took human life, but rather because it contradicted the right of the head of a family to make the decisions for the group under his power.[42]

As had happened with adultery, the state could not remain indifferent to the increase of abortion. If the defense of family morality was a question of public interest, so was abortion. Abortion was believed to have such immediately disastrous consequences for the family that it could no longer be merely a private affair.

EXCLUSION FROM THE *VIRILIA OFFICIA*

Even during the era of the greatest expansion of women's rights, Roman society maintained certain fundamental principles designed to contain female emancipation. Foremost were the principles of family morality. Next was the notion of the natural incapacity of women to participate in the governing of the state. Everything to do with administration and government was part of the *virilia officia,* duties that only men, by definition, were able to perform.

Cicero had said, "quanta erit infelicitas urbis ullius, in qua virorum officia mulieres occupabunt"—how unhappy will be the city where women hold the offices of men.[43] The mere thought that, once the strict limit of the sex roles had been surpassed, women could even accede to public office was reason for gloomy predictions. But the danger was averted: "to guarantee modesty," women were forbidden *postulare pro aliis* (to plead cases for others) and hold the *virilia officia* (*Digesta* 3.1.1.5). "Foeminae," was the solemnly sanctioned principle, "ab omnibus officiis civilibus vel publicis remotae sunt"—women shall not have access to any civil or public offices, and therefore they could not be judges or take part in administration (*Digesta* 50.17.2). Excluded from "male" territory, women who had tried to escape from the "female" territory were once again imprisoned there. When the crisis worsened, the state tightened its reins, polishing off the old laws and imposing models of behavior that had been ignored.

The old image of the *materfamilias,* which even in the centuries of emancipation had always been held up against the new and disturbing image of the emancipated woman, became again the obligatory choice of women. Christianity made no small contribution toward women's return to subordinate status.

CHRISTIAN CHASTITY

The teaching of Christ had been revolutionary, albeit not without contradiction. It is enough to recall his reply to Mary, who at the wedding at Cana (in the Gospel according to John) asked for a miracle. "Ti emoi kai soi?" Jesus answered—"don't interfere." Despite the contradictions of this new and liberating teaching, the society of the late Empire praised those points that echoed the ancient misogyny and that would eventually create a new, onerous subordination.

Christ had said that to remarry after repudiating one's wife would be adultery, and that it was also adultery to marry a woman who had been repudiated. In only one case was repudiation allowed: if the wife was an adulteress (there is no reference to male adultery). In this case, however, it is not clear whether remarriage was allowed (Matt. 19:9; Mark 10:11). To disciples who wondered if it would be better not to marry, Jesus answered:

> Not all men can accept this saying, but only those to whom it is given. For some are eunuchs because they are born so, and some are eunuchs

because they were made so by men, and some have made eunuchs of themselves for the sake of the kingdom of heaven. Let those accept it who can. (Matt. 19:11–12, trans. A. E. Harvey and M. R. Lefkowitz)

For Christ, then, virginity, which helped one to attain divine grace, had to be a choice. But his speech can be interpreted differently. The phrase translated as "Let those accept it who can," reads in Greek, "o dunamenos chorein, choreito." *Chorein* means "understand with the intellect," but translated by Jerome in the Vulgate, it reads, "qui potest capere, capiat." There the phrase is interpreted in the sense of "he who is able to do so (that is, remain chaste), let him do so," and thus it becomes the basis for subsequent Christian prescriptions for chastity and the celibacy of priests. Chastity was a superior state, to which all should aspire in fleeing the temptations of the flesh.

Many elements contributed to the spread of this ascetic vision. The Cynic and Stoic doctrines (for which liberation from the instincts was a primary objective) as well as Christian customs influenced the ideal of virginity. Paul had written:

> If a man has a partner in celibacy and feels that he is not behaving properly toward her, if, that is, his instincts are too strong for him; and something must be done, he may do as he pleases; there is nothing wrong in it; let them marry. But if a man is steadfast in his purpose, being under no compulsion, and has complete control of his own choice; and if he has decided in his own mind to preserve his partner in her virginity, he will do well. Thus, he who marries his partner does well, and he who does not will do better. (1 Cor. 7:36–38)

Paul probably did not address his exhortations to the fathers of virgins, as is often thought.[44] He referred to their fiancés and alluded to an ascetic practice which was beginning to appear at that time and which was to spread quickly. By the second century the practice of "spiritual marriage" would have many adherents. This practice entailed living in chastity with virgin girls (called *parthenoi syneisactoi* or *virgines subintroductae*); it soon degenerated into unions that were anything but chaste and was condemned by Irenaeus and Tertullian, among others.

Despite the possible interpretations of this passage, one thing is certain. Marriage clearly was regarded as inferior to virginity as a remedy against the evils that derived from the temptation of the flesh. In this connection Gnosticism becomes important. "Gnosis" (knowledge) allowed one to know the reasons for evil in the world. The Gnostics (bearers of this knowledge) were therefore able to conquer evil and to teach others to do the same. Given that evil arose from the sin of Adam (who introduced the bipolarity between the sexes, which had not existed before), spiritual "regeneration" was linked to the elimination of sexuality. The Encratites (the followers of Saturninus), the Severians, and the Naasenes practiced abstinence and preached it with particular vigor: women and marriage, they said, were the work of Satan.[45]

The praise of chastity was to grow in the centuries to follow. In the fourth century, Gregory of Nazianzus told young girls:

> Let marriage be praised for you, but before marriage, virginity. Marriage is an indulgence of the passions, purity is splendor. Marriage is also the root of virginity pleasing to God: but still it is slavery to the flesh and passion . . . may the good God confirm you, may fasting empty you; vigils, prayers, tears, sleeping on the ground, love all turned around legitimately toward God, who will put to sleep every desire for unholy things.[46]

But it was especially due to the cult of Mary (which spread rapidly, particularly after Christianity's recognition as state religion by Constantine) that chastity was exalted and proposed as the highest model of behavior. The Church Fathers worried no small amount about the virginity of the mother of Christ. After having spoken of her *vulva reserata,* they propounded the theory of the *uterus clausus,* in order to maintain her "eternal virginity" (*ante partum, in partu,* and *post partum*). This became dogma at the Lateran Council of 649, and was confirmed by the Council of Tolentine in 675. The hypothesis posed some problems which were resolved, however. The brothers and sisters of Jesus mentioned in the Gospels became stepbrothers and stepsisters (Joseph's children from a previous marriage). Later they were said to be his cousins.

Mary's sexuality had been established, but that was not enough. Every reference to sex in relation to her character was to disappear. In the thirteenth century a dispute arose. In contrast with the Dominicans, the Franciscans maintained that Mary was conceived without sin by Anne, her mother. The hypothesis was welcomed by Pope Sixtus IV in 1476; with the bull *Cum Praecelsa,* it became dogma in 1854 under Pius IX, and it was providentially confirmed in 1858 when the Blessed Virgin appeared at Lourdes to Bernadette Soubirous as the "immaculate conception."[47]

But let us return to the Roman Empire. Perhaps the success of this model was not due only to Christian preaching. Perhaps the ascetic proposal actually found affirmation in the daily practice of sexual relations, in the way in which average men and women had long been experiencing their relationship with the body and with sex.[48] This is difficult to prove and difficult to rule out, yet chastity, so highly praised, was practiced as an arduous but gratifying conquest of the body by men and women alike. The ideal had particular consequences in the lives of women, however.

THE CHURCH FATHERS: THE DEMONIZATION OF WOMEN

The demonization of all women except the Virgin Mary was in sharp contrast to the exaltation of the ascetic model and chastity. Unlike Mary, women were both flesh and matter. Hostile to all that was instinct and passion, immersed in Platonic and Neoplatonic culture, the Fathers praised the refusal of sex. It was viewed as an evil linked to human nature, to be conquered (or at least controlled). And this was one good function they intended for marriage—to control the impulses, to channel the instincts, in a union within which, once again, woman (seen as procreatrix) was inexorably subordinated and identified as inferior.

A few references chosen from the long list of the Church Fathers' invectives against women will suffice. "Woman," said Tertullian, "you are the gate of the devil" (*De cultu foeminarum* 1.1.2). Clement of Alexandria wrote, "it is a shameful thing for every woman merely to think that she is a woman," and "women must seek wisdom, like men, even if men are superior and have first place in every field, at least if they are not too effeminate."[49] For Origen, "he is truly male who ignores sin, which is to say female fragility," and "woman represents the flesh and the passions, while man represents reason and intellect."[50] According to John Chrysostom, "the mind of woman is somewhat infantile."[51]

It was with Augustine, perhaps, that Christianity reached its peak of misogyny. Conversion was viewed by Augustine as liberation from desire, from the temptations of the flesh; the state of grace could be achieved solely by exorcising women. "There is nothing I must flee more than the conjugal bed," he wrote in the *Soliloquy*. "Nothing throws the mind of man into more confusion than the flattery of women and that contact of bodies without which the bride does not let herself be possessed." He concluded, "Since you have no other way to have children, consent to the work of the flesh only with sorrow, because it is a punishment of that Adam from whom we descend."[52]

The ancient cry of Hippolytus ("If only we could have children without the help of women!") and the idea of Metellus Numidicus (marriage as evil necessary for the purpose of having children) return, now united with the idea of woman as temptation, as instrument of evil and sin.

Centuries had passed since Jesus preached love and equality. The political, social, and economic conditions were different, but the essential idea was the same. Founded on new presuppositions, misogyny, this constant of ancient culture, was to reconfirm itself in Christian ideology. And in the centuries to come, its consequences for the female condition were to be confirmed by canon law. In 1140, the Decree of Gratian confirmed that "est ordo naturalis in hominibus, ut foeminae serviant viris"—the subordination of women to men is in the natural order of things.[53] Man is "imago et gloria Dei," woman "non est gloria aut imago Dei."[54] From which results "quaemadmodum viris foeminas subditas, et poene famulas esse lex voluerit uxores"—that the law established that women shall be subordinated, and that wives shall be virtually slaves of their husbands.[55]

But let us resume the thread of our discussion of the Empire, to conclude it with a sketch of the Byzantine Empire.

Eleven

The Byzantine Empire

t has been said that Byzantine women, who were protected by the law as much as if not more than men, held a position rarely surpassed in history.[1] But the facts indicate that the status of women was much less than one of privilege.

At first sight one element seems to confirm the hypothesis of women's determining presence in the society. Designated by the title Augusta or Basilissa (Queen), the Byzantine empress was crowned as was the emperor. If she received the crown with the emperor, the ceremony took place in the church; if she became Augusta later (for example, if she married the emperor after he had been crowned), the coronation was held in the imperial palace. The empresses participated not only in public ceremonies but also, in a way, in government. Theodora, for example, sat in the councils called by Justinian. She even spoke in councils, although before doing so, she used to beg the council's pardon.[2]

If the emperor was too young or otherwise disqualified from ruling, the Augusta acted as regent. For example, Pulcheria replaced her young brother (not only wives could be crowned empresses, but also the mothers, sisters, and daughters of emperors). Sophia replaced her husband Justin II when he became insane.

171

When an emperor died, moreover, the empress had the right to nominate his successor. Pulcheria designated Marcian, Ariadne designated Anastasius, and Zoe made emperors of her several husbands. Sometimes when the Basilissa was the only surviving holder of power she did not want to give it up; then she did not name a new emperor at all. Irene had her son blinded and governed alone. This created questions of protocol because the case was so exceptional; it was decided to call her "emperor" in official documents.[3]

But how little effect the existence of female holders of political power can have on the lives of ordinary women is something we have already discussed with regard to the Hellenistic period. And the story of the Byzantine Empire seems to offer further confirmation. The legislation of the Byzantine Empire (besides certain attempts at innovation made by the Isaurians) was inspired, at least in private matters, by the desire to reconfirm the principles of Justinianic law (which, as we have seen, wanted women strictly bound to their familiar role). The Byzantine emperors tended to view marriage as indissoluble. Although divorce was still allowed they tried to discourage it. The family had to be protected against the danger of breaking down; the value of devotion and filial obedience had to be reaffirmed. And this, as always in history, translated itself into laws that discriminated against women.

Within marriage the husband was the head; the wife was only *boethos,* or "help."[4] Only in the *Eclogue* of Leo III and Constantine V (A.D. 726) do we find a provision that takes the maternal role into consideration, giving it a value equal to the paternal role. The mother too, says the *Eclogue,* must consent to the marriage of her children.[5] But the law was not destined to last. Basil I (A.D. 867–886)—the same emperor who annulled the marriage of a girl who married without the consent of her father and called a similar marriage "fornication"—in his prescriptive work *Procheiros* cancelled every reference to the mother's consent.[6]

In the matter of divorce and adultery, it is superfluous to say that the rules for male and female behavior were different. The wife (and not the husband, obviously) was considered guilty if she slept outside the home or if she frequented the baths, racetrack, or theater. The husband could obtain a divorce on those grounds. A wife could not leave a husband who had been condemned for adultery.[7] We should understand that the term *adulterer* when applied to a man did not signify a man who betrayed his wife (a fact irrelevant to law). Only the woman (wife, fiancée, or concubine) was bound to conjugal fidelity. A man was an adulterer if (regardless of his own marital status) he had sexual relations with the wife, fiancée, or concubine of another.[8]

Leo VI (A.D. 886–912) established that women could not be witnesses in any cases that did not involve so-called female issues (such as the birth of a child) in order not to "cross the natural boundaries that separate the sexes."[9] The *Peira* of Eustatius Romanus (a collection of judiciary decisions rendered between 950 and 1034, which shows how Leo IV's codification—called the *Basilici*—was applied in practice) says that women could not carry out judiciary actions except in explicitly provided hypotheses; women merely suspected of having a lover could not make wills in favor of that man; mothers who became guardians of children after their father's death lost that role if they remarried; and a wife's nonvirginity—duly communicated to the man's friends after the wedding night—was grounds for divorce.[10] Then there were the protective laws. Because of her weakness and ignorance, a woman could, to a cerain extent, avoid fulfilling obligations which she had assumed and could be excused for her ignorance of the law.[11]

Overall, we see a series of provisions that are not very compatible with the idea of equality between the sexes and of the social importance of women. And it is no accident that (besides the empresses, whose situations are scarcely typical of "common" women's) in the centuries of the Empire there existed very few female figures of intellectual standing.[12]

Only two women have left traces in Byzantine literature. The poetess Casia (or Icasia) was born around 810. Anna Comnena, eldest daughter of Alexis Comnenus, was born in 1083. She wrote fifteen books on the life of her father.

Of the life of Casia (which K. Krumbacher considered a "beautiful tale") this is what we know. Like all the beautiful and noble girls of her time, Casia participated in a sort of contest to become the wife of the emperor Theophilus. She was apparently the most beautiful of all the girls, and Theophilus spoke to her first. He commented that women had done much evil. "They have, however," she replied, "been the occasion for much good as well." The reply was too spirited for Theophilus, who moved away, turning his back on her. Casia, humiliated, withdrew to a convent where she spent the rest of her life.[13]

The "beautiful tale" of Casia speaks for itself, as does the work of Anna Comnena, a woman without doubt of exceptional culture and artistic gifts.[14] The female figures in her work (all imperial) are praised first for their devotion to motherhood. "Nothing is equal to maternal love," she wrote. "There is no defense stronger than a mother, her prayers for her child are an invincible guardian and support." At the same time, the greatest praise Anna manages to give a woman is that "she was not at all feminine; she had none of the weaknesses that women usually display." Anna shared completely, needless to say, the opinion held by the men of her time of women and their role.[15]

"The world was dying," goes a proverb of the time, "and my wife continued to beautify herself."[16] As always, when they are not dangerous (as evident in Theophilus' remark to Casia) women are futile, unable to understand important problems and incapable of seeing beyond their "feminine" world. That world was identified by means of the negative connotations that a centuries-old tradition had attributed to it.

So what were the female virtues? According to Michael Psellus (1018–1097?), the best ornament for a woman was silence (nothing new here since the time of Pericles). If she absolutely had to speak, she should at least see that only her husband heard her.[17]

That is not all. The ever more vicious tone of those who saw women as the instrument of the devil echo the social perception of female inferiority. Saint Simeon Stylites (A.D. 521–592), the pillar ascetic, erected a barrier around his pillar to keep women away from him.[18] Nilus of Rossano (d. 1004) declared that it "is better to converse with a serpent than with a woman." He accused the monks of his monastery of having sullied the church by letting women in. He saw a young nun on a path one day and, to keep her from getting too near, hit her with his cane and put her to flight.[19]

Obviously this has been only a brief picture of Byzantine society. Yet it seems possible to conclude, on the basis of the few sketches given here, that in the centuries following the fall of the Western Empire the status of women deteriorated inexorably. The centuries of emancipation were far away. The reversal of the trend, which accompanied the decline of the Empire, meant that once again women were confined to a role that, for a brief moment, they had believed they could escape. The family, the home, and motherhood (without the rights that motherhood should bring) was once more the only horizon of their lives. The only alternative (as for Casia) was the convent.

Conclusion

The picture of the female condition that we have tried to reconstruct may seem pessimistic, especially compared with other reconstructions that take discrimination for granted and emphasize the importance and dignity of the role of women in family life. But I believe that that approach is absolutely unacceptable with reference to both Greece and Rome.

To speak of social recognition of the "female" role and of women's power, however mediated and occult, in Greek history is altogether unfounded. The function of women in Greece was exclusively that of reproducing citizens, if they were free, and servile labor, if they were slaves. The much more important job of training the new generations (given the inadequacy of women, who had no education and were completely shut out of the male world) was entrusted to men. And because it was carried out according to an ideology that considered women inferior, the Greek *paideia* perpetuated a misogyny that excluded the female sex not only from social and political life but also from the world of reason, and consequently from that of love, which, as communication of experience, found its highest expression in relationships between men. In other words, with the fulfillment of her biological function, the

Greek woman had realized her only form of participation (and even that was controlled by others) in the life of the *polis*.

If the condition of Roman women was better in this respect, there are other reasons why the role they were given in the family should not be viewed as benign. In Rome, unlike Greece, women's functions were not limited to the purely "natural" one of childbirth: female duty was more complicated and certainly more important in the eyes of society. In educating their children to make "citizens" of them, Roman women fulfilled a cultural duty of primary importance. The performance of this duty required that they participate in some way in the life of men (whence their greater freedom, which was essentially aimed at this goal) and involved the recognition of a dignity never attributed to Greek women. But precisely because of its importance to the state, their responsibilities of wife and mother impeded Roman women from leaving the confines of an inflexible role. It made them project every hope of fulfillment to the performance of a duty which, because they perceived it as absolute, became the instrument of their annulment as persons.

This, it seems to me, is the first lesson that the history of Greek and Roman women can teach us. But another aspect of this history is very instructive: it demonstrates that the process of emancipation is reversible. During politically, economically, and culturally happy times, the women who lived in the period of Rome's greatest expansion obtained the formal recognition of a near total equality. Even if they were thwarted by an ideology that rejected women's new image and interpreted every freedom as license and dissolution, some women (the socially privileged) did manage to achieve a new model of life. But it is not by chance that the fall of the Empire coincided with the reemergence of misogyny, to which the teachings of the Church Fathers also made a significant contribution. The ground women had won was lost; women were once again pushed back to the "female" world, characterized, as always, by subservience.

The third lesson of the history of the female condition in antiquity is that it allows identification of the moment when a practice of discrimination of centuries' duration was rationalized and presented for the first time as necessary, inevitable, and eternal.

It was during the centuries of the Greek *polis* that the assertion of the "difference" between men and women was codified. Identified by Aristotle with matter, while men were form and spirit, women were classified as "inferior" because of their "natural" difference. That difference, well beyond the confines of Greek history, has been the fundamental theory that has been used to justify every case of discrimination. By appealing to the "difference," the theoreticians of female inferiority of every epoch have opposed women's entry into the world of intellect and reason.

This "difference" was understood by the Greeks as a bipolarity determined a priori and codified as universal human nature, in which male and female are eternally opposed. Instead of inspiring reflection on the need to respect differences between individuals— whether male or female—the theory of natural difference has been and may continue to be the rationalization for every sort of discrimination.

These are the reasons why I have stressed the aspects of women's presumed incapacity and their exclusion, though I have tried, where possible, to collect the hopeful moments, the recognitions, and the conquests. In the name of the "difference," entire generations of unknown women have passed nameless through Greek and Roman history, and not only because their individual names could not be spoken. Annulled as individuals because of their gender, these women, who populated and produced citizens for cities and empires, have been canceled from history.

Abbreviations Used in the Notes

Standard abbreviations for classical references used in the notes are from the *Oxford Classical Dictionary*.

AAN	*Atti della Accademia di Scienze morali e politiche della Società nazionale di Scienze, Lettere ed Arti di Napoli*
AAntHung	*Acta Antiqua Academiae Scientiarum Hungaricae*
AC	*L'Antiquité Classique*
AI	*Acta Iranica: Encyclopédie permanente des études iraniennes*
AJAH	*American Journal of Ancient History*
AJP	*American Journal of Philology*
Annales ESC	*Annales Économie, Sociétés, Civilisations*
ANRW	*Aufstieg und Niedergang der römischen Welt: Geschichte und Kultur Roms im Spiegel der neueren Forschung*
BICS	*Bulletin of the Institute of Classical Studies of the University of London*
BIDR	*Bollettino dell'Istituto di Diritto romano*
Chiron	*Chiron: Mitteilungen der Kommission für alte Geschichte und Epigraphik des Deutschen Archäologischen Instituts*

CJ	*Classical Journal*
CP	*Classical Philosophy*
CPh	*Classical Philology*
CQ	*Classical Quarterly*
DWF	*Donna Woman Femme*
Iura	*Iura: Rivista internazionale di Diritto romano e antico*
JHS	*Journal of Hellenic Studies*
JJP	*Journal of Juristic Papyrology*
JMS	*Journal of Mithraic Studies*
JRS	*Journal of Roman Studies*
Labeo	*Labeo: Rassegna di Diritto romano*
Latomus	*Latomus: Revue d'études latines*
LIMC	*Lexicon Iconographicum Mythologiae Classicae*
MD	*Materiali e Discussioni per l'analisi dei testi classici*
MEFR	*Mélanges d'Archéologie et d'Histoire de l'École Française de Rome*
NDI	*Novissimo Digesto Italiano*
QS	*Quaderni di Storia*
QUCC	*Quaderni Urbanati di Cultura classica*
RAL	*Rendiconti della Classe di Scienze morali, storiche e filologiche dell'Accademia dei Lincei*
RD	*Revue Historique de Droit français et étranger*
RE	*Paulys Real-Encyclopädie der klassischen Altertumswissenschaft*
REA	*Revue des Études Anciennes*
REG	*Revue des Études Grecques*
REL	*Revue des Études Latines*
RFIC	*Rivista di Filologia e di Istruzione Classica*
RhM	*Rheinisches Museum*
RIDA	*Revue Internationale des Droits de l'Antiquité*
RIL	*Rendiconti dell'Istituto Lombardo, Classe di Lettere, Scienze morali e storiche*
RISG	*Rivista italiana per le scienze giuridiche*
RSJB	*Recueils de la Société Jean Bodin*
RSI	*Rivista Storica Italiana*
SDHI	*Studia et Documenta Historiae et Iuris*

SMSR	*Studi e materiali di storia delle religioni*
SO	*Symbolae Osloenses, auspiciis Societatis Graeco-Latinae*
StudRom	*Studi Romani: Rivista bimestrale dell'Istituto di Studi Romani*
TLS	*Times Literary Supplement*
ZSS, RA	*Zeitschrift der Savigny-Stiftung für Rechtsgeschichte, romantische Abteilung*

Notes

Preface

1. For an idea of the number and diversity of the problems being studied today, not to mention the research methods and approaches, it will suffice to cite some of the most recently published, or forthcoming, studies (others will be cited further on) that I used in preparing the manuscript for translation.

Since 1981, the following have appeared, beginning with France: N. Loraux, *Les enfants d'Athéna: Idées athéniennes sur la citoyenneté et la division des sexes* (Paris, 1981); A. Rousselle, *Porneia: De la maîtrise du corps à la privation sensorielles, II–IV siècles de l'ère chrétienne* (Paris, 1983); and C. Mossé, *La femme dans la Grèce antique* (Paris, 1983). The proceedings of the March 1981 conference held at Strasbourg, together with those of an earlier meeting, have been published as E. Lévy, ed., *La femme dans les sociétés antiques* (Strasbourg, 1983). In September 1982, at Perpignan, the Société Internationale F. de Visscher pour l'Histoire des Droits de l'Antiquité dedicated its thirty-sixth session to "La condition juridique de la femme dans le monde antique."

In June 1983 the Colloque de Saint Maximin was held on the topic "Une histoire des femmes est-elle possible?"—proceedings forthcoming from Éditions Rivages. Going beyond (but still including) the ancient world, the Groupe de Recherches Interdisciplinaire d'Étude des Femmes has published two volumes of the Travaux de l'Université de Toulouse–Le Mirail entitled *La dot, la valeur des femmes* (ser. A, vol. 21) (Toulouse, 1982) and *La femme et la mort* (ser. A, vol. 21) (Toulouse, 1982) and *La femme et la*

185

mort (ser. A, vol. 27) (Toulouse, 1984). Finally, at the Centre de recherches comparées sur les sociétés anciennes of the École pratique des hautes Études, N. Loraux is directing a research project on "Masculin et feminin en Grèce et ailleurs."

The following have appeared in English: M. R. Lefkowitz, *Heroines and Hysterics* (London, 1981); H. P. Foley, ed., *Reflections of Women in Antiquity* (New York, London, and Paris, 1981); M. R. Lefkowitz and M. B. Fant, eds., *Women's Life in Greece and Rome* (*WLGR*) (Baltimore and London, 1982); S. Humphreys, *The Family, Women, and Death: Comparative Studies* (London, 1983); and A. Cameron and A. Kuhrt, eds., *Images of Women in Antiquity* (Detroit and London, 1983).

In Italy: the acts of the "Ottave giornate filologiche genovesi," held in February 1980 and dedicated to "Misoginia e maschilismo in Grecia e a Roma" (Genoa, 1981); A. Giallongo, *L'immagine della donna nella cultura greca* (Rimini, 1981); G. Arrigoni, *Camilla amazzone e sacerdotessa di Diana* (Milan, 1982); E. Cavallini, *Donne e amore da Saffo ai tragici* (Venice, 1982); I. Savalli, *La donna nella società della Grecia antica* (Bologna, 1983); S. Campese, P. Manuli, and G. Sissa, *Madre Materia: Sociologia e biologia della donna greca* (Turin, 1983); G. Arrigoni, ed., *Le donne in Grecia* (Bari, 1985); M. Vegetti and S. Humphreys, eds., *La donna antica* (Turin, forthcoming); also forthcoming, two monograph issues of the journals *Memoria: Rivista di storia della donna* (Turin, 1981) and *DWF* (*Donna Woman Femme*) (1986).

Finally, in Germany: B. Wagner, *Zwischen Mythos und Realität; Die Frau in der frügriechischen Gesellschaft* (Frankfurt am Main, 1982).

Introduction

1. See S. Campese and S. Gastaldi, eds., *La donna e i filosofi: Archeologia di un'immagine culturale* (Bologna, 1977), pp. 52 ff.; and S. Campese, "Donna, casa, città nell'antropologia di Aristotele," in S. Campese, P. Manuli, and G. Sissa, *Madre Materia,* pp. 15 ff.

2. T. Hobbes, *Leviathan* 2, 20; or, *The Matter, Form, and Power of a Commonwealth, Ecclesiastical and Civil* (London, Glasgow, and New York, 1885). See also Hobbes, *Elements of Natural and Political Law,* vol. 2, chap. 4, p. 2. On this point see G. Conti Odorisio, "La teoria del matriarcato in Hobbes," *DWF* 1.3 (1976): 21 ff.; "Matriarcato e patriarcalismo nel pensiero politico di Hobbes e Locke," in I. Magli, ed., *Matriarcato e potere delle donne* (Milan, 1978), pp. 37 ff.; and the considerations already treated by me, and presented here, in "Cenni storici," introduction to *Donne e diritto* (= *Lessico politico delle donne,* vol. 1) (Milan, 1978).

3. J. T. Lafitau, *Moeurs des sauvages amériquains comparées aux moeurs des premiers temps* (Paris, 1724), pp. 69 and 89–92.

4. P. G. Cabanis, *Rapports du physique et du moral de l'homme* (Paris, 1813), 1: 274. On the hypotheses of Cabanis, see S. Moravia, *La scienza dell'uomo nel Settecento* (Bari, 1978), pp. 50 ff. With specific reference to the problems of women, see I. Magli, *La donna un problema aperto* (Florence, 1974), pp. 9 ff.

5. D. Livingstone, *Missionary Travels and Researches in Southern Africa* (London, 1857).

6. J. J. Bachofen, *Das Mutterrecht* (Stuttgart, 1861). For a translation see *Myth, Religion, and Mother Right: Selected Writings of J. J. Bachofen,* trans. R. Manheim (Princeton, N.J., 1967).

7. J. F. McLennan, *Primitive Marriage* (Edinburgh, 1865); and *Studies in Ancient Society* (London, 1876).

8. L. H. Morgan, *Ancient Society* (London, 1877).

9. We will return to the *Oresteia* in chapter 5.

10. For a famous example of demographic history, see P. Goubert, *Beauvais et le Beauvaisis de 1600 à 1730* (Paris, 1960), partial revision *Cent mille provinciaux au dix-septième siècle* (Paris, 1968). On this type of research, and more generally on the revival of historical studies, see J. Le Goff's introductory essay to *La nouvelle histoire* (Paris, 1979). On women specifically, among the numerous studies inspired by nontraditional methods, see, for example, on various periods, vols. 27.4–5 (1972) and 30.4 (1975) of *Annales ESC;* and J. Goody, J. Thirsk, and E. P. Thompson, eds., *Family and Inheritance: Rural Society in Western Europe, 1200–1800* (Cambridge, 1976). For a theoretical discussion of the problem relative not only to women but also to all "marginalized" peoples, see B. Vincent, ed., *Les Marginaux et les ésclus dans l'histoire* (Paris, 1979); and J. C. Schmitt, "La storia dei marginali," in Le Goff, ed., *La nouvelle histoire.*

11. See Humphreys, *The Family, Women, and Death;* and her earlier "Family Tombs and Tomb Cult in Ancient Athens: Tradition or Traditionalism?" *JHS* 100 (1980): 96 ff.

12. See, for example, the sources of this type collected in Lefkowitz and Fant, eds., *WLGR;* and noted by M. R. Lefkowitz in "Princess Ida, the Amazons, and a Women's College Curriculum," *TLS* (Nov. 27, 1981): 1399–1401 = *Women in Greek Myth* (Baltimore, 1986), pp. 15–29.

13. D. M. Schaps, *Economic Rights of Women in Ancient Greece* (Edinburgh, 1979), esp. pp. 89 ff., to whose theory we will return, maintains that in the classical period custom was more advanced than law. S. G. Cole, "Could Greek Women Read and Write?" in Foley, ed., *Reflections,* pp. 219 ff., has reconstructed the proportions of the literate and the illiterate in Greek Egypt and established that women were largely illiterate, leading me to believe that the genuine freedom of the women was more limited than what was theoretically recognized by law. See S. B. Pomeroy, *Women in Hellenistic Egypt: From Alexander to Cleopatra* (New York, 1985).

187

14. The attempts to demonstrate that a difference existed between political status and social status of women in reality leave a number of problems. I am thinking in particular of the statement by J. Le Gall that women, though not citizens, were still registered at birth in the phratry of their fathers. See "Un critère de differenciation sociale, la situation de la femme," in *Recherches sur les structures sociales dans l'antiquité classique* (Paris, 1970), pp. 257 ff. But, as J. Gould has shown, this statement is not corroborated in the sources; see "Law, Custom and Myth: Aspects of the Social Position of Women in Classical Athens," *JHS* 100 (1980): 37 ff., esp. pp. 40, 42. Different and rather more flexible are the positions of C. Mossé and R. di Donato, "Status e/o funzione: Aspetti della condizione della donna-cittadina nelle orazioni civili di Demostene," *QS* 17 (1983): 151 ff.; and of D. M. Schaps, "Women in Greece in Wartime," *CPh* 77 (1982): 193–213. From the attitude of Greek women during wars Schaps concludes that "citizen women did not see themselves as an entirely disenfranchised group." I think it is possible to agree with this statement, and with Schaps's claim that "the sympathy between women and men was greater than we might perhaps have expected from a society so heavily patriarchal." Nevertheless, great caution is needed when generalizing such observations, although it may be valid in exceptional circumstances to extend them to times of peace and daily life.

Chapter 1 Matriarchy in Prehistory, Myth, and History

1. See the nineteenth-century literature outlined in the notes of the Preface; for further information on the literature of that period, see E. Cantarella, "J. J. Bachofen tra storia del diritto romano e scienze sociali," *Sociologia del diritto,* 3rd ed. (1982), pp. 111 ff., republished with some modifications as the preface to J. J. Bachofen, *Introduzione al diritto materno* (Rome, 1983). Of the paleoethnologists, see G. Patroni, *La preistoria,* vol. 1 (Milan, 1937); P. Laviosa Zambotti, *Il Mediterraneo, l'Europa, l'Italia durante la preistoria* (Turin, 1954); and *Origini e diffusione della civiltà* (Milan, 1957). The historians who believed in the matriarchy in Greece and Rome will be cited later. For conditions of life in the Paleolithic Age, see M. Sahlins, *L'economia dell'età delle pietre* (Milan, 1980).

2. On the chronology and geography of the Neolithic Age, see R. Furon, *Manuale di preistoria* (Turin, 1961), pp. 237 ff.; F. Rittatore, *Oriente antico (Nuova storia universale dei popoli e delle civiltà)* (Turin, 1969), pp. 53 ff.; and E. Boulding, *The Underside of History: A View of Women through Time* (Boulder, Colo., 1976). On the Neolithic Age in Italy, see G. Luraschi, *Comum oppidum* (Como, 1974), pp. 218 ff. On the history of agriculture and its consequence for women's roles, see the investigations of D. Forni, "Rendiconti delle ricerche condotte dal centro di museologia

agraria nel periodo ottobre 1978–novembre 1979," in *Rivista di storia dell'agricoltura* 3 (1979): 170 ff. According to Forni, agriculture derived from the practice of burning vegetation in order to capture wild herbivores. *Pirolimax,* the matrix of the domestic grasses, would have originated from such burning, to be later cultivated with the plow. Agriculture, in other words, would have been invented by men as hunters, although it was later developed by women. See now also G. Barker, *Prehistoric Farming in Europe* (Cambridge, 1985).

3. On primitive societies with maternal law see R. Fox and I. Magli, *Matriarcato e potere delle donne* (Milan, 1978). On maternal law among the ancient peoples of the Mediterranean, cf. Boulding, *The Underside of History,* pp. 140 ff.

4. The hypothesis is sustained by, among others, R. Briffault, *The Mothers,* vol. 3 (London, 1927), I, pp. 338 ff.; G. Thomson, *Studies in Ancient Greek Society: The Prehistoric Aegean* (London, 1949), pp. 147 ff.; U. Pestalozzi, *Religione mediterranea* (Venice, 1954); and M. Marconi, "La primitiva espressione del divino nella religione mediterranea," *RIL* 79 (1945–46): 247 ff. An interesting criticism and up-to-date discussion of the hypothesis of the matriarchy is Wagner, "Die Frage des Matriarchats," in *Zwischen Mythos und Realität,* pp. 13 ff.

5. For example, R. Willets, *Aristocratic Society in Ancient Crete* (London, 1955).

6. On this point, see C. G. Thomas, "Matriarchy in Early Greece," *Arethusa* 6.2 (1973): 173 ff., who tentatively concludes that maternal law may have existed in Crete.

7. For basic information on the Mycenaean kingdoms, see J. Chadwick, *The Mycenaean World* (London, 1976).

8. P. DiFidio, "La donna e il lavoro nella Grecia arcaica," *DWF* 12–13 (1979): 188 ff. On the female condition in Mycenae, see P. Carlieri, "La femme dans la société mycénienne d'après les archives en linéaire B," in E. Lévy, ed., *La femme dans les sociétés antiques,* pp. 9 ff. J. C. Billigmeier and J. A. Turner, "The Socio-economic Roles of Women in Mycenaean Greece: A Brief Survey from Evidence in the Linear B Tablets," in Foley, ed., *Reflections,* pp. 1 ff., on the other hand, emphasize the female presence in all sectors of activity, the importance of the female priestly role, and the participation of women in the distribution of lands.

9. So R. J. Carlier, "Voyage en Amazonie grecque," *AAntHung* 27 (1979): 381 ff. See Lefkowitz, "Princess Ida, the Amazons, and a Women's College Curriculum." P. Devambez, "Amazones," *LIMC* 1.1 (1981): 642–43; and *Dictionnaire des mythologies* (Paris, 1981) s.v. "Amazons." On mythological inversion in general, see F. Hartog, *Le miroir d'Hérodote: Essai sur la représentation de l'autre* (Paris, 1980), pp. 225 ff.

10. So W. Burkert, "Jason, Hypsipyle, and New Fire at Lemnos: A Study

in Myth and Ritual," *CQ* 20 (1970): 1 ff. On the Lemnians (whose myth is narrated in Ap. Rhod. *Argon.* 1.696 ff.) see also G. Dumézil, *Le crime des Lemniennes* (Paris, 1924); and M. Detienne, *The Gardens of Adonis: Spices in Greek Mythology,* trans. J. Lloyd (Atlantic Highlands, N.J., 1977; first published Paris, 1972), pp. 117 ff.

11. The myth of the daughters of Proetos is in Hesiod (fr. 26–29 Rz.). On the significance of the foul odor and of illnesses, see A. Brelich, *Paides e parthenoi* (Rome, 1969), pp. 472–73; and Detienne, *The Gardens of Adonis,* p. 104.

12. M. Detienne, in "Mythes grecques et analyse structurale: Controverses et problèmes," in *Il mito greco* (Atti Conv. internaz. Urbino, 1973) (Rome, 1977), p. 74. See also M. Detienne, *Dionysos Slain* (Baltimore and London, 1979), pp. xii–xiii; B. Gentili and G. Paioni, eds., *Il mito Greco: Guida storica e critica* (Bari, 1974); "Repenser la mythologie," in M. Izard and P. Smith, eds., *La fonction symbolique: Essai d'anthropologie* (Paris, 1979), pp. 71 ff.; and *L'invention de la mythologie* (Paris, 1983). A different approach is found in M. Eliade, *Aspects du myth* (Paris, 1963); *Traité d'histoire des religions* (Paris, 1968); and in G. S. Kirk, *Myth: Its Meaning and Function in Ancient and Other Cultures* (Berkeley, Calif., 1970).

13. For the sources, see E. Ciarceri, *Storia della Magna Grecia,* vol. 1 (Milan, 1924), pp. 82 ff.; and J. Bérard, *La Magna Grecia* (Turin, 1963), pp. 146 ff.

14. Cf. P. Vidal-Naquet, "Slavery and the Rule of Women in Tradition, Myth, and Utopia," in *The Black Hunter* (Baltimore, 1986); also in R. L. Gordon, ed., *Myth, Religion, and Society* (Cambridge and Paris, 1981), pp. 187–200. S. G. Pembroke, "Locres et Tarente: Le rôle des femmes dans le fondation de deux colonies grecques," in *Annales ESC* 25.4 (1970): 1240 ff.; D. Briquel, "Tarente, Locres, les Scythes, Thera, Rome: Précedents antiques au thème de l'amant de Lady Chatterley?" *MEFR* 86 (1974): 673 ff.; R. Van Compernolle, "Le mythe de la gynécocratie-doulocratie argienne," in *Hommages à C. Préaux* (Brussels, 1975), pp. 355 ff. On matriarchy in general (and apart from the woman–slave relationship in myth), see the studies in which S. G. Pembroke has demonstrated the impossibility of documenting matriarchy's existence in one of the countries most frequently considered "matriarchal," namely Lycia: "Last of the Matriarchs: A Study in the Inscriptions of Lycia," *Journal of Economic and Social History of the Orient* 8 (1965): 217 ff.; and "Women in Charge: The Function of Alternatives in the Early Greek Tradition and the Ancient Idea of Matriarchy," *Journal of the Warburg and Courtauld Institutes* 30 (1976):1–35.

15. On the possible connection between homosexuality and male initiation in Cretan traditions and in myth, discussed in chapter 6, see B. Sergent, *L'homosexualité dans la mythologie grecque* (Paris, 1984).

16. On Spartan initiations, see Brelich, *Paides e parthenoi,* pp. 113 ff.; C. Calame, *Les choeurs de jeunes filles en Grèce archaïque,* vol. 2 (Rome, 1977); and "Helène (le culte d') et l'initiation feminine in Grèce," in *Dictionnaire des mythologies.*

17. Ar. *Lys.* 641–45.

18. See Brelich, *Paides e parthenoi,* p. 229. Also see the observations of P. Vidal-Naquet, "Recipes for Greek Adolescence," in *The Black Hunter,* also in Gordon, ed., *Myth, Religion, and Society,* pp. 163 ff., esp. p. 178, on *Lys.* 638–47: ". . . we must understand this speech as ideological: Athenian women were not properly speaking citizens, and young girls who were not citizens-to-be whom the city had to take through the stages of an educative initiation." On female initiation rites, see H. Lloyd-Jones, "Artemis and Iphigenia," *JHS* 103 (1983): 87–102; W. Burkert, "Kekropidensage und Arrhephoria," *Hermes* 94 (1966): 1–25. Vidal-Naquet, even if only at the ideological level, sees in the passage confirmation that "the sole civic function of women was to give birth to children" (Gordon, pp. 178–79).

Chapter 2 Origins of Western Misogyny

1. On the problem of historicity see L. E. Rossi, "I poemi omerici come testimonianza di poesia orale," in R. Bianchi Bandinelli, ed., *Origini e sviluppo della città: Il medioevo greco (Storia e civiltà dei Greci,* vol. 1) (Milan, 1978), pp. 73 ff.; the anthology edited by M. Vegetti, *Oralità, scrittura, spettacolo* (Turin, 1983); and, on lyric, B. Gentili, *Poesia e pubblico nella Grecia antica* (Bari, 1984).

2. See especially E. A. Havelock, *Preface to Plato* (Cambridge, Mass., 1978); and *The Greek Concept of Justice from Its Shadow in Homer to Its Substance in Plato* (Cambridge, Mass., 1978). According to Havelock, Homer had an "institutional" role in the *paideia.* With some revision, the following paragraphs on the Homeric age are taken from E. Cantarella, *Norme e sanzione in Omero* (Milan, 1979), pp. 44 ff.; see also "La nascita della conscienza," *Labeo* (1984).

3. S. Butler, *The Authoress of the Odyssey* (London, 1922; reprinted 1967; first published 1892).

4. G. Germain, *Homère* (Paris, 1955), p. 133.

5. But see recently the correct observations of Di Fidio, "La donna e il lavoro," p. 211, who brings to light the connections between the female condition and the house, and the already evident subordination of women.

6. On the beauty of Homeric women, see the observations of H. Montsacré, *Autour du corps heroïque: Masculin, feminin, et souffrance dans l'Iliade* (Paris, 1983), for an interesting attempt to tone down the habitual opposition of males and females and to show interaction between the two worlds at different levels.

7. S. B. Pomeroy, "Andromaque, un exemple méconnu du matriarcat," *REG* 88 (1975):16–19; and *Goddesses, Whores, Wives, and Slaves* (New York, 1975), pp. 22–23.

8. According to M. Arthur, "The Divided World of *Iliad* VI," in Foley, ed., *Reflections,* pp. 19–44, the conversation between Hector and Andromache tones down the opposition between male and female that is characteristic of the poems in order to make room for a dialectic relationship between the world of war and that of women. This, it seems to me, is in some way true, if only because of the locale of the encounter, namely, "un lieu frontière où chacun est séparé de la sphère à laquelle il appartient et où s'opère la continuité entre les deux mondes," to quote P. Schmitt-Pantel in *Annales ESC* 5–6 (1982):1017.

9. Cf. E. Cantarella, "Ragione d'amore: Preistoria di un difetto femminile," *Memoria* 1 (1981):1 ff.

10. Cf. Montsacré, *Autour du corps heroïque,* pp. 236 ff.

11. *Od.* 2.90–92. Cf. M. M. Mactoux, *Pénélope, Légende et Mythe* (Ann. Litt. Univ. Besançon, 175) (Paris, 1975).

12. *Od.* 1.215–16. For the doubts of Athena, Nestor, and Odysseus, respectively, see *Od.* 2.274–75, 3.122–23, and 16.300.

13. On the placement of women "halfway between the animal, the bestial evil against which nothing can be done, and the super-human, that is where the virtuous wife is found," see E. Pellizer, "La sposa funesta nei racconti di Ulisse," *Prospettive Settanta* 2 (1976):120 ff.

14. Cf. M. I. Finley, "Marriage, Sale and Gift in the Homeric World," *RIDA* 2 (1955):167–94, reprinted in *Economy and Society in Ancient Greece* (New York, 1981), pp. 233–45; W. K. Lacey, "Homeric *eedna* and Penelope's *kurios,*" *JHS* 86 (1966):55 ff.

15. On Homeric marriage see J. Scheid, "Il matrimonio omerico," *Dialoghi di Archeologia* 1 (1979):60 ff.; and M. Weinsanto, "L'évolution du mariage de l'Iliade à l'Odyssée," in Lévy, ed., *La femme dans les sociétés antiques,* pp. 45 ff. According to Weinsanto, the *Odyssey* values marriage more than the *Iliad* and presents a less fluid situation, in which personal statuses (wife/concubine, legitimate/illegitimate child) were more precisely defined than in the *Iliad.*

16. On women as transmitters of power, see A. Tourraix, "La femme et le pouvoir chez Hérodote," *Dialogue d'histoire ancienne* 2 (1976):369 ff., who reads in certain stories in Herodotus the traces of a vanished matrilineal succession, but see Tourraix's criticism of Annequin, pp. 387 ff.

17. M. Woronoff, "La femme dans l'univers épique (*Iliad*)" in Lévy, ed., *La femme dans les sociétés antiques,* pp. 33 ff., maintains that the female condition in the *Iliad* was not so subordinate and that women, although rarely intervening, had a certain weight in public affairs. Though particularly relevant to Trojan women (whose condition does not seem very

different from that of Greek women), this opinion is very difficult to accept.

18. Cf. G. Patroni, *Commenti mediterranei all'Odissea di Omero* (Milan, 1950), pp. 322 ff. and 911 ff.

19. The hypothesis of a "great dignity" on the part of Homeric women returns, often, in the reconstructions of those who, fully aware of the misogyny of the Greeks, place its birth in the epoch after that of the poems. See, for example, M. Arthur, "Liberated Women: The Classical Era," in R. Bridenthal and C. Koonz, eds., *Becoming Visible: Women in European History* (Boston, 1977), pp. 60 ff.

20. Cf. J. P. Vernant, "The Myth of Prometheus in Hesiod," in Gordon, ed., *Myth, Religion, and Society,* pp. 43–66; N. Loraux, "Sur la race des femmes et quelques unes de ses tribus," *Arethusa* 11 (1978):43 ff., now in *Les enfants d'Athéna*; G. Arrighetti, "Il misoginismo di Esiodo," in *Misoginia e machilismo in Grecia e Roma* (Genoa, 1981), pp. 27–48, and M. B. Arthur, "Cultural Strategies in Hesiod's *Theogony*: Law, Family and Society," *Arethusa* 15 (1982):1–2 (= *Texts and Contexts: American Classical Studies in Honor of J. P. Vernant,* pp. 63–82).

21. *WD* 61. In the *Theogony,* "made of earth": cf. 571.

22. For the gift of seduction, cf. *Th.* 571–73; for the capacity to seduce, 572.

23. Cf. *Th.* 585. On the same theme, see Loraux, "Sur la race des femmes."

24. Fr 24 Bergk (*Poetae lyrici graeci,* III).

25. Cf. 7.21–42. On the fragment, see H. Lloyd-Jones, *Females of the Species: Semonides on Women* (London, 1975), whose translation is reproduced here. On lines 27–42, see E. Pellizer, "La donna del mare: La dike amorosa 'assente' nel giambo di Semonide sopra le donne," *QUCC* 32 (1979):29 ff.

26. Loraux, "Sur la race des femmes."

Chapter 3 Exclusion from the Polis

1. It is not possible here to address the complex problem of the origin of the *polis,* which has been the object of endless debates and which—in synthesis—revolves around two points: the Mycenae–Homer relationship, that is, the discussion of possible continuities between the pre- and post-Mycenaean Greek world, and the debate on the nature of the Homeric social centers, considered by some to be prepolitical and by others political. On the first problem, see P. Vidal-Naquet, "Homère et le monde mycénien: à propos d'un livre récent et d'une polémique ancienne," 18 *Annales ESC* (July-August 1963): pp. 703 ff.; and G. Pugliese Carratelli, "Dal regno miceneo alla polis," in *Scritti sul mondo antico* (Naples, 1976), pp. 135 ff. On the second problem, from the extensive literature I cite

V. Ehrenberg, "When Did the Polis Rise?" in F. Gschitzner, ed., *Zur griechischen Staatskunde* (Darmstadt, 1969), pp. 3 ff.; W. Hoffman, "Die Polis bei Homer," ibid., pp. 13 ff.; F. Gschitzner, "Stadt und Stamm bei Homer," *Chiron* 1 (1971):1 ff.; Carratelli, "Dal regno miceneo alla polis"; and R. Bianchi Bandinelli, ed., *Origini e sviluppo della città: Il medioevo greco* (*Storia e civiltà dei Greci*, vol. 1); B. Quiller, "The Dynamics of Homeric Society," *SO* 56 (1981):109 ff.; W. C. Runciman, "Origins of State, the Case of Archaic Greece," *Comparative Studies in Society and History* 24 (1982):351 ff.

2. P. Vidal-Naquet, "Slavery and the Rule of Women," in *The Black Hunter*; also in Gordon, ed., *Myth, Religion, and Society*, pp. 187–200, esp. p. 188: "The Greek club in its classical form was marked as a double exclusion: the exclusion of women, which made it a 'men's club'; and the exclusion of slaves, which made it a 'citizen's club.'" But see the recent observations of L. Gallo, "La donna greca e la marginalità," *QUCC* 18 (1984): 7–51, who favors a more nuanced position that takes account of a possible discrepancy between laws and social practice—perhaps the relationship between domestic space (reserved for women) and external space (reserved for men) did not necessarily involve prejudice against the female sex. Gallo also points out that the variety of the Greek experience may discourage any generalization from the Athenian experience. I have taken all these circumstances into consideration, but they do not seem to invalidate the hypothesis of "exclusion."

3. See E. Cantarella, *Studi sull'omicidio in diritto greco e romano* (Milan, 1976), pp. 84–85, with bibliography.

4. The text of the law, renewed in 409–408 B.C. and inscribed on a marble stele, was found in 1843 during the excavations for the Metropolitan Church of Athens and is currently preserved in Athens in the Epigraphical Museum, inventory number EM 6602. Published in *Inscriptiones Graecae* 1² 115, it was republished in R. Stroud, *Drakon's Law on Homicide* (Berkeley and Los Angeles, 1968).

5. See E. Cantarella, *Studi sull'omicidio*, pp. 131 ff., esp. for public action, p. 154, and for the sanctions against women, pp. 156–57.

6. Lys. *de caede Herat.* par. 29.

7. See Ar. *Clouds* 1083–84, *Plutus* 168, *Ach.* 849; and *Suda* s.v. *paratilletai* and *raphanis*. On public action for adultery, see E. Ruschenbusch, *Untersuchungen zur Geschichte des attischen Strafrechts* (Cologne, 1968).

8. Lys. *de caede Herat.* 2, and Xen. *Hiero* 3.3.

9. Ael. *VH* 13.24.

10. Heraclid. Pont. in Arist. Fr. 611–42 Rose. On the passage, and more generally on humiliating punishments for adultery imposed by other cities,

cf. P. Schmitt-Pantel, *L'âne, l'adultère et la cité: Le charivari* (Paris, 1972), pp. 117 ff.

11. The text of the law (discovered in 1884 by the Italian archaeological expedition) was published in *Inscriptiones Creticae,* vol. 4, *Tituli Gortynii* (Rome, 1950) and republished by R. F. Willetts, *The Law Code of Gortyn* (Berlin, 1967). The part relating to adultery is 2.20–28.

12. This hypothesis is that of U. E. Paoli, "La legislazione sull'adulterio nel diritto di Gortina," in *Studi in onore di G. Funaioli* (Rome, 1955), pp. 306 ff.; and "Gortina (diritto di)" in *NDI.* On various other problems posed by the text, see (besides Willetts, cited in note 11) L. Gernet, "Observations sur la loi de Gortyne," in *Droit et Société en Grèce ancienne* (Paris, reprinted 1955), pp. 21 ff.

13. Xen. *Resp. Laced.* 1.4. Cf. Eur. *Andr.* 595 ff.

14. Plato *Laws* 1.637 c, and Arist. *Pol.* 2.9.126 b.

15. Plut. *Laced. Apophthegm.* 240 ff., and Ael. *VH* 12.21.

16. Plut. *Lyc.* 14.8.

17. An overall portrait of the condition of Spartan women can be found in J. Redfield, "The Women of Sparta," *CJ* 73 (1977–78): 146–61; and P. Cartledge, "Spartan Wives: Liberation or Licence?" *CQ* 31 (1981): 84 ff.

18. Arist. *Pol.* 7.14.10.1335 b.

19. Posidippus *Hermaphr.* fr. 11 Kock.

20. Ar. *Frogs* 1190; Plato *Minos* 315 d.

21. On the practice of exposure in Greece, which has been the subject of much discussion, see the opposing positions of D. Engels, "The Problem of Female Infanticide in the Graeco-Roman World," *CPh* 75 (1980):112 ff., who holds that it was not frequent, and W. V. Harris, "The Theoretical Possibility of Extensive Infanticide in the Graeco-Roman World," *CQ* 32 (1982):114 ff., who maintains instead the theory of its diffusion, linked to the young age of marriage for Roman girls (on which see K. Hopkins, "The Age of Roman Girls at Marriage," *Population Studies* 18 [1965]:309 ff.). Among the earlier bibliography, amply cited by Harris, see at least P. A. Brunt, *Italian Manpower 225 B.C.–A.D. 14* (Oxford, 1971), pp. 148 ff.; and P. Salmon, *Population et depopulation dans l'Empire romain* (Brussels, 1974), pp. 70 ff.

22. The *promnéstria* or *promnestris*; cf. Ar. *Clouds* 41 ff.; Xen. *Mem.* 2.6.36; and Plato *Tht* 149 d–150 d.

23. Plut. *Sol.* 23.

24. Eur. *Hel.* 283.

25. Dem. *Aphob.* 1.4 ff.

26. Xen. *Oec.* 7.5. The problem of the best age to contract marriage was much debated by the Greeks. According to Hesiod (*WD* 6–95 ff.), the woman should marry in the fifth year after puberty, and the man at age thirty. For Plato the ideal ages were sixteen to twenty for the woman and

twenty-five to thirty for the man (*Laws* 7.772 d–e). For Aristotle, as very young women frequently died in childbirth, marriage should be contracted between a woman of eighteen and a man of thirty-seven (*Pol.* 7.1135). In practice, marriage followed puberty almost immediately, and puberty was reached, on average, at age thirteen or fourteen. See D. W. Amundsen and C. J. Diers, "The Age of Menarche in Classical Greece," *Human Biology* 41 (1969):125 ff.

27. Cf. for example *Anth. Pal.* 6.59–276, 277, 280. For a different approach to the role of Artemis in the transition from virginity to marriage, see Brelich, *Paides e parthenoi,* pp. 229 ff.; and Vidal-Naquet, "Recipes for Greek Adolescence," in *The Black Hunter* and in Gordon, ed., *Myth, Religion, and Society,* pp. 163 ff.

28. Hesych. s.v. *gamon, éthe,* and *protélia;* Ari. *Lys.* 378; Eur. *Phoen.* 347 and *Schol.* ad loc.

29. Eur. *IA* 722; Isaeus *De Cir. hered.* 9; *Poll.* 10.33; Ar. *Peace* 1316 ff.

30. Hesych. s.v. *anakaluptérion.* On the nuptial rites, in much more detail, see A. Roveri, "La vita familiare nella Grecia antica," in *Enciclopedia classica* 1.3 (Turin, 1959), pp. 392 ff.

31. On Athenian marriage, see E. Hruza, *Beiträge zur Geschichte des griechischen und römischen Familienrechts,* vol. I (Erlangen and Leipzig, 1893); W. Erdmann, *Die Ehe im alten Griechenland* (Munich, 1934); U. E. Paoli, "Matrimonio (diritto greco)," in *Enciclopedia italiana* 22 (1936):578 ff.; and "Famiglia (diritto greco)," *NDI* 8 (1961); H. J. Wolff, "Marriage Law and Family Organization in Ancient Athens," *Traditio* 2 (1944):43 ff., now in *Beiträge zur Rechtsgeschichte Altgriechenlands und des hellenistischrömischen Aegypten* (Weimar, 1961), pp. 155 ff.; Finley, "Marriage, Sale and Gift in the Homeric World"; E. Cantarella, "La *eggue* prima e dopo di Solone nel diritto matrimoniale attico," *RIL* 98 (1964):121 ff.; A.R.W. Harrison, *The Law of Athens: The Family and Property* (Oxford, 1968); W. K. Lacey, *The Family in Classical Greece* (Ithaca and London, 1968); J. P. Vernant, "Marriage," in *Myth and Society* (London, 1980), pp. 45 ff.; E. Bickerman, "La conception du mariage à Athènes," *BIDR* ser. 3, 17 (1976): 1 ff.; J. Modrzejewski, "La structure juridique du mariage grec," in *Scritti in onore di Orsolina Montevecchi* (Bologna, 1981), pp. 231 ff.; and finally, J. Redfield, "Notes on the Greek Wedding," *Arethusa* 15.1–2 (1982): 181–201.

32. Cf. Cornelius Nepos *Cim.* 1.2–3 and *Praefatio;* Dem. *Eubul.* 20; Plut. *Them.* 32.1–2.

33. So Erdmann, *Die Ehe,* pp. 68–85. On the rule, see also Harrison, *The Law,* who maintains that no rational explanation has ever been offered for the lawfulness of marriage between uterine siblings (pp. 22–23); and Lacey, *The Family in Classical Greece,* p. 108.

34. Ar. *Eccl.* 818–22; *Wasps* 788–90.

35. Isaeus *de Pyrr. hered.* 14.

36. V. Ehrenberg, *The People of Aristophanes* (Cambridge, Mass., 1951), p. 27 n. 2.

37. Lys. *Sim.* 6.

38. K. J. Dover, *Greek Popular Morality in the Time of Plato and Aristotle* (Oxford, 1974), p. 69.

39. On the whole story and its legal aspects see U. E. Paoli, "Il reato di adulterio (*moicheia*) in diritto attico," *SDHI* 16 (1950): 123 ff.; and E. Cantarella, "L'omicidio legittimo e l'uccisione del *moichos* in diritto attico," in *Studi sull'omicidio,* pp. 128 ff.

40. For reproval by society for this act, see Eur. *Med.* 226 ff. For the Alcibiades episode, see Andoc. *Alcib.* 14, and Plut. *Alc.* 8.4 ff.

41. On the institution, see Harrison, *The Law of Athens,* pp. 30 ff.

42. On the system of succession, see U. E. Paoli, "L'archisteia nel diritto successorio to attico," *SDHI* 2 (1936): 77 ff.; and "Successioni (diritto greco)," in *NDI*; J. W. Jones, *The Law and Legal Theory of the Greeks* (Oxford, 1956), pp. 191 ff.; and Harrison, *The Laws.* On the dowry, see P. Dimakis, "A propos du droit de proprieté de la femme mariée sur les biens dotaux d'après le droit grec ancien," in *Symposion* 1974 (*Vorträge zur griechischen und hellenistischen Rechtypeschichte*) (Cologne, 1979), pp. 227 ff.; Schaps, *Economic Rights of Women in Ancient Greece,* pp. 74–88 and 99–104; C. Leduc, "Reflexions sur le système matrimonial athénienne à l'époque de la cité état (VI–IV siècles avant J.C.)," in *La dot, la valeur des femmes* (ser. A, t-21, "Le grief") (Toulouse, 1982), pp. 7 ff.; and C. Mossé, *La femme dans la Grèce antique* (Paris, 1983), app. 1: "Hedna, pherne, proix: le problème de la dot en Grèce ancienne," pp. 145 ff.

43. On the condition of the heiress, see L. Gernet, "Sur l'epiclérat," *REG* 34 (1921): 337–83; U. E. Paoli, "La legittima aferesi dell'*epikleros* nel diritto attico," in *Miscellanea Mercati,* vol. 5 (Vatican City, 1946); E. Karabelias, *L'epiklérat attique* (Thesis, Paris, 1974); and "Recherches sur la condition juridique et sociale de la femme unique dans le monde grec excepte Athènes" (mimeograph, Paris, 1980); D. M. Schaps, "Women in Greek Inheritance Law," *CQ* 25 (1975): 53 ff.; and *Economic Rights of Women in Ancient Greece,* pp. 25 ff. According to Schaps, legislation on the heiress can be seen in a different light. Given that the woman could not marry without the consent of her guardian, and given that the heiress's guardian, who as nearest relative had a vested interest in not consenting to marriage, would try to prevent the estate from leaving the family, the law would have forced the guardian's marriage to the heiress so that she would not be left without a husband. But the hypothesis, though interesting, seems difficult to accept, if only because the relative had the right but not the duty to marry the heiress.

44. Dem. *Macartatus* 59.

45. Plut. *Sol.* 20.4; see Lacey, *The Family in Classical Greece,* pp. 89–90.

The passage is interpreted incorrectly by F. Le Corsu, *Plutarque et les femmes* (Paris, 1981), p. 13, who maintains that the law of Solon was applicable to all husbands and not just to those who had married an *epikleros*. He concludes that "les lois de Solon, en ce qui concernent les femmes, semblent tenir compte de leur dignité" (p. 14).

46. On the status of the Spartan heiress (called *patrouchos* or *epipamatis*), see Hdt. 6.57.4 and 130 (relatives had the right to marry her only if she was not married already). At Gortyn, where she was called *patroikos* and where her status was regulated by a law mentioned earlier, she could refuse marriage with the relative by giving him half her inheritance. Cf. U. E. Paoli, "Gortina (diritto di)," *NDI*. On inheritance in the cities of Magna Graecia, see Diod. Sic. 18.3–4; and A. Maffi, "*IC* IV, 72 col. II, 16–20, Plut., *Sol.* 23, 1–2 e le leggi sulle donne," in *Sodalitas scritti in onore di A. Guarino* (Naples, 1984–85), IV, pp. 153 ff.

47. [Dem.] *Against Neaera* 122.

48. For the possible coexistence of wife and concubine under the same roof, see Antiph. *de Venef.* 17 ff.

49. Diog. Laert. 2.2.6.

50. Pomeroy, *Goddesses, Whores, Wives, and Slaves*, p. 88. But see Harrison, *The Law of Athens*, pp. 16–17; Wolff, *Marriage Law*, p. 85 n. 195; and J. W. Fitton, "That Was No Lady, That Was . . . ," *CQ* 64 (1970): 56–66.

51. On the status of children born out of wedlock, see D. M. MacDowell, "Bastards as Athenian Citizens," *CQ* 26 (1976): 88–91; and P. J. Rhodes, "Bastards as Athenian Citizens," *CQ* 28 (1978): 89 ff., with different opinions as to their right of citizenship.

52. For the limit on prices see Arist. *Ath. Pol.* 52.2, and Hyperid. *pro Euxen.* 3. For the tax, see Aeschin. *In Tim.* 119 ff.

53. See E. Cantarella, "Prostituzione (diritto greco)," *NDI*, with bibliography.

54. Fr. 122 Snell.

55. Simon fr. 104 a Diehl: "And these prayed to divine Aphrodite for the warlike Greeks and the warlike citizens: and Aphrodite refused to give the Medes the Acropolis of the Hellenes."

56. The word *politis*, female citizen, appears only twice in the sources: Dem. 57.43 and [Dem.] 59.107. For a different opinion on the point, see D. M. MacDowell, *The Law of Classical Athens* (Ithaca, 1978).

57. On citizenship, see U. E. Paoli, "Lo stato di cittadinanza in Atene," in *Studi di diritto attico,* vol. 3 (Florence, 1930; reprinted Milan, 1974), pp. 258 ff.; and C. Hignett, *A History of the Athenian Constitution to the End of the Fifth Century B.C.* (Oxford, 1952; reprinted 1975), with more information on the Periclean decree (p. 343 ff.).

58. See Campese, Manuli, and Sissa, *Madre Materia*.

Notes to Pages 53–56

Chapter 4 Philosophers and Women

1. On these themes, see Campese and Gastaldi, eds., *La donna e i filosofi*; and J. Rostand, *Maternità e biologia* (Paris, 1968), pp. 7 ff. On Greek gynecology, see P. Manuli, "Fisiologia e patologia del femminile negli scritti ippocratici dell'antica ginecologia greca," in *Hippocratica: Actes colloque hippocratique de Paris, 4–9 Septembre 1978* (Paris, 1980), pp. 393 ff.; A. Rousselle, "Observation féminine et idéologie masculine: Le corps de la femme d'après les médecins grecs," *Annales ESC* 35 (1980): 1089 ff.; and *Porneia*, pp. 37 ff.; M. R. Lefkowitz, "The Wandering Womb," in *Heroines and Hysterics*, pp. 12–25; and P. Manuli, "Donne mascoline, femmine sterili, vergini perpetue: La ginecologia greca tra Ippocrate e Sorano," in Campese, Manuli, and Sissa, *Madre Materia*.

2. See a differing opinion in G. Raepsaet, "Sentiments conjugaux à Athènes aux Vᵉ et VIᵉ siècles avant notre ère," *AC* 50 (1981): 677 ff.; and in Mossé, *La femme*, app. 4: "La femme greque et l'amour." We will return to this problem shortly.

3. A. Schmidt, *Das Perikleische Zeitalter*, vol. 1 (Jena, 1877), pp. 90 ff.

4. The dialogue is repeated in Cic. *Inv. Rhet.* 1.31.

5. So R. Flacelière, "Le féminisme dans l'ancienne Athènes," in *Comptes rendus de l'Académie des inscriptions et belles lettres* (Paris, 1971), pp. 698 ff., esp. 702. Flacelière puts Aspasia in the difficult-to-accept context of a sort of Athenian feminist movement, already suggested in "D'un certain feminisme grec," *REA* 64 (1962): 109 ff.

6. For an interesting reconstruction of the figure of Aspasia, see G. De Sanctis, *Pericle* (Milan, 1944), pp. 188 ff.

7. The rumor is recounted in Plut. *Per.* 13.15. That Aspasia was a hetaera, and apart from that of no importance, is also the opinion of U. von Wilamowitz-Moellendorff, *Aristoteles und Athen*, vols. 1 and 2 (Berlin, 1893), 1: 263 n. 7; 2: 99 n. 35. According to him, her name, "the desired one," was evidence of this status.

8. Phidias in particular was suspected of arranging Pericles' meetings with women in his workshop (Plut. *Per.* 13.15), and was accused of having withheld part of the ivory from the construction of the chryselephantine statue of Athena, Anaxagoras was accused of "impiety" for his ideas on the sun and the moon, which were incompatible with the belief that they were divinities. On the evident link between these accusations and Phidias' and Anaxagoras' relationships with Pericles, see De Sanctis, *Pericle*, pp. 243 ff.

9. Xen. *Oec.* 7.26–27. The translations from this work are by Carnes Lord, reprinted in *WLGR*, pp. 100–104.

10. The account occupies chapters 7–10. On the jobs performed effectively by women in the house and outside, see P. Herfst, *Le travail de la femme dans la Grèce ancienne* (Diss., Utrecht, 1922). With particular

199

reference to the wife of Ischomachos, see Savalli, *La donna nella società della Grecia antica,* pp. 104 ff.

11. Diog. Laert. 6.12.

12. Ibid. 6.72. On the phrase of Diogenes (in Diog. Laert. 6.52), who, having seen some women hanged from a tree, is supposed to have said, "If only all trees bore these fruits," see Brelich, *Paides e parthenoi,* p. 444 n. 2.

13. Cf. D. Wender, "Plato: Misogynist, Paedophile and Feminist," *Arethusa* 6.1 (1973): 75 ff. For a more general exposition of the philosophical theories on women, see B. Tovery and G. Tovery, "Women's Philosophical Friends and Enemies," *Social Quarterly* 55 (1974): 589 ff.; and J. Annas, "Plato's *Republic* and Feminism," *Philosophy* 51 (1976): 307 ff.

14. Plato *Rep.* 5.451 c–457 b; 466 e–467 a. On women "guardians" (whom Plato "desexualized"), cf. A. W. Saxonhouse, "The Philosopher and the Female in the Political Thought of Plato," *Political Theory* 9.2 (1976): 195 ff. See also Wender, "Plato."

15. *Laws* 5.742 c; 6.744 e–d; 7.773 b; 774 a–b; 783–85 b; 7.720 a–d; 808 a–b; 11.923 c–925 d; 930 a–d; 937 a.

16. Ibid. 6.780 a–781 d; 7.789 e–790 b.

17. *Tim.* 42 b–c. Trans. M. R. Lefkowitz.

18. U. von Wilamowitz-Moellendorff, *Platon, sein Leben und seine Werke* (Berlin, 1959), pp. 312–13 and 573.

19. See H. Kelsen, "Platonic Love," *American Imago* 3 (1942): 3 ff., for a hypothesis on the relationship between Plato and his mother.

20. G. Sissa, "Il corpo della donna: Lineamenti di una ginecologia filosofica," in Campese, Manuli, and Sissa, *Madre Materia.* See also S. Campese, "Donna, casa, città nell'antropologia di Aristotele," in *Madre Materia,* on the social and material consequences of this "gynecology," on which more later.

On the "animal" aspect, the passivity, and the negative characteristics attributed by Aristotle to the female sex, see also S. Saïd, "Feminin, femme et femelle dans les grands traités biologiques d'Aristote," in Lévy, ed., *La femme dans les sociétés antiques,* p. 93.

21. Arist. *Gen. An.* 728 a. See also M. Vegetti, *Il coltello e lo stilo* (Milan, 1979), pp. 125 ff.

22. Arist. *Pol.* 1. (A). 5.1254 b. The translations of the passages from the *Politics* and the *Apology* are by Benjamin Jowett.

23. Ibid. 1(A).13.1260 a.

24. Ibid. 1(A).12.1259 b.

25. Ibid. 1(A).5.1254 b. Cf. 1 (A).12.1259 b.

26. Ibid. 1(A).13.1260 a. The line from Sophocles is *Ajax* 293.

27. *Pol.* 2(A).9.1269 b.

28. Plato *Ap.* 19 b–c and 24 b–c.

29. Cf. Dover, *Greek Popular Morality,* and W. den Boer, *Private Morality in Greece and Rome* (Leiden, 1979).

30. On the relationship between, for example, the poet and his audience, specifically the reaction of the public to themes that could involve a questioning of female behavior, see now M. R. Lefkowitz, "Influential Women," in Cameron and Kuhrt, eds., *Images,* pp. 49–64.

Chapter 5 Women and Literature

1. A. W. Gomme, "The Position of Women in Athens in the Fifth and Fourth Centuries," *CPh* 20 (1925): 1 ff. On analogous positions, see also D. C. Richter, "The Position of Women in Classical Athens," *CJ* 67 (1971): 1 ff.; and H. D. Kitto, *The Greeks* (London, 1951), pp. 255 ff.

2. Pomeroy, *Goddesses, Whores, Wives, and Slaves,* pp. 93 ff.

3. Translations of Aeschylus are by H. Lloyd-Jones; the translations of Euripides in the following pages are by M. R. Lefkowitz.

4. On the female role in tragedy, see M. Shaw, "The Female Intruder: Women in Fifth-Century Drama," *CPh* 70 (1975): 255–66. Shaw sees in tragedy a reevaluation of the values of the *oikos,* that is, female, with respect to those of the city, represented by men. But see also the reservations of H. P. Foley, "The Female Intruder Reconsidered: Women in Aristophanes' *Lysistrata* and *Ecclesiazusae,*" *CPh* 77 (1982): 1–21; and "The Concept of Women in Athenian Drama," in Foley, ed., *Reflections,* pp. 127–68; and M. R. Lefkowitz, "Women's Heroism," in *Heroines and Hysterics,* pp. 1–11. On the *Oresteia* in particular, see F. I. Zeitlin, "The Dynamics of Misogyny: Myth and Mythmaking in the *Oresteia,*" *Arethusa* 11.1–2 (1978): 179 ff.

5. E. Benveniste, "La légende des Danaïdes," *Revue de l'Histoire des Religions* 136 (1949): 129–38.

6. Soph. *Ant.* 806–14, 877–81. On the character of Antigone, who "far from being unconventional or independent . . . is only doing what her family might have expected of her," see Lefkowitz, "Influential Women," in Cameron and Kuhrt, eds., *Images,* pp. 49–64, esp. pp. 54 ff.

7. Among the many investigators of the relationship between women and nature, the savage element, and animality (that is, everything opposed to civilization, which is represented by man) see, *inter alios,* S. B. Ortner, "Is Female to Male as Nature Is to Culture?" in M. L. Rosaldo and L. Lamphere, eds., *Woman, Culture and Society* (Stanford, 1974), pp. 67 ff.; and N. C. Mathieu, "Homme-culture et femme-nature?" *L'homme* (1973): 101 ff. With reference to the Greek world, see J. Gould, "Law, Custom and Myth," *JHS* 100 (1980), pp. 57 ff.

8. On the life of Euripides, with an evaluation of the sources, and with reference to attitude toward women, see M. R. Lefkowitz, *The Lives of the Greek Poets* (Baltimore, 1981), pp. 88 ff. and 163 ff.

9. On this subject, see C. Nancy, "Euripide et le parti des femmes," in Lévy, ed., *La femme dans les sociétés antiques,* pp. 73 ff.

10. See Foley, "The Female Intruder Reconsidered"; F. I. Zeitlin, "Travesties of Gender and Genre in Aristophanes *Thesmophoriazusae,*" in Foley, ed., *Reflections,* pp. 169–217; and Lefkowitz, "Influential Women," pp. 49–64, esp. pp. 54 ff.

11. On the inversion of the sex roles in comedy (where the typically male facility of speech is separated from "virility") see D. Lanza, *Lingua e discorso nell'Atene delle professioni* (Naples, 1979), pp. 40 ff.

12. Cf. R. Cantarella, *Letteratura greca* (Milan, 1972), pp. 229 ff.

13. On the poetry of Sappho as "female" poetry, distinguished from male lyric by its different mode of feeling love and expressing eroticism, see E. S. Stigers, "Sappho's Private World," in Foley, ed., *Reflections,* pp. 45–61; and J. Winkler, "Gardens of Nymphs: Public and Private in Sappho's Lyrics," in Foley, ed., *Reflections,* pp. 63–89.

14. Fr. 36 Diehl = Lobel-Page (LP) 22, lines 9–14. The translations of Sappho, as of all women poets that follow, are by M. R. Lefkowitz.

15. Fr. 98 Diehl = LP 96, lines 1–17.

16. Fr. 96 Diehl = LP 94, lines 1–20 (*WLGR* no. 41).

17. Fr. 50 Diehl = LP 47.

18. Fr. 137 Diehl = LP 131.

19. Fr. 2 Diehl = LP 31 (*WLGR* no. 2).

20. Fr. 15 Diehl (*WLGR* no. 8).

21. Paus. 9.22.3; Corinna 654 *PMG.* See R. Cantarella, *Letteratura greca,* pp. 142 ff.

22. Paus. 2.20.8.

23. On Praxilla, see A. Lesky, *History of Greek Literature,* trans. J. Willis and C. Detter (New York, 1966), 1: 180–81.

24. Erinna 1 GP = *Anth. Pal.* 7.710 (*WLGR* no. 10).

25. Ar. *Lys.* 1237; cf. *Wasps* 1245–47 = 912 *PMG.*

26. *Anth. Pal.* 4.1.9 = Meleager I.5 GP.

27. *Anth. Pal.* 7.190 = Anyte xx GP.

28. *Anth. Pal.* 16.228 = Anyte xviii GP = Anth. Planud. 228.

29. *Anth. Pal.* 6.265 = Nossis iii GP.

30. *Anth. Pal.* 7.718 = Nossis xi GP.

31. *Anth. Pal.* 4.1.9 = Meleager I.9–10 GP.

32. *Anth. Pal.* 5.170 = Nossis i GP.

Chapter 6 Homosexuality and Love

1. E. Bethe, "Die dorische Knabenliebe, ihre Ethic, ihre Idee," *RhM* 62 (1907): 438–75.

2. Cf., for example, R. Flacelière, *Love in Ancient Greece* (Paris, 1971),

p. 63. For ample bibliography, see the preface to K. J. Dover, *Greek Homosexuality* (London, 1978); and B. Sergent, *L'homosexualité dans la mythologie grecque* (Paris, 1984).

3. So Raepsaet, "Sentiments conjugaux," p. 680, who agrees with Gallo, *La donna greca e la marginalità*, n. 76. Regarding the presumed "legal reproval," Raepsaet refers to the opinion of Lacey, *The Family in Classical Greece*, p. 158, who bases his statements on sources for male prostitution, which, as we shall see, has nothing to do with repression of homosexuality. Social judgment is discussed later.

4. Raepsaet, p. 680; and Flacelière, *Love*, p. 6. According to the latter, "les milieux populaires des paysans et des artisans étaient probablement fort peu touchés par la contagion de ces moeurs, qui semblent avoir été liées à une sorte de *snobisme*."

5. See K. J. Dover, "Classical Greek Attitudes to Sexual Behavior," *Arethusa* 6 (1973): 59–73.

6. See the investigation of Sergent, *L'homosexualité*. On pp. 300–301 there is a review of all the myths of this type, with indications of the area of their provenience.

7. Plato *Symp.* 180 a; Aeschylus fr. 135, 136 Radt. See Sergent, *L'homosexualité*, pp. 285 ff. (with bibliography, p. 286 n. 4); and pp. 237 ff., for references to Ganymede in the *Iliad* and in the Homeric *Hymn to Aphrodite*.

8. Strabo 10.4.21 = Eph. *FGrH* 70 F. 149.21. On gifts that by law lovers had to give to loved ones, and on the possibility (disputable) of tracing them back to the well-known Indo-European "functional tripartition," see Sergent, *L'homosexualité*, pp. 15 ff.

9. Plut. *Lyc.* 17.1. Cf. Xen. *Ages.* 2.1, *Constitution of Sparta* 2.12 ff. Lycurgus wanted to regulate homosexual relationships by law.

10. Cf. A. van Gennep, *The Rites of Passage*, trans. M. B. Vizedom and G. L. Caffee (Chicago, 1960; first published Paris, 1909).

11. H. Jeanmaire, *Couroi et couretes* (Lille, 1939); L. Gernet, *The Anthropology of Ancient Greece*, trans. J. Hamilton and B. Nagy (Baltimore and London, 1981; first published in Paris, 1968), in particular "Dolon le Loup." See also Brelich, *Paides e parthenoi*; P. Vidal-Naquet, "The Black Hunter and the Origin of the Athenian *Ephebia*," and "Recipes for Greek Adolescence," *The Black Hunter*, also in Gordon, ed., *Myth, Religion and Society*, pp. 147–62, pp. 163–85; Calame, *Les choeurs*; B. Lincoln, *Emerging from the Chrysalis* (Cambridge, Mass., 1981), pp. 71–90.

12. This is the central thesis of Sergent, *L'homosexualité*.

13. This and all other translations from Plato are by Benjamin Jowett.

14. Ar. *Birds* 131–45; *Knights* 1384–86, *Thesm.* 35; *Wasps* 578.

15. Xen. *Hiero* 1.33.

16. Xen. *Ages.* 5.4.

17. Lysias *Sim.*
18. Theoc. *Id.* 2.44–150.
19. Ovid *Met.* 4.285. Hermaphroditus is also mentioned by Theophr. *Char.* 16.
20. Plut. *Thes.* 20.
21. Macrob. *Sat.* 3.8.2.
22. Plut. *De mul. vir.* 245 e.
23. Plut. *Quaest. Graec.* 304 e.
24. Plut. *Lyc.* 15.5.
25. H. Licht, *Sexual Life in Ancient Greece* (New York, 1949), pp. 124 ff.
26. Ar. *Frogs* 55–57, trans. B. B. Rogers (Loeb Classical Library).
27. Plut. *Pel.* 18.
28. Plato *Symp.* 218 d.
29. A. Gouldner, *Enter Plato* (New York and London, 1965), esp. pp. 52 ff. The situation was different in Rome, where the citizens expressed their virility in active homosexual relationships with slaves; but see P. Veyne, "L'homosexualité à Rome," in P. Ariès, ed., *Sexualités occidentales* (Paris, 1982).
30. The most interesting source on the subject of penal repression and of male prostitution is the oration of Aeschines, *Against Timarchus*.
31. See B. Gentili, "Le vie di eros nella poesia dei tiasi femminili e dei simposi," and "La veneranda Saffo," in *Poesia e pubblico nella Grecia antica,* pp. 101 ff.; pp. 285 ff.
32. *Suda* s.v. "Sappho" (C 107 Adler).
33. Fr. 55 L-P (trans. M. R. Lefkowitz).
34. Plut. *Lyc.* 18.9.
35. Calame, *Les Choeurs,* pp. 428–29.
36. G. Devereux, "The Nature of Sappho's Seizure in fr. 31 LP as Evidence of Her Inversion," *CQ* 20 (1970): 17 ff.; and "Greek Pseudo-homosexuality and the Greek Miracle," *SO* 42 (1967): 70 ff. On the Sappho fragment, and for the discussion raised by Devereux's theories, see G. A. Privitera, "Ambiguità, antitesi analogia nel fr. 31 LP di Saffo," *QUCC* 8 (1969): 37 ff.; F. Maniere, "Saffo: Appunti di metodologia generale per un approccio psichiatrico," *QUCC* 14 (1972): 46 ff.; and Calame, *Les Choeurs,* p. 430 and n. 160.
37. Devereux, "Nature," p. 31; *WLGR,* no. 4.
38. Dover, *Greek Homosexuality,* p. 181.

Chapter 7 The Hellenistic Age: New Images, Old Stereotypes

1. On Hellenism, see W. W. Tarn and G. I. Griffith, *Hellenistic Civilization,* 3rd ed. (London, 1952); A. Momigliano, "Introduzione all'ellenismo," *RSI* 82 (1970): 781 ff.; and *Alien Wisdom: The Limits of*

Hellenization (London 1975); R. Bianchi Bandinelli, ed., *Storia e civiltà dei Greci* (Milan, 1977–79), vols. 4 (*La società ellenistica*) and 5 (*La cultura ellenistica*); P. Lévêque, *Il mondo ellenistico* (Rome, 1980).

2. For a comprehensive view of the question (in addition to the specific contributions cited in the following notes) see C. Préaux, "Le statut de la femme à l'époque hellénistique, principalemente en Égypte," *RSJB* 11, *La femme* (Brussels, 1959), pp. 127–75.; and C. Vatin, *Recherches sur le mariage et la condition de la femme marié à l'époque hellénistique* (Paris, 1970). More briefly, but also on the new and better conditions, M. B. Arthur, " 'Liberated' Women: The Classical Era," in *Becoming Visible: Women in European History*, ed. R. Bridenthal and C. Koonz (Boston, 1979), pp. 73 ff. On the condition of women in Egypt, cf J. Pirenne, "Le statut de la femme dans l'ancienne Égypte," *RSJB* 11, pp. 63 ff.; and now Pomeroy, *Women in Hellenistic Egypt.*

3. *IG* 9.2.62.

4. See J. Robert and L. Robert, *Bulletin épigraphique* 76, inscription no. 170 = Pleket 2.

5. *I. Priene*, no. 208 = Pleket 5.

6. See (in addition to Préaux), V. Arangio-Ruiz, *Persone e famiglia nel diritto dei papiri* (Pubbl. Univ. Cattol. S. Cuore, ser. 2, vol. 26) (Milan, 1930); E. Ziebarth, "Ehe im Recht der Papyri," *RE* suppl. 7 (1940), 169; and J. Modrzejewski, "Droit de famille dans les lettres privées d'Egypte," *JJP* 9–10 (1955–56): 339 ff.

7. *BGU* 1052 and *PGiess.* 2. Cf. R. Taubenschlag, *The Law of Graeco-Roman Egypt in the Light of the Papyri* (Warsaw, 1955).

8. *POxy.* 1273 (260 B.C.) and *PEleph.* 1 (113 B.C.). Cf. Modrzejewski, "Droit de famille"; and R. Taubenschlag, "Die Materna Potestas im gräko-ägyptischen Recht," in *Opera Minora*, vol. 2 (Warsaw, 1959), pp. 323 ff.

9. Préaux, "Le statut," pp. 143 ff.

10. Ibid.

11. *POxy.* 97 (A.D. 115–16). When marriage ended not by death but by divorce, the alimentary obligation fell, as a rule, on the father. Cf. *POxy.* 497, pp. 6 ff. (second century A.D.); *POxy.* 265, 19–26 (81–95 A.D.).

12. *POxy.* 237, col. 7.1.12. Cf. Préaux, "Le Statut," p. 163.

13. *POxy.* 744.

14. Cole, "Could Greek Women Read and Write?"

15. S. B. Pomeroy, "The Education of Women in the Fourth Century and in the Hellenistic Period," *AJAH* 2 (1977): 51 ff.; and *Women in Hellenistic Egypt.*

16. Préaux, "Le Statut," pp. 171–72.

17. Dittenberg. *SIG²*, no. 578.

18. Plutarch gives a profile of Olympias in *Alexander* 2.

19. Diod. Sic. 19.67; see the reconstruction of this character by G. H.

Macurdy, "The Political Activities and the Name of Cratesipolis," *AJP* 50 (1929): 273 ff.

20. G. H. Macurdy, *Hellenistic Queens* (Baltimore, 1932), p. 125.

21. On Cleopatra, see E. Will, *Histoire politique du monde hellénistique,* vol. 2 (Nancy, 1967), pp. 445 ff.

22. See Macurdy, *Queens;* the observations of Préaux, "Le statut," pp. 134 ff.; Pomeroy, *Goddesses, Whores, Wives, and Slaves,* 131 ff.; and now Lefkowitz, "Influential Women," in Cameron and Kuhrt, eds., *Images,* pp. 49–64 = *Women in Greek Myth,* pp. 80–94.

23. See A. W. Gomme and F. H. Sandbach, eds., *Menander: A Commentary* (Oxford, 1973), pp. 21 ff.

24. On the characters of New Comedy, see R. Cantarella, *Letteratura greca,* pp. 396 ff.; and E. Fantham, "Sex, Status and Survival in Hellenistic Athens: A Study of Women in New Comedy," *Phoenix* 29 (1975): 44 ff.

25. A. Körte, "Ménandros," *RE* 15.1 (1931), 720 ff.; H. J. Mette, "Ménandros," *RE* suppl. 12 (1970), 854 ff.; and A. Borgogno, "Aspis e epikleros," *RFIC* II s. 98 (1970): 275 ff.

26. Karabelias, *L'épiclerat attique* (Paris, 1974), 234 ff.; "L'épiclerat dans la comédie nouvelle et dans les sources latines," *Symposium* (1971). See *Vorträge zur griechischen und hellenistischen Rechtsgeschichte* (Cologne, 1971), pp. 215 ff., for a discussion of the possibility of using the Roman *palliata* as source for knowledge about Hellenistic law and, therefore, for integrating information on the female condition in this period.

27. See Gomme and Sandbach, eds., *Menander,* p. 328 = *WLGR* no. 38.

28. *Frag. Grenfellianum* 8–16. On women in Theocritus, see F. T. Griffiths, "Home before Lunch: The Emancipated Woman in Theocritus," in Foley, ed., *Reflections,* pp. 247–73.

29. *CAF* vol. 3, p. 1691, fr. 1109.

30. *Anth. Pal.* 7.455. The author of the epitaph is Leonidas, born in Tarentum ca. 320–315 B.C.

31. *Anth. Pal.* 5.175. The author of the invective is Meleager, born at Gadara in Syria at the end of the second century B.C.

32. Herod. 5.74–76. On the misogyny of Hellenistic literature, see Vatin, "Recherches," pp. 17 ff.

33. Stob. 68.1. Cf. *WLGR* no. 37 = Menander fr. 333 Koerte.

Chapter 8 The Hypothesis of Matriarchy

1. For Liguria see E. Sereni, *Comunità rurali nell'Italia antica* (Rome, 1955). For Etruria see the works cited in the following notes. On the origins of Rome, see A. Momigliano, "An Interim Report on the Origins of Rome," *JRS* 53 (1963); 95 ff.; A. Alföldi, *Early Rome and the Latins* (Ann Arbor, Mich., 1965); R. M. Ogilvie, *Early Rome and the Etruscans* (London,

1976). For an overview of the literature, see C. Ampolo, ed., *La città antica: Guida storica e critica* (Bari, 1980).

2. On female divinities at Rome and on their cults, see G. Dumézil, *Déesses latines et mythes védiques* (Brussels, 1956); and *Archaic Roman Religion: With an Appendix on the Religion of the Etruscans*, trans. P. Krapp (Chicago, 1970; first published 1966); J. Gagé, *Matronalia: essai sur les dévotions et les organisations culturelles des femmes dans l'ancienne Rome*, Collection Latomus 60 (Brussels, 1963), pp. 101 ff.; G. Radke, *Die Götter Alteritaliens* (Münster, 1965); and the classic G. Wissowa, *Religion und Kultus der Römer*, 2nd ed. (Munich, 1912).

3. The hypothesis goes back to Bachofen, especially *Die Sage von Tanaquil* (Heidelberg, 1870); see selections from *The Myth of Tanaquil* in *Myth, Religion, and Mother Right*, trans. R. Manheim, pp. 21–46.

4. A. Momigliano, "Tre figure mitiche: Tanaquilla, Gaia Cecilia e Acca Larenzia," in *Quarto contributo alla storia degli Studi classici e del mondo antico* (Rome, 1969), pp. 455 ff.

5. Theopompus in Ath. *Deipnosophistai* 12.517 D–518 B.

6. On Etruscan women, see L. Bonfante Warren, "The Women of Etruria," *Arethusa* 6.1 (1973): 91 ff., who, while denying that Etruscan society was "matriarchal" in the sense intended by Bachofen, points out the social prestige enjoyed by women. See also L. Bonfante Warren, "Etruscan Women: A Question of Interpretation," *Archaeology* 26 (1973): 242 ff.; "Etruscan Couples and Their Aristocratic Society," in Foley, ed., *Reflections*, pp. 323–41; and, finally, M. Sordi, "La donna etrusca," in *Misoginia e maschilismo*, pp. 49 ff., who, while ruling out matriarchy, speaks of "matrilineal descendence."

7. Y. Thomas, "Mariages endogamiques à Rome: Patrimoine, pouvoir et parenté dans l'époque archaïque," *RD* 58 (1980): 345 ff., reproposes the hypothesis of the transmission of royal power by marriage with the daughter of the king. A. Borghini, "Elementi di denominazione matri-lineare alle origini di Roma: logica di una tradizione," forthcoming in *MD*, who, departing from the legend of Aeneas in Latium and moving along the lines traced by J. G. Frazer, suggests that the group that obtained women from another (whether only one, as in the case of king's daughters, or a group, such as the Sabine women) would have given up its name, assuming the matrilineal denomination.

8. Serini, *Comunità rurali*, p. 262.

9. Cf. Magli, ed., *Matriarcato e potere delle donne*, p. 61.

10. G. Franciosi, *Clan gentilizio e strutture monogamiche*, vol. 1 (Naples, 1978), pp. 239 ff. In a different sense, see O. Szemerenyi, "Studies in the Kinship Terminology of the Indo-European Languages," *AI* 16 (1977): 159 ff.; and Ph. Moreau, "La terminologie latine et indoeuropéenne de la parenté et le système de parenté et d'alliance à Rome: Question de

methode," *REL* 56 (1978): 41 ff. According to Moreau, the Latin terminology presents no classificatory element. See also my remarks in "Storia del diritto e antropologia sulla *gens* romana," *Labeo* 28 (1982): 322 ff.

11. It will suffice to record the names of J. F. McLennan and A. Kroeber, who address the problem in, respectively, *Primitive Marriage*, and *Classificatory System of Relationship* (1909) = *The Nature of Culture* 2:19, 175 ff.

12. Franciosi, *Clan gentilizio*, vol. 1, pp. 222 ff.

13. Cf. G. Dumézil, *Déesses latines et mythes védiques*, pp. 9 ff.; and *Archaic Roman Religion*.

14. Cf. M. Bettini, "Su alcuni modelli antropologici della Roma più arcaica: Designazione linguistiche e pratiche culturali," parts I and II, *MD* 1 (1978): 123 ff., and 2 (1979): 9 ff. Other explanations in Gagé, *Matronalia*; and F. Castagnoli, "Il culto della Mater Matuta e della Fortuna nel Foro Boario," *StudRom* 27 (1979): 145 ff. On the inscription discovered on 13 October 1977 in the sanctuary of the goddess at Satricum, published in *Lapis satricanus: Archaeological, Epigraphical, Linguistic and Historical Aspects of the New Inscription from Satricum* = *Scripta minora*, vol. 5 of the Istituto Olandese (Rome, 1980), see M. Guarducci, "L'epigrafe arcaica di Satricum e Publio Valerio," *RAL* 35 (1980): 479 ff.

15. Respectively, *FGrH* 90 F 103 (D) and *FGrH* 90 F 104 (3).

16. Pembroke, "Women in Charge," p. 5. On Herodotus and women, see also V. Ando, "La comunanza delle donne in Erodoto," in *Philias charin, Miscellanea di studi classici in onore di E. Manni*, vol. 1 (Rome, 1980), pp. 85 ff.; and C. Dewald, "Women and Culture in Herodotus' *Histories*," in Foley, ed., *Reflections*, pp. 91–125.

17. Cf. F. Hartog, *Le Miroir d'Hérodote: Essai sur la représentation de l'autre* (Paris, 1908).

18. Pembroke, "Women in Charge," p. 35.

19. On these ceremonies, see E. Pais, *Storia di Roma*, vol. 2 (Rome, 1926), pp. 357 ff.; and Dumézil, *Archaic Roman Religion*, p. 264. On the Lupercalia, in particular, see Dion. Hal. 1.80.1; Ovid *Fasti* 2.19–36, 267–452; Plut. *Ant.* 12, *Rom.* 21, *Caes.* 61; and C. Ulf, *Das römische Lupercalienfest: Ein Modelfall für Methodeprobleme in der Altertumswissenschaft* (= *Impulse der Forschung* 38) (Darmstadt, 1982), with an ample collection of various opinions and a large bibliography.

20. E. Reed, *Problems of Women's Liberation: A Marxist Approach* (New York, 1969); "In Defence of Engels on Matriarchy," in *Feminism and Socialism* (New York, 1972); and *Women's Evolution: From Matriarchal Clan to Patriarchal Family* (New York, 1975). On the believers in the matriarchy see Evelyn Ackworth, *The New Matriarchy* (London, 1965).

21. The political interest of feminist groups in the problem has led to the creation of study centers such as the Matriarchy Study Group (Flat 6, Guilford Street, London WC 1) and the Foundation for Matriarchy (P.O.

Box 271, Pratt Station, Brooklyn, NY 11205).

22. For more detail see my introduction to the Italian translation of Bachofen, *Il potere femminile*, pp. 10 ff.; and my "J. J. Bachofen tra storia del diritto romano e le scienze sociali," *Sociologia del diritto* 3 (1982): 111 ff. = *Presentazione di J. J. Bachofen*, E. Cantarella, ed., *Introduzione al diritto materno* (Rome, 1983); see also selections from *Mother Right* in *Myth, Religion, and Mother Right*, trans. R. Manheim, pp. 69–207.

23. W. Reich, *The Invasion of Compulsory Sex-Morality* (New York, 1971).

24. Bachofen, *Mother Right*, pp. 24 ff.

25. E. Jones, *Essays in Applied Psychoanalysis*, vol. 2 (New York, 1964).

26. J. Evola, introduction to *Le madri e la virilità olimpica* (Milan, 1949), p. 16.

Chapter 9 The Period of the Kings and the Republic

1. *Digesta* 50.16.195.2. On the Roman *familia* and the powers of the *pater*, see the fundamental V. Arangio-Ruiz, *Istituzioni di diritto romano*, 14th ed. (Naples, 1976), pp. 426 ff.; and L. Capogrossi Colognesi, *Enciclopedia del diritto*, s.v. *Patria potestas*, vol. 22 (1982), pp. 242 ff. On women's status see also R. Villers, "Le statut de la femme à Rome jusqu'à la fin de la Republique," *RSJB*, vol. 11, 1, pp. 177 ff.

2. See Article 316 of the Italian Civil Code.

3. Cf. E. A. Hoebel, *Il diritto nelle società primitive* (Bologna, 1973), with bibliography for the problem in the Greek world.

4. Juv. 4.25 and Aul. Gell. 10.10. On the *sponsalia* cf. J. Gaudemet, "La conclusion des fiançailles Rome à l'époque pre-classique," *RIDA* 1 (1948): 79 ff.; and "L'originalité des fiançailles romaines," *Iura* 6 (1955): 46 ff., now in *Études de droit romain*, vol. 3 (Naples, 1979), pp. 3 ff. and 21 ff., respectively; E. Volterra, "Osservazioni intorno agli antichi sponsali romani," in *Scritti C. A. Jemolo*, vol. 5 (Milan, 1963), pp. 639 ff.; and s.v. "Sponsali" in *NDI* 18 (1971): 34 ff.

5. There is some debate on the age of Roman girls at marriage. According to M. Durry, in many cases marriage took place before puberty: Durry, "Le mariage des filles impubères à Rome," *Comptes rendus de l'Académie des inscriptions* (1955): 84 ff.; and "Auto-critique et mise au point," *RIDA* 3 (1956): 227 ff., both now in "Mélanges Durry," *REL* 47 bis (1969): 16 ff. and 27 ff., respectively. See also Hopkins, "The Age of Roman Girls at Marriage," 309 ff.; D. Gourevitch, *Le mal d'être femme* (Paris, 1984), pp. 109 ff.; and J.-P. Neraudau, *Être enfant à Rome* (Paris, 1984), pp. 256 ff.

6. Dion. Hal. 2.25.6 attributes the law to Romulus.

7. M. Durry, "Les femmes et le vin," *REL* 33 (1955): 108 ff.

8. See L. Minieri, "Vini usus foeminis ignotus," *Labeo* 28 (1982): 150 ff., who maintains that the ban, although motivated also by fear of adultery,

was an autonomous ban inspired by the need for a broader preventive control of family morals. Interesting, though not convincing, is the hypothesis of G. Piccaluga, "Bona dea: Due contributi allo studio del suo culto," *SMSR* 35 (1964): 203 ff., according to whom the wine forbidden to women would have been only the *temetum,* wine used for ritual purposes, and the reason for the prohibition would have been the fear that when women drank the wine they would begin to prophesy and, perhaps, more generally speak of things of which they should not have spoken.

9. This is the hypothesis proposed by P. Noailles, "Les tabous du mariage dans le droit primitif des Romains," in *Fas et Ius: Études de droit romain* (Paris, 1948), p. 1.

10. This is the explanation given by Aul. Gell. *NA* 10.23.1 and Pliny *NH* 14.13.89–90. A different explanation can be found in G. Franciosi, *Clan gentilizio,* vol. 2 (Naples, 1980), pp. 132 ff., who believes the practice to be a relic of an ancient votive surrender of women at marriage, according to a hypothesis of Bachofen in *Mutterrecht.*

11. Plut. *Rom.* 22.3 and Pliny *NH* 39.18.6. On abortion, see E. Nardi, *Procurato aborto nel mondo greco romano* (Milan, 1971).

12. Cf. P. Bonfante, *Corso di diritto romano,* vol. 6 (Rome, 1930), p. 96.

13. The legend is retold in Livy 1.4.6–7, Dion. Hal. 1.84, and Aul. Gell. 7.75–77. The thesis that the story reveals the status of Etruscan women has been maintained by V. Scialoja in *Rendiconti Lincei* (1905) 141 ff. The Romanness of the figure of Acca has been maintained by E. Pais, *Storia di Roma,* vol. 1 (Rome, 1926), pp. 311 ff.; by E. Volterra, "Sulla capacità del *populus* romano di essere istituito erede," *Studi Sassaresi* 16 (1937) (= *Scritti F. Mancaleoni*), pp. 203 ff.; and "Sulla capacità delle donne far testamento," *BIDR* 48 (1942): 74 ff.; and by Momigliano, *Tre figure mitiche.*

14. E. Peruzzi, *Origini di Roma,* vol. 1 (Florence, 1970), p. 75.

15. Ibid., pp. 49 ff.

16. Gaius *Inst.* 2.226 ff. On the real scope of the law, its application, and its consequences for the history of female emancipation, see P. Vigneron, "L'antiféministe' loi Voconia et les 'Schleichwege des Lebens,'" *Labeo* 29 (1983): 140 ff.

17. Cf. Arangio-Ruiz, *Istituzioni di diritto romano,* pp. 443 ff.; and E. Volterra, *Istituzioni di diritto romano* (Rome, 1961) p. 715.

18. *Digesta,* 48.5.23 (22).4. On the *lex Iulia,* cf. D. Daube, "The Lex Julia concerning Adultery," *Irish Jurist* 7 (1972): 373 ff.; E. Cantarella, "Adulterio, omicidio legittimo e causa d'onore in diritto romano," in *Studi sull'omicidio,* pp. 163 ff. See A. Reichlin, "Approaches to the Sources on Adultery at Rome," in Foley, ed., *Reflections,* pp. 379–404, for the problems of social attitude, actual applications of the law, and the possibilities of evading it.

19. With the sole exception of the elegiac poets, on whose attitudes see

F. della Corte, "Le *leges Iuliae* e l'elegia romana," *ANRW* 2.30.1 (1982): 531 ff.

20. I. Kajanto, *L'onomastique latine* (Paris, 1977), pp. 184 ff.

21. G. Bonfante, "Il nome della donna nella Roma arcaica," *RAL* 35 (1980): 3–10.

22. This is the hypothesis already cited of Peruzzi, *Le origini di Roma,* pp. 99 ff.

23. R. I. Menager, "Systèmes onomastiques, structures familiales et classes sociales dans le monde gréco-romain," *SDHI* 46 (1980): 146 ff.

24. According to Q. Mucius Scaevola (cited by Val. Max., in Julius Paris' epitome), the *praenomen* was given women when they married (males received theirs when they took the *toga virilis*). But Festus, s.v. *Lustrici dies;* Plut. *Quaest. Rom.* 102 (288 c); and Macrob. *Sat.* 1.16.36 maintain instead that the *praenomen* was given at the purification, that is, the eighth day after a girl's birth and the ninth after a boy's.

25. Menager, "Systèmes onomastiques," p. 203.

26. On the Etruscan system of nomenclature, see, among others, the classic by M. Cristofani, *Introduzione allo studio dell'Etrusco* (Florence, 1923); and the more recent M. Torelli, *Storia degli Etruschi* (Bari, 1981), pp. 71 ff.

27. The praise of the Bona Dea is in Varro (in Lactant. *Div. Inst.* 1.22).

28. M. I. Finley, "The Silent Women of Rome," in *Aspects of Antiquity: Discoveries and Controversies,* 2nd. ed. (New York, 1978; first published London, 1968), p.131. See also D. M. Schaps, "The Woman Least Mentioned," *CQ* 27 (1977): 323–30.

29. On the trial see C. Hermann, *Le rôle judiciaire et politique des femmes sous la république romaine* (= *Collection Latomus* 67) (Brussels, 1964).

30. See C. Gallini, *Protesta e integrazione nella Roma antica* (Bari, 1970), p. 31.

31. This does not mean that the Bacchanalia can be interpreted only in terms of "feminist" revolt, according to the hypothesis put forth by Hermann, *Le rôle judiciaire.* As Gallini, *Protesta,* rightly notes, p. 5, women were only one of the components of a vaster and more complex movement in which all the "marginalized" classes expressed their dissatisfaction. Against the simplistic hypothesis of a feminist revolt, see too G. Franciosi, *Clan gentilizio,* vol. 1, pp. 51–52; and C. Bellu, "Alcune considerazioni sulla condizione giuridica della donna nell'età Repubblicana," *Studi economico-giuridici dell'Università di Cagliari* 49 (1979): 151 ff.

32. Cf. Jerome *Against Jovinianus* 1.49 P. L. Migne 23.281 (318), quoting the third-century pope Xystus or Sixtus II: "The wise man must love his own wife with judgment, not with affection."

33. On the population crisis, its long duration, and its outcome, see M. I. Finley, "Manpower and the Fall of Rome," in *Aspects of Antiquity,* p. 153 ff.; Salmon, *Population et depopulation;* E. Patlagean, "La limitation de

la féconidité dans la Haute-Époque byzantine," *Annales ESC* (1969): 1353 ff. The role played in this direction in the following centuries by asceticism and praise of chastity will be discussed later; see A. Rousselle, *Porneia: De la maîtrise du corps à la privation sensorielle.* On contraceptive methods (mentioned in the Republican period by, among others, Lucr. 4.1268–77 and later by Pliny *NH* 29.27.85), see Pomeroy, *Goddesses, Whores, Wives, and Slaves,* pp. 166–68; and now Gourevitch, *Le mal,* pp. 195 ff. With particular reference to the Empire, see also K. Hopkins, "Contraception in the Roman Empire," *Studies in Society and History* 8 (1965–66): 124 ff. On abortion, see Nardi, *Procurato aborto;* and Gourevitch, *Le mal,* pp. 206 ff.

34. On the "myth" of Lucretia, its origins and fortune, and the way it has been interpreted and elaborated through the centuries, see I. Donaldson, *The Rape of Lucretia: A Myth and Its Transformations* (Oxford, 1982).

35. Plut. *Ti. Gracch.* 1.3–7, and *C. Gracch.* 4.4 and 19; *WLGR* no. 145–47. In H. Dessau, ed., *Inscriptiones Latinae Selectae (ILS),* however, the inscription is recorded as "Cornelia, wife of Africanus and mother of the Gracchi." On the personages cited thus far, see P. Gide, *Étude sur la condition privée de la femme* (Paris, 1885), pp. 100 ff., who sees in their history the proof of women's greater importance in public as well as private life.

36. On the episode, see R. Flacelière, "Caton d'Utique et les femmes," in *Mélanges Heurgon,* vol. 1 (Rome, 1976), pp. 293 ff.

37. Plut. *Cato Min.* 25.1–12 and 52.5–6. For the accusation of avidity, see 52.6

38. Cf. E. Malcovati, *Donne di Roma antica* (fasc. 8.1) (*Quaderni di studi romani, Istituto di Studi romani,* 1945).

39. Cic. *Cael.* 20 ff., and Plut. *Cic.* 29c; cf. *WLGR* no. 155. For an attempt to reconstruct the relationship between Cicero and the women of his family, see T. Carp, "Two Matrons of the Late Republic," in Foley, ed., *Reflections,* pp. 343–54. The conclusions are perhaps a bit optimistic on the conditions of women in the late Republic, who Carp maintains were not "silent" (M. I. Finley's designation), but capable of deciding the questions that affected them personally, even if they were defined and defined themselves "in terms of their connection with a male figure" (p. 353). On women's family relationships, see now J. P. Hallett, *Fathers and Daughters in Roman Society* (Princeton, N.J., 1984).

40. Orelli 4617; 4624–27; 4639; 4644; cf. *WLGR* no. 139, 143.

41. *CIL* 6.15.346 (= *ILS* 8403); *WLGR* no. 134; trans. R. Lattimore, *Themes in Greek and Latin Epitaphs.*

42. *Laudatio quae dicitur Turiae* in *Fontes iuris romani anteiustiniani* vol. 3, *Negotia* (Florence, 1953), pp. 209 ff. = *WLGR* no. 207; N. Horsfall, "Some Problems in the *Laudatio Turiae,*" *BICS* 30 (1983): 85–98. For a reconstruction of the story, see L. Storoni Mazzolani, *Una moglie* (Palermo,

1982). On the respect women enjoyed and the roles they could play, see on the *Laudatio,* Gaudemet, "Le statut de la femme," pp. 191 ff., esp. 193.

43. Cf. D. Daube, *Civil Disobedience in Antiquity* (Edinburgh, 1972), pp. 23 ff., who explains the difference between the heroic gestures of transgression of Greek women, intended to question male values, and those of Roman women, intended to confirm and defend them.

Chapter 10 The Principate and the Empire: The Emancipation of Women?

1. See Gaius, *Inst.* 3.17, for the end of gentile law. On the transformation of the family and its consequences on the female condition, see Gaudemet, "Le statut de la femme," p. 191.

2. On this theme, see A. M. Rabello, *Effetti personali della "patria potestas,"* vol. 1 (Milan, 1979), pp. 22 ff.

3. For the provinces, Constantine recognized the validity of the sale of the exposed child as a slave in A.D. 322 (*Cod. Theod.* 11.27.2).

4. On marriage and related problems, see J. Gaudemet, "Le mariage en droit romain—*Iustum matrimonium,*" *RIDA* 2 (1949): 309 ff.; and "Originalité et destin du mariage romain," in *Studi P. Koschaker, L'Europa e il diritto romano* (Milan, 1954), pp. 513 ff., both republished in *Société et mariage* (Strasbourg, 1980), respectively, pp. 46 ff. and 140 ff. See also R. Orestano, *La struttura giuridica del matrimonio dal diritto classico al diritto giustiniano* (Milan, 1951); E. Volterra, *La conception du mariage d'après les juristes romains* (Padua, 1940); and *Lezioni di diritto romano* (Rome, 1960–1961); s.v. "Matrimonio (dir. rom.)," in *NDI,* vol. 10 (Turin, 1964), pp. 330 ff.; "La conventio in manum e il matrimonio romano," *RISG* 95 (1968); 205 ff.; "Matrimonio," in *Enciclopedia del diritto,* vol. 25 (1975), pp. 726 ff.; "Precisazioni in tema di matrimonio classico," *BIDR* 78 (1975): 245 ff.; and "Ancora sulla struttura del matrimonio classico," in *Festscrift U. von Luetow* (Berlin, 1980), pp. 147 ff.; O. Robleda, *El matrimonio en derecho romano* (Rome, 1970); D. Daube, "Aspects of informal marriage," *RIDA* 25 (1978); C. W. Westrup, *Introduction to Early Roman Law. Comparative Sociological Studies: The Patriarchal Joint Family* (Copenhagen and London, 1944); A. Watson, *The Law of Persons in the Later Roman Republic* (Oxford, 1947); and finally, for important observations on the role of the instrument of political and patrimonial solidarity assumed by the institution of marriage in the last centuries of the Republic, see Y. Thomas, "Mariages endogamiques à Rome: Patrimoine, pouvoir et parenté depuis l'époque archaïque," *RD* 58 (1980): 345 ff.

5. For the formula for repudiation, see Mart. 10.41, where it is spoken by a woman. We will return to this subject.

6. On the patrimonial relationships between spouses, see M. Garcia Garrido, *Ius uxorium: El régimen patrimonial de la mujer casado en derecho*

romano (Rome and Madrid, 1958). See also H. Kupiszewski, "Osservazioni sui rapporti patrimoniali tra fidanzati in diritto romano classico: 'Dos' e 'donatio,' " *Iura* 29 (1978): 114 ff.

7. On the dowry and its evolution, see Arangio-Ruiz, *Istituzioni di diritto romano*, pp. 685 ff.; and K. Kagan, "The Nature of Dowry in Roman Law: Rights of Husband and Wife," *Tulane Law Review* 20 (1944–45): 55 ff.

8. On the evolution of *tutela*, see P. Zannini, *Studi sulla tutela muliebre* (Turin, 1976); and G. MacCormack, "The Liability of the Tutor in Classical Roman Law," *Irish Jurist* 5 (1970): 369 ff.

9. Cf. T. Masiello, *La donna tutrice* (Naples, 1979), with bibliography.

10. G. Fau, *L'emancipation féminine à Rome* (Paris, 1978), pp. 195 ff. On this period see also A. del Castillo, *La mujer romana y sus intentos de emancipación durante el siglo I d.C.* (Granada, 1975); *La emancipación de la mujer romana en el siglo I d.C.* (Granada, 1976); "Apuntes sobre la situación de la mujer en la Roma imperial," *Latomus* 38 (1979): 173 ff. V. A. Sirago, *Femminismo a Roma nel Primo Impero* (Catanzaro, 1983), identifies emancipation and "feminism." On these subjects there is much to debate. On the limits of emancipation, and on the prices that Roman women had to pay for it, see the just observations of Gourevitch, *Le mal,* pp. 19 ff.

11. For the ban, cf. *Digesta* 3.1.1.5. On Afrania, see E. Ciccotti, *Donne e politica negli ultimi anni della Roma repubblicana* (Milan, 1895), and *WLGR* no. 205.

12. Quint. *Inst. Or.* 1.1.6; for Hortensia see *WLGR* nos. 205, 206.

13. In Tib. 3 = *WLGR* no. 133.

14. *Historia Augusta, Vita Elag.* 3; *WLGR* no. 240; also see Gagé, *Matronalia,* pp. 101 ff.; and J. Straub, "Senaculum, id est mulierum senatus," in *Bonner Historia Augusta Colloquium 1964–65* (Bonn, 1966), pp. 221–40.

15. See S. Mazzarino, *La fine del mondo antico* (Milan, 1959), pp. 141–42.

16. From another inscription we know of one Appuleia, who apparently worked in a shop with her husband. Cf. Dessau *ILS* 6408a (*WLGR* no. 210), on which see Lefkowitz, "Influential Women," in Cameron and Kuhrt, eds., *Images,* pp. 49–64 = *Women in Greek Myth* (80–94); and more generally E. Lyding Will, "Women in Pompeii," *Archaeology* 33 (1979): 34 ff.

17. Cf. J. Carcopino, *Daily Life in Ancient Rome: The People and the City at the Height of the Empire,* trans. E. O. Lorimer (London, 1941; first published 1917), p. 209; and Fau, *L'emancipation,* pp. 193 ff.; *WLGR* no. 182, 183. On midwives and other female medical practitioners, see Gourevitch, *Le mal,* pp. 217 ff.

18. Cic. *Off.* 1.42. See J. Maurin, "*Labor matronalis:* aspects du travail féminine à Rome," in Lévy, ed., *Les femmes dans les sociétés antiques,* pp. 139

ff., who comments on the different valuation of male and female work. *Otium* was considered negative for women (but not for men) in that it was a sign of neglected female duties and a possible cause of dissoluteness.

19. The following poetry extracts are from Juvenal, *The Sixteen Satires*, trans. P. Green (Baltimore, 1974; first published 1967).

20. Ovid *Am.* 2.14; Sen. *Helv.* 16.3; Aul. Gell. *NA* 12.1.8–9.

21. Soranus deals with the problem in the *De anima* 25.4.6, and in *Gynaikeia* 1.19.60–63. His theories were taken up by Aëtius in *De re medica* 16.16–17. On his theories, and more generally on physicians' attitudes toward abortion, see the already-cited works of Manuli, Rousselle, and Gourevitch. Maximus *Peri katarchon* 145 ff.

22. On the fact that abortion was prohibited to married women, see R. Crahay, "Les moralistes anciens et l'avortement," *AC* 10 (1942): 11 ff.; and Gourevitch, *Le mal*, pp. 210 ff.

23. Arria, *WLGR* no. 150.

24. See Gagé, *Matronalia*, pp. 251 ff. On the cults reserved for women and the cult privileges of *univirae*, see M. Humbert, *Le remariage à Rome* (Milan, 1972), pp. 42 ff.

25. On the contrast between social practice, the demographic legislation, and the persistent model of the *univira*, see M. Humbert and M. Penta, "La *viduitas* nella condizione della donna romana," *AAN* 91 (1980): 341 ff.

26. Val. Max. 8.15.12. On the episode of Helvia and its possible interpretations, see Gagé, *Matronalia*, pp. 264 ff.

27. On trials of Vestal Virgins, see A. Fraschetti, "Le sepolture rituali nel Foro Boario," in *Le délit religieux dans la cité antique* (= *Coll. École Française de Rome* 48) (Rome, 1981), pp. 51 ff.

28. Trans. P. Green; on Bona Dea cf. *WLGR* no. 247.

29. So F. Guizzi, *Aspetti giuridici del sacerdozio romano: Il sacerdozio di Vesta* (Naples, 1968), p. 200. Still interesting is G. Giannelli, *Il sacerdozio delle Vestali romane* (Florence, 1913), but now see M. Beard, "The Sexual Status of Vestal Virgins," *JRS* 70 (1980): 12–27; T. Cornell, "Some Observations on the *crimen incestis*," in *Le délit religieux dans la cité antique*, pp. 27 ff.; and G. Radke, "Die Dei Penates und Vesta in Rom," *ANRW* 2.17.1, 343 ff.

30. R. Schilling, *La religion de Venus depuis les origines jusqu'au temps d'Auguste* (Paris, 1954; reprinted 1982). On Isis, see F. Dunand, *Le culte d'Isis dans le bassin orientale de la Méditerranée*, 3 vols. (Leiden, 1973). On other cults, cf. M. J. Vermaseren, *Cybele and Attis: The Myth and the Cult* (London, 1977), pp. 38 ff; and J. Champeaux, *Fortuna: Recherches sur le culte de Fortuna à et dans le monde romain des origines à la mort de César* (= *Coll. École Française à Rome* 64) (Rome, 1982). On the spread of the cult of the Magna Mater, see J. Bremmer, "The Legend of Cybele's Arrival in

Rome," in *Studies in Hellenistic Religions,* ed. M. J. Vermaseren (Leiden, 1979), pp. 9 ff.; and J. Gérard, "Légende et politique autour de la Mère des Dieux," *REL* 58 (1980): 153 ff.

31. Cf. L. Friedlander, *Roman Life and Manners under the Early Empire,* vol. 1 (London, 1968), pp. 225 ff.

32. J. Geremias, *Jerusalem au temps de Jésus* (French translation) (Paris, 1967). On Jewish marriage more particularly, see B. Cohen, *Jewish and Roman Law: A Comparative Study,* vol. 1 (New York, 1966), pp. 279 ff.; Z. W. Falk, "Ueber die Ehe in der biblischen Prophetien," *Zeitschrift für systematische Theologie* 90 (1973): 36 ff.; and B. Patai, *L'amour et le couple au temps biblique* (Paris, 1967). On women, more specifically, see J. Pirenne, "Le statut de la femme dans la civilisation hébraique," *RSJB* 11 (1959): 107 ff.; and D. Daube, "Johanan Ben Beroqa and Women's Rights," *ZSS, RA* 99 (1982): 22 ff.

33. On Paul's opinion of women, see A. Cumming, "Pauline Christianity and Greek Philosophy: A Study of the Status of Women," *Journal of the History of Ideas* 34 (1973): 517–28.

34. On the conception of women and marriage in the preaching of Christ and in the gospels, see F. Bolgiani, *Il matrimonio cristiano,* vol. 1 (Turin, 1972), pp. 136 ff. Cf. also G.E.M. de Ste. Croix, *The Class Struggle in the Ancient Greek World* (Ithaca and London, 1981), pp. 103–11.

35. The theory of natural selection in reverse as determining cause of the crisis was held by O. Seeck, in *Geschichte des untergangs der antiken welt* (1921) and was exposed, expounded, and criticized by Mazzarino, *La fine del mondo antico,* pp. 128 ff.

36. The most important relevant provisions are contained in the *Novellae* 22 (of A.D. 535) and 117 (of A.D. 542) of Justinian. In *Novella* 74, moreover, Justinian tends to consider the nuptial benediction as proof of the existence of the marriage. For a different point of view on the Christian concept of marriage and on its influence on the conception and legal regulation of Roman marriage, see Orestano, *La struttura giuridica,* pp. 258 ff.; J. Gaudemet, "Droit romain et principes canoniques en matière de mariage au Bas-Empire," in *Studi Albertario,* vol. 2 (Milan, 1953), pp. 173 ff. (= *Société et mariage,* pp. 116 ff.); *L'église dans l'Empire romain (IV et V siècles)* (Paris, 1958); "L'interpretation du principe d'indissolubilité du mariage chrétien au cours du premier millenaire," *BIDR* 81 (1978): 11 ff. (= *Société et mariage,* pp. 230 ff.); O. Robleda, "Intorno alla nozione di matrimonio nel diritto romano e nel diritto canonico," *Apollinaris* 50 (1977): 172 ff.; A. Montan, "La legislazione romana sul divorzio: Aspetti evolutivi e influssi cristiani," *Apollinaris* 53 (1980): 161 ff.; and F. P. Casavola, "Sessualità e matrimonio nelle Novelle giustinianee," in *Mondo classico e cristianesimo* (Rome, 1982), pp. 183 ff.

37. All that follows in the text on the repression of adultery in imperial

legislation, Romano-barbarian law, and intermediate law is expounded more fully in E. Cantarella, *Adulterio, omicidio legittimo e causa d'onore* (Milan, 1976), pp. 161 ff.

38. *Lex Rom. Vis.*—Paulus *Sent.* 2.27.1 (Haenel).

39. *Ep. Aeg.*, ed. Haenel, p. 372.

40. In Giovanni Novizzano d'Asti, *Silvae nuptialis libri sex* (Venice, 1573), vol. 1, p. 372, par. 102.

41. The rescript has not come down to us directly but can be reconstructed from the references of three jurists: Triphoninus (in *Digesta* 48.19.39), Ulpian (in *Digesta* 48.8.8), and Marcianus (in *Digesta* 47.11.4).

42. On the very significant fact that the unmarried woman could abort, see Crahay, *Les moralistes anciens et l'avortement*; and Gourevitch, *Le mal*, pp. 210 ff.

43. In Lactant. *Ep.* 33(38).5.

44. On the interpretation of the passage and what precedes it, see M. Craveri, *La vita di Gesù* (Milan, 1979; first ed. 1966), pp. 223 ff.

45. On the Gnostics, see F. Adorno, *La filosofia antica*, vol. 2, 3rd ed. (Milan, 1972), pp. 440 ff. On their continence and their beliefs about sex, see Craveri, *La vita di Gesù*, pp. 225 ff.; and A. di Nola, *Cristo segreto, Ascesi e rivoluzione sessuale nel cristianesimo nascente* (Rome, 1980), pp. 55 ff.

46. On Gregory of Nazianzus and his work, see R. Cantarella, *Poeti bizantini*, vol. 2 (Milan, 1948), pp. 54 ff. On praise of virginity in general, see J. A. McNamara, "Sexual Equality and the Cult of Virginity in Early Christian Thought," *Feminist Studies* 3.3–4 (1976): 145 ff.

47. Cf. Craveri, *La vita di Gesù*, p. 28, with further references to the process of "hyperdulia" of the Virgin Mary, who was declared by the Council of Trent (1546) to be immune from any sin, even venial; declared assumed into heaven, body and soul, by Pius XII in 1950; indicated by some theologians at the Mariological congress in Lourdes in 1958 as "mediatrix," which means that without her intervention God could not grant any grace to men; and finally in 1964 proposed by the Polish Cardinal Wyszynski (during Vatican II) as "mother of the Church."

48. This is the thesis held by Rousselle, *Porneia*.

49. Migne, P. G. 8.429 (*Paedagogus*); 8.1275 (*Stromata*).

50. Ibid. 12.188 (*in Levit.*); 12.305 (*in Exod.*).

51. Ibid. 42.148 (*in Epist. ad Ephes.*).

52. Ibid. 32.878 (*Soliloq.*); 38.347–48 (*Sermo* 51).

53. Canon 33, quaest. 5, caus. 12.

54. Canon 33, quaest. 5, caus. 13.

55. Canon 33, quaest. 5, caus. 14.

Chapter 11 The Byzantine Empire

1. So states G. Buckler, "Women in Byzantine Law, about 1100 A.D.," *Byzantion* 11 (1936): 391 ff., esp. 393. On the Byzantine empire and civilization, of the vast literature we will cite only A. A. Vasiliev, *History of the Byzantine Empire*, trans. and revised by S. Ragozin (Madison, Wis., 1928–29); S. Runciman, *Byzantine Civilisation* (London, 1933); *The Byzantine Empire*, vol. 4 of *Cambridge Medieval History* (Cambridge, 1966); and H. Ahrweiler, *L'idéologie politique de l'empire byzantine* (Paris, 1975). On the female condition in particular, see S. Lambros, "E gyné para tois byzantinois," *Neos Hellenomnemon* 17 (1923): 259 ff.; and J. Beaucamp, "La situation juridique de la femme à Byzance," *Actes du colloque sur "La femme dans les civilisations des XI–XIII s."* (= *Cahiers de civilisation médiévale* 20.2–3 [1977]: 145 ff.). See also A. E. Laiou, "The Role of Women in Byzantine Society," *XVI Internationaler Byzantinistenkongress, Akten* 1.1 (Vienna, 1981) (= *JOB* 31.1, p. 233 ff.); section 4.4 of *Akten* 2, entirely dedicated to the female condition; and J. Herren, "In Search of Byzantine Women: Three Avenues of Approach," in Cameron and Kuhrt, eds., *Images*, pp. 167–206.

2. Procop. *De Bello Persico* 1.230 (Loeb).

3. See Runciman, *Byzantine Civilisation*, pp. 68–69. On the struggle for power between Irene and her son, see J. B. Bury, *A History of the Later Roman Empire (395 A.D.–850 A.D.)*, vol. 2 (London, 1889; reprinted Amsterdam, 1966), pp. 483 ff.

4. So the emperor Leo VI states several times in his legislation; see *Novellae* 31, 98, and 112, which (like all the legal works cited in this paragraph) can be found in the collection *Ius graecoromanum*, edited by C. E. Zachariae von Linghenthal (reprinted Aalen, 1962).

5. *Ecloga* 1.1.

6. *Procheiros* 1.3 and 1.6.

7. Cf. *Ecloga* 2.13, 17, and 27; and *Ecloga privata aucta* 2.21.

8. On the penalty for adultery, see F. Goria, *Studi sul matrimonio dell'adultera nel diritto giustinianeo e bizantino* (Turin, 1975), esp. pp. 182–85; and J. Beaucamp, *La situation juridique*, pp. 156 ff.

9. Cf. *Nov.* 48. The theme is developed in *Peira* 30.11.

10. *Peira* 64.1–2, 8, 9–11, 19–20; 25.30; 16.7 and 25.68; 49.5.

11. See Beaucamp, *La situation juridique*, p. 175. For a study of the Roman roots of the notion of female weakness, see J. Beaucamp, "Le vocabulaire de la faiblesse féminine dans les textes juridiques romaines du III au VI siècles," *RD* 54 (1976): 485 ff. A different evaluation of the Byzantine attitude is that of P. I. Zepos, "Disposizioni e consuetudini bizantini e postbizantine a protezione dell'onore della donna," in *Studi*

Volterra, vol. 4 (Milan, 1971), pp. 615 ff. See also C. Mango, *Byzantium* (London, 1980), pp. 225–27.

12. On the empresses and their role, see E. A. Fisher, "Theodora and Antonina in the *Historia Arcana:* History and/or Fiction," *Arethusa* 11 (1978) 255 ff., who brings to light the differences between the imperial condition and that of the "common" women. The latter were segregated, says Fisher, no less than Greek women of the classical period. On the lack of instruction of Byzantine women, see Runciman, *Byzantine Civilisation,* pp. 230–31.

13. On Casia, see K. Krumbacher, *Geschichte der byzantinischen Literatur,* 2nd ed. (Munich, 1897); and R. Cantarella, *Poeti bizantini,* vol. 2, p. 164.

14. Cf. G. Buckler, *Anna Comnena* (London, 1929).

15. *Alex.* 3.6.4–6; 15.3.2.

16. K. Krumbacher, *Sammlung byzantinischer Sprichwörter, Sitzungsberichte,* vol. 2 (Munich, 1887), n. 45.

17. Psellus *Chron.* 7.4.9.

18. On Simeon Stylites see Krumbacher, pp. 144 ff.

19. Ibid., p. 195. On the episodes cited in the text, see A. Ducellier, *Il dramma di Bisanzio* (Naples, 1980), p. 21.

Index

Parental authority, modern concept
  of, 115
Parmenides, 52
Pastimes of girls, 45
paterfamilias, 104, 109, 115, 117
Paternity, 29, 30–32, 115
patria potestas, 113, 115–16, 121,
  135, 136
Patroclus, 78
Paul, Saint, 157–58, 167
Paullina, 156
Pelops, 78
Pembroke, S., 108
Penelope, 26–27, 27–28, 29–30, 32–
  33
Perfume, 159
Pericles, 51, 54, 126
Phaedra, 69
Phidias, 55
Philip II, of Macedon, 92
Philosophers, female, 56
Phintys, 57
Phyle of Priene, 91
Physicians, female, 142
pia (faithful), 132
Pindar, 50, 73
Plato, 57, 58–59, 78; *Laws,* 58;
  Menexenus, 55; *Republic,* 58, 59;
  Symposium, 80–82, 83–85;
  Timaeus, 59
Plebeian women, cults for, 151, 152
Pliny the Younger, 135, 150
Plutarch, 54, 57, 79, 89, 128, 148,
  153, 154
Poets, female, 86–87, 91, 147. See
  also *names of poets*
Poisoning trials, 126, 128
polis, 57, 177, 179; decline of, 70, 90;
  exclusion of women from, 38–51
Political power of women, 70–71, 92,
  103–4. *See also* Empresses, Byzan-
  tine; Magistrates, female; Queens
Polygamy, 31, 108
Pomeroy, S. B., 63
Pompeia, 153
Pompeii, 142
Pontifex Maximus, 155

Poor women, 46, 146
Poppaea Sabina, 148
Poseidon, 78
Posidippus, 44
potnia, 12, 102
praenomen. See Nomenclature, Roman
Praxilla, 74
Prodigies: warning against women,
  152; women readers of, 102
Prometheus, 34
Promiscuity, 108
Prostitution, prostitutes, 50–51, 116,
  119, 151; in temples, 50. *See also*
  Hetaerae
Protective legislation, 173
Protectiveness of men toward women,
  104
Ptolemy XIII, 92
Ptolemy XIV, 92
Ptolemy XV, 92
Public speaking by women, 141, 171
pudica (modest), 132
Pudicitia (Chastity), 151, 152, 157
Pulcheria, 171–72
Punishment, 30, 32, 51, 126; of men,
  51, 163; of Vestals, 155; of women,
  117–18. *See also* Adultery
Pythagoras, 56

Queens: Byzantine, 171–72; Egyptian,
  93, 141; Etruscan, 103; Ptolemaic,
  92
Quintilian, 131

Reclining at dinner, 103
Recognition of children by father, 115
Religion. *See* Female divinities and
  cults
Remarriage, 122
Repression, sexual, 127
Reproduction, 52–53, 59, 65, 109
Repudiation, 41, 118, 166. *See also*
  Divorce
repudium. See Divorce; Repudiation
Right of life and death, of man over
  woman, 32, 109, 113

ANCIENT SOCIETY AND HISTORY

The series Ancient Society and History offers books, relatively brief in compass, on selected topics in the history of ancient Greece and Rome, broadly conceived, with a special emphasis on comparative and other nontraditional approaches and methods. The series, which includes both works of synthesis and works of original scholarship, is aimed at the widest possible range of specialist and nonspecialist readers.

Published in the series:
Eva Cantarella, PANDORA'S DAUGHTERS: The Role and Status of Women in Greek and Roman Antiquity
Alan Watson, ROMAN SLAVE LAW
John E. Stambaugh, THE ANCIENT ROMAN CITY
Géza Alföldi, THE SOCIAL HISTORY OF ROME
Giovanni Comotti, MUSIC IN GREEK AND ROMAN CULTURE